D1175195

DATE DUE

THE BLACK DEATH

THE BLACK DEATH

Joseph P. Byrne

Greenwood Guides to Historic Events of the Medieval World
Jane Chance, Series Editor

GREENWOOD PRESS
Westport, Connecticut • London

Library of Congress Cataloging-in-Publication Data

Byrne, Joseph Patrick.
    The black death / Joseph P. Byrne.
       p. cm.—(Greenwood guides to historic events of the medieval world)
    Includes bibliographical references and index.
    ISBN 0-313-32492-1 (alk. paper)
    1. Black Death—History. I. Title. II. Series.
  RC172.B976   2004
  614.5'732—dc22   2004043640

British Library Cataloguing in Publication Data is available.

Library of Congress Catalog Card Number: 2004043640
ISBN: 0-313-32492-1

First published in 2004

Greenwood Press, 88 Post Road West, Westport, CT 06881
An imprint of Greenwood Publishing Group, Inc.
www.greenwood.com

Printed in the United States of America

The paper used in this book complies with the
Permanent Paper Standard issued by the National
Information Standards Organization (Z39.48-1984).

10 9 8 7 6 5 4 3 2 1

CONTENTS

Photo essay follows Chapter 5.

Series Foreword

The Middle Ages are no longer considered the "Dark Ages" (as Petrarch termed them), sandwiched between the two enlightened periods of classical antiquity and the Renaissance. Often defined as a historical period lasting, roughly, from 500 to 1500 C.E., the Middle Ages span an enormous amount of time (if we consider the way other time periods have been constructed by historians) as well as an astonishing range of countries and regions very different from one another. That is, we call the "Middle" Ages the period beginning with the fall of the Roman Empire as a result of raids by northern European tribes of "barbarians" in the late antiquity of the fifth and sixth centuries and continuing until the advent of the so-called Italian and English renaissances, or rebirths of classical learning, in the fifteenth and sixteenth centuries. How this age could be termed either "Middle" or "Dark" is a mystery to those who study it. Certainly it is no longer understood as embracing merely the classical inheritance in the west or excluding eastern Europe, the Middle East, Asia, or even, as I would argue, North and Central America.

Whatever the arbitrary, archaic, and hegemonic limitations of these temporal parameters—the old-fashioned approach to them was that they were mainly not classical antiquity, and therefore not important—the Middle Ages represent a time when certain events occurred that have continued to affect modern cultures and that also, inevitably, catalyzed other medieval events. Among other important events, the Middle Ages saw the birth of Muhammad (c. 570–632) and his foundation of Islam in the seventh century as a rejection of Christianity which led to the imperial conflict between East and West in the eleventh and twelfth centuries. In western Europe in the Middle Ages the foundations for modern nationalism and modern law were laid and the concept of romantic love arose in the Middle Ages, this latter event partly one of the indirect consequences of the Crusades. With the shaping of national identity came the need to defend boundaries against invasion; so the castle emerged as a military outpost—whether in northern Africa, during the Crusades, or in Wales, in the eleventh century, to defend William of Normandy's newly acquired provinces—to satisfy that need. From Asia the invasions of Genghis Khan changed the literal and cultural shape of eastern and southern Europe.

In addition to triggering the development of the concept of chivalry and the knight, the Crusades influenced the European concepts of the lyric, music, and musical instruments; introduced to Europe an appetite for spices like cinnamon, coriander, and saffron and for dried fruits like prunes and figs as well as a desire for fabrics such as silk; and brought Aristotle to the European university through Arabic and then Latin translations. As a result of study of the "new" Aristotle, science and philosophy dramatically changed direction—and their emphasis on this material world helped to undermine the power of the Catholic Church as a monolithic institution in the thirteenth century.

By the twelfth century, with the centralization of the one (Catholic) Church, came a new architecture for the cathedral—the Gothic—to replace the older Romanesque architecture and thereby to manifest the Church's role in the community in a material way as well as in spiritual and political ways. Also from the cathedral as an institution and its need to dramatize the symbolic events of the liturgy came medieval drama—the mystery and the morality play, from which modern drama derives in large part. Out of the cathedral and its schools to train new priests (formerly handled by monasteries) emerged the medieval institution of the university. Around the same time, the community known as a town rose up in eastern and western Europe as a consequence of trade and the necessity for a new economic center to accompany the development of a bourgeoisie, or middle class. Because of the town's existence, the need for an itinerant mendicancy that could preach the teachings of the Church and beg for alms in urban centers sprang up.

Elsewhere in the world, in North America the eleventh-century settlement of Chaco Canyon by the Pueblo peoples created a social model like no other, one centered on ritual and ceremony in which the "priests" were key, but one that lasted barely two hundred years before it collapsed and its central structures were abandoned.

In addition to their influence on the development of central features of modern culture, the Middle Ages have long fascinated the modern age because of parallels that exist between the two periods. In both, terrible wars devastated whole nations and peoples; in both, incurable diseases plagued cities and killed large percentages of the world's population. In both periods, dramatic social and cultural changes took place as a result of these events: marginalized and overtaxed groups in societies rebelled against imperious governments; trade and a burgeoning middle class came to the fore; outside the privacy of the family, women began to have a greater role in Western societies and their cultures.

How different cultures of that age grappled with such historical change is the subject of the Greenwood Guides to Historic Events of the Medieval World. This series features individual volumes that illuminate key events in medieval world history. In some cases, an "event" occurred during a relatively limited time period. The troubadour lyric as a phenomenon, for example, flowered and died in the courts of Aquitaine in the twelfth century, as did the courtly romance in northern Europe a few decades later. The Hundred Years War between France and England generally took place during a precise time period, from the fourteenth to mid-fifteenth centuries.

In other cases, the event may have lasted for centuries before it played itself out: the medieval Gothic cathedral, for example, may have been first built in the twelfth century at Saint-Denis in Paris (c. 1140), but cathedrals, often of a slightly different style of Gothic architecture, were still being built in the fifteenth century all over Europe and, again, as the symbolic representation of a bishop's seat, or chair, are still being built today. And the medieval city, whatever its incarnation in the early Middle Ages, basically blossomed between the eleventh and thirteenth centuries as a result of social, economic, and cultural changes. Events—beyond a single dramatic historically limited happening—took longer to affect societies in the Middle Ages because of the lack of political and social centralization, the primarily agricultural and rural nature of most countries, difficulties in communication, and the distances between important cultural centers.

Each volume includes necessary tools for understanding such key events in the Middle Ages. Because of the postmodern critique of authority that modern societies underwent at the end of the twentieth century, students and scholars as well as general readers have come to mistrust the commentary and expertise of any one individual scholar or commentator and to identify the text as an arbiter of "history." For this reason, each book in the series can be described as a "library in a book." The intent of the series is to provide a quick, in-depth examination and current perspectives on the event to stimulate critical thinking as well as ready-reference materials, including primary documents and biographies of key individuals, for additional research.

Specifically, in addition to a narrative historical overview that places the specific event within the larger context of a contemporary perspective, five to seven developmental chapters explore related focused aspects of the event. In addition, each volume begins with a brief chronology and ends with a conclusion that discusses the consequences and impact of the event. There are also brief biographies of twelve to twenty key individuals (or places or buildings, in the book on the cathedral); primary documents from the period (for example, letters, chronicles, memoirs, diaries, and other writings) that illustrate states of mind or the turn of events at the time, whether historical, literary, scientific, or philosophical; illustrations (maps, diagrams, manuscript illuminations, portraits); a glossary of terms; and an annotated bibliography of important books, articles, films, and CD-ROMs available for additional research. An index concludes each volume.

No particular theoretical approach or historical perspective characterizes the series; authors developed their topics as they chose, generally taking into account the latest thinking on any particular event. The editors selected final topics from a list provided by an advisory board of high school teachers and public and school librarians. On the basis of nominations of scholars made by distinguished writers, the series editor also tapped internationally known scholars, both those with lifelong expertise and others with fresh new perspectives on a topic, to author the twelve books in the series. Finally, the series editor selected distinguished medievalists, art historians, and archaeologists to complete an advisory board: Gwinn Vivian, retired professor of archaeology at the University of Arizona Museum; Sharon Kinoshita, associate professor of French literature, world literature, and cultural studies at the University of California–Santa Cruz; Nancy Wu, associate museum educator at the Metropolitan Museum of Art, The Cloisters, New York City; and Christopher A. Snyder, chair of the Department of History and Politics at Marymount University.

In addition to examining the event and its effects on the specific cultures involved through an array of documents and an overview, each volume provides a new approach to understanding these twelve events. Treated in the series are: the Black Death; the Crusades; Eleanor of Aquitaine, courtly love, and the troubadours; Genghis Khan and Mongol rule; Joan of Arc and the Hundred Years War; Magna Carta; the medieval castle, from the eleventh to the sixteenth centuries; the medieval cathedral; the medieval city, especially in the thirteenth century; medieval science and technology; Muhammad and the rise of Islam; and the Puebloan society of Chaco Canyon.

The Black Death, by Joseph Byrne, isolates the event of the epidemic of bubonic plague in 1347–52 as having had a signal impact on medieval Europe. It was, however, only the first of many related such episodes involving variations of pneumonic and septicemic plague that recurred over 350 years. Taking a twofold approach to the Black Death, Byrne investigates both the modern research on bubonic plague, its origins and spread, and also medieval documentation and illustration in diaries, artistic works, and scientific and religious accounts. The demographic, economic, and political effects of the Black Death are traced in one chapter, the social and psychological patterns of life in another, and cultural expressions in art and ritual in a third. Finally, Byrne investigates why bubonic plague disappeared and why we continue to be fascinated by it. Documents included provide a variety of medieval accounts—Byzantine, Arabic, French, German, English, and Italian—several of which are translated for the first time.

The Crusades, by Helen Nicholson, presents a balanced account of various crusades, or military campaigns, invented by Catholic or "Latin" Christians during the Middle Ages against those they perceived as threats to their faith. Such expeditions included the Crusades to the Holy Land between 1095 and 1291, expeditions to the Iberian Peninsula, the "crusade" to northeastern Europe, the Albigensian Crusades and the Hussite crusades—both against the heretics—and the crusades against the Ottoman Turks (in the Balkans). Although Muslim rulers included the concept of jihâd (a conflict fought for God against evil or his enemies) in their wars in the early centuries of Islam, it had become less important in the late tenth century. It was not until the middle decades of the twelfth century that jihâd was revived in the wars with the Latin Christian Crusaders. Most of the Crusades did not result in victory for the Latin Christians, although Nicholson concedes they slowed the advance of Islam. After Jerusalem was destroyed in 1291, Muslim rulers did permit Christian pilgrims to travel to holy sites. In the Iberian Peninsula, Christian rulers replaced Muslim rulers, but Muslims, Jews, and dissident Christians were compelled to convert to Catholicism. In northeastern Europe, the Teutonic Order's campaigns allowed German colonization that later encouraged twentieth-century German claims to land and led to two world wars. The Albigensian Crusade wiped out thirteenth-century aristocratic families in southern France who held to the Cathar heresy, but the Hussite crusades in the 1420s failed to eliminate the Hussite heresy. As a result of the wars, however, many positive changes occurred: Arab learning founded on Greek scholarship entered western Europe through the acquisition of an extensive library in Toledo, Spain, in 1085; works of western European literature were inspired by the holy wars; trade was encouraged and with it the demand for certain products; and a more favorable image of Muslim men and women was fostered by the crusaders' contact with the Middle East. Nicholson also notes that America may have been discovered because Christopher Columbus avoided a route that had been closed by Muslim conquests and that the Reformation may have been advanced because Martin Luther protested against the crusader indulgence in his Ninety-five Theses (1517).

Eleanor of Aquitaine, Courtly Love, and the Troubadours, by ffiona Swabey, singles out the twelfth century as the age of the individual, in which a queen like Eleanor of Aquitaine could influence the development of a new social and artistic culture. The wife of King Louis VII of France and later the wife of his enemy Henry of Anjou, who became king of England, she patronized some of the troubadours, whose vernacular lyrics celebrated the personal expression of emotion and a passionate declaration of service to women. Love, marriage, and the pursuit of women were also the subject of the new romance literature, which flourished in northern Europe and was the inspiration behind concepts of courtly love. However, as Swabey points out, historians in the past have misjudged Eleanor, whose independent spirit fueled their misogynist attitudes. Similarly, Eleanor's divorce and subsequent stormy marriage have colored ideas about medieval "love courts" and courtly love, interpretations of which have now been challenged by scholars. The twelfth century is set in context, with commentaries on feudalism, the tenets of Christianity, and the position of women, as well as summaries of the cultural and philosophical background, the cathedral schools and universities, the influence of Islam, the revival of classical learning, vernacular literature, and Gothic architecture. Swabey provides two biographical chapters on Eleanor and two on the emergence of the troubadours and the origin of courtly love through verse romances. Within this latter subject Swabey also details the story of Abelard and Heloise, the treatise of Andreas Capellanus (André the Chaplain) on courtly love, and Arthurian legend as a subject of courtly love.

Genghis Khan and Mongol Rule, by George Lane, identifies the rise to power of Genghis Khan and his unification of the Mongol tribes in the thirteenth century as a kind of globalization with political, cultural, economic, mercantile, and spiritual effects akin to those of modern globalization. Normally viewed as synonymous with barbarian destruction, the rise to power of Genghis Khan and the Mongol hordes is here understood as a more positive event that initiated two centuries of regeneration and creativity. Lane discusses the nature of the society of the Eurasian steppes in the twelfth and thirteenth centuries into which Genghis Khan was born; his success at reshaping the relationship between the northern pastoral and nomadic society with the southern urban, agriculturalist society; and his unification of all the Turco-Mongol tribes in 1206 before his move to conquer Tanquit Xixia, the Chin of northern China, and the lands of Islam. Conquered thereafter were the Caucasus, the Ukraine, the Crimea, Russia, Siberia, Central Asia, Afghanistan, Pakistan, and Kashmir. After his death his sons and grandsons continued, conquering Korea, Persia, Armenia, Mesopotamia, Azerbaijan, and eastern Europe—chiefly Kiev, Poland, Moravia, Silesia, and Hungary—until 1259, the end of the Mongol Empire as a unified whole. Mongol rule created a golden age in the succeeding split of the Empire into two, the Yuan dynasty of greater China and the Il-Khanate dynasty of greater Iran. Lane adds biographies of important political figures, famous names such as Marco Polo, and artists and scientists. Documents derive from universal histories, chronicles, local histories and travel accounts, official government documents, and poetry, in French, Armenian, Georgian, Chinese, Persian, Arabic, Chaghatai Turkish, Russian, and Latin.

Joan of Arc and the Hundred Years War, by Deborah Fraioli, presents the Hundred Years War between France and England in the fourteenth and fifteenth centuries within contexts whose importance has sometimes been blurred or ignored in past studies. An episode of apparently only moderate significance, a feudal lord's seizure of his vassal's land for harboring his mortal enemy, sparked the Hundred Years War, yet on the face of it the event should not have led inevitably to war. But the lord was the king of France and the vassal the king of England, who resented losing his claim to the French throne to his Valois cousin. The land in dispute, extending roughly from Bordeaux to the Pyrenees mountains, was crucial coastline for the economic interests of both kingdoms. The series of skirmishes, pitched battles, truces, stalemates, and diplomatic wrangling that resulted from the confiscation of English Aquitaine by the French form the narrative of this Anglo-French conflict, which was in fact not given the name Hundred Years War until the nineteenth century.

Fraioli emphasizes how dismissing women's inheritance and succession rights came at the high price of unleashing discontent in their male heirs, including Edward III, Robert of Artois, and Charles of Navarre. Fraioli also demonstrates the centrality of side issues, such as Flemish involvement in the war, the peasants' revolts that resulted from the costs of the war, and Joan of Arc's unusually clear understanding of French "sacred kingship." Among the primary sources provided are letters from key players such as Edward III, Etienne Marcel, and Joan of Arc; a supply list for towns about to be besieged; and a contemporary poem by the celebrated scholar and court poet Christine de Pizan in praise of Joan of Arc.

Magna Carta, by Katherine Drew, is a detailed study of the importance of the Magna Carta in comprehending England's legal and constitutional history. Providing a model for the rights of citizens found in the United States Declaration of Independence and Constitution's first ten amendments, the Magna Carta has had a role in the legal and parliamentary history of all modern states bearing some colonial or government connection with the British Empire. Constructed at a time when modern nations began to appear, in the early thirteenth century, the Magna Carta (signed in 1215) presented a formula for balancing the liberties of the people with the power of modern governmental institutions. This unique English document influenced the growth of a form of law (the English common law) and provided a vehicle for the evolution of representative (parliamentary) government. Drew demonstrates how the Magna Carta came to be—the roles of the Church, the English towns, barons, common law, and the parliament in its making—as well as how myths concerning its provisions were established. Also provided are biographies of Thomas Becket, Charlemagne, Frederick II, Henry II and his sons, Innocent III, and many other key figures, and primary documents—among them, the Magna Cartas of 1215 and 1225, and the Coronation Oath of Henry I.

Medieval Castles, by Marilyn Stokstad, traces the historical, political, and social function of the castle from the late eleventh century to the sixteenth by means of a typology of castles. This typology ranges from the early "motte and bailey"—military fortification, and government and economic center—to the palace as an expression of the castle owners' needs and purposes. An introduction defines the various contexts—military, political, economic, and social—in which the castle appeared in the Middle Ages. A concluding interpretive essay suggests the impact of the castle and its symbolic role as an idealized construct lasting until the modern day.

Medieval Cathedrals, by William Clark, examines one of the chief contributions of the Middle Ages, at least from an elitist perspective—that is, the religious architecture found in the cathedral ("chair" of the bishop) or great church, studied in terms of its architecture, sculpture, and stained glass. Clark begins with a brief contextual history of the concept of the bishop and his role within the church hierarchy, the growth of the church in the early Christian era and its affiliation with the bishop (deriving from that of the bishop of Rome), and the social history of cathedrals. Because of economic and political conflicts among the three authorities who held power in medieval towns—the king, the bishop, and the cathedral clergy—cathedral construction and maintenance always remained a vexed issue, even though the owners—the cathedral clergy—usually held the civic responsibility for the cathedral. In an interpretive essay, Clark then focuses on Reims Cathedral in France, because both it and the bishop's palace survive, as well as on contemporary information about surrounding buildings. Clark also supplies a historical overview on the social, political, and religious history of the cathedral in the Middle Ages: an essay on patrons, builders, and artists; aspects of cathedral construction (which was not always successful); and then a chapter on Romanesque and Gothic cathedrals and a "gazetteer" of twenty-five important examples.

The Medieval City, by Norman J. G. Pounds, documents the origin of the medieval city in the flight from the dangers or difficulties found in the country, whether economic, physically threatening, or cultural. Identifying the attraction of the city in its *urbanitas,* its "urbanity," or the way of living in a city, Pounds discusses first its origins in prehistoric and classical Greek urban revolutions. During the Middle Ages, the city grew primarily between the eleventh and thirteenth centuries, remaining essentially the same until the Industrial Revolution. Pounds provides chapters on the medieval city's planning, in terms of streets and structures; life in the medieval city; the roles of the Church and the city government in its operation; the development of crafts and trade in the city; and the issues of urban health, wealth, and welfare. Concluding with the role of the city in history, Pounds suggests that the value of the city depended upon its balance of social classes, its need for trade and profit to satisfy personal desires through the accumulation of wealth and its consequent economic power, its political power as a representative body within the kingdom, and its social role in the rise of literacy and education and in nationalism. Indeed, the concept of a middle class, a bourgeoisie, derives from the city—from the *bourg,* or "borough." According to Pounds, the rise of modern civilization would not have taken place without the growth of the city in the Middle Ages and its concomitant artistic and cultural contribution.

Medieval Science and Technology, by Elspeth Whitney, examines science and technology from the early Middle Ages to 1500 within the context of the classical learning that so influenced it. She looks at institutional history, both early and late, and what was taught in the medieval schools and, later, the universities (both of which were overseen by the Catholic Church). Her discussion of Aristotelian natural philosophy illustrates its impact on the medieval scientific worldview. She presents chapters on the exact sciences, meaning mathematics, astronomy, cosmology, astrology, statics, kinematics, dynamics, and optics; the biological and earth sciences, meaning chemistry and alchemy, medicine, zoology, botany, geology and meteorology, and geography; and technology. In an interpretive conclusion, Whitney demonstrates the impact of medieval science on the preconditions and structure that permitted the emergence of the modern world. Most especially, technology transformed an agricultural society into a more commercial and engine-driven society: waterpower and inventions like the blast furnace and horizontal loom turned iron working and cloth making into manufacturing operations. The invention of the mechanical clock helped to organize human activities through timetables rather than through experiential perception and thus facilitated the advent of modern life. Also influential in the establishment of a middle class were the inventions of the musket and pistol and the printing press. Technology, according to Whitney, helped advance the habits of mechanization and precise methodology. Her biographies introduce major medieval Latin and Arabic and classical natural philosophers and scientists. Extracts from various kinds of scientific treatises allow a window into the medieval concept of knowledge.

The Puebloan Society of Chaco Canyon, by Paul Reed, is unlike other volumes in this series, whose historic events boast a long-established historical record. Reed's study offers instead an original reconstruction of the Puebloan Indian society of Chaco, in what is now New Mexico, but originally extending into Colorado, Utah, and Arizona. He is primarily interested in its leaders, ritual and craft specialists, and commoners during the time of its chief flourishing, in the eleventh and twelfth centuries, as understood from archaeological data alone. To this new material he adds biographies of key Euro-American archaeologists and other individuals from the nineteenth and twentieth centuries who have made important discoveries about Chaco Canyon. Also provided are documents of archaeological description and narrative from early explorers' journals and archaeological reports, narratives, and monographs. In his overview chapters, Reed discusses the cultural and environmental setting of Chaco Canyon; its history (in terms of exploration and research); the Puebloan society and how it emerged chronologically; the Chaco society and how it appeared in 1100 c.e.; the "Outliers," or outlying communities of Chaco; Chaco as a ritual center of the eleventh-century Pueblo world; and, finally, what is and is not known about Chaco society. Reed concludes that ritual and ceremony played an important role in Chacoan society and that ritual specialists, or priests, conducted ceremonies, maintained ritual artifacts, and charted the ritual calendar. Its social organization matches no known social pattern or type: it was complicated, multiethnic, centered around ritual and ceremony, and without any overtly hierarchical political system. The Chacoans were ancestors to the later Pueblo people, part of a society that rose, fell, and evolved within a very short time period.

The Rise of Islam, by Matthew Gordon, introduces the early history of the Islamic world, beginning in the late sixth century with the career of the Prophet Muhammad (c. 570–c. 632) on the Arabian Peninsula. From Muhammad's birth in an environment of religious plurality—Christianity, Judaism, and Zoroastrianism, along with paganism, were joined by Islam—to the collapse of the Islamic empire in the early tenth century, Gordon traces the history of the Islamic community. The book covers topics that include the life of the Prophet and divine revelation (the Qur'an) to the formation of the Islamic state, urbanization in the Islamic Near East, and the extraordinary culture of Islamic letters and scholarship. In addition to a historical overview, Gordon examines the Caliphate and early Islamic Empire, urban society and economy, and the emergence, under the Abbasid Caliphs, of a "world religious tradition" up to the year 925 C.E.

As editor of this series I am grateful to have had the help of Benjamin Burford, an undergraduate Century Scholar at Rice University assigned to me in 2002–2004 for this project; Gina Weaver, a third-year graduate student in English; and Cynthia Duffy, a second-year graduate student in English, who assisted me in target-reading select chapters from some of these books in an attempt to define an audience. For this purpose I would also like to thank Gale Stokes, former dean of humanities at Rice University, for the 2003 summer research grant and portions of the 2003–2004 annual research grant from Rice University that served that end.

This series, in its mixture of traditional and new approaches to medieval history and cultures, will ensure opportunities for dialogue in the classroom in its offerings of twelve different "libraries in books." It should also propel discussion among graduate students and scholars by means of the gentle insistence throughout on the text as primal. Most especially, it invites response and further study. Given its mixture of East and West, North and South, the series symbolizes the necessity for global understanding, both of the Middle Ages and in the postmodern age.

Jane Chance, Series Editor
Houston, Texas
February 19, 2004

PREFACE

The Black Death presents students (myself included) not only with a medieval phenomenon of great complexity and fascination, but with a mirror for our own time. In 1966 the Rand Corporation, a political and scientific think-tank, commissioned a study of the Black Death with the intent of determining the possible social effects of thermonuclear war: would society dissolve into chaos if the Soviets dropped the bomb? The researcher's answer was "no": history suggested that society and government would survive even huge death tolls and the shocks they brought.[1] Now, forty years later, both professionals, such as historians, physicians, biologists, and epidemiologists, and the general public have developed a stronger and broader interest in the medieval Plague. This is largely due to the contemporary threat of many "new" diseases and the potential for deadly epidemics. Nature seems to menace humanity as never before with Ebola, SARS, AIDS, West Nile Virus, and flesh-eating bacteria, while anthrax, smallpox, and even bubonic plague appear to be in the arsenals of terrorists and rogue states, ready to be unleashed in support of one or another political agenda. Biologically speaking, the world seems to be a very dangerous place.

And yet, some 650 years ago large parts of Europe, North Africa, and the Middle East underwent a biological attack that swiftly wiped out somewhere around 35 percent of the population. In a large village of 1,000 people, graves for about 350 of them had to be dug, and the 350 laid to rest, and the 350 mourned, all over about four months' time. Rand was right to see the parallel. The human spirit was put to an enormous test, but, all in all, it survived the shock and laid the groundwork for the modern age. Like a neutron bomb, the Plague destroyed people but left the physical world otherwise untouched.

The interest of many historians is focused on the aftermath of the first outbreak of the Plague in 1347–52. What were the psychic, spiritual, intellectual, economic, political, social, and cultural effects of the initial strike? How, then, did people react to the subsequent outbreaks, which occurred about once a decade in any given place until the medieval world turned modern? What was the relationship of the Black Death to the fall of feudalism and the rise of vernacular literature, humanism, the Renaissance, and the Reformation? Questions about the Black Death go deeper still, as historians and scientists today argue about the very nature and origin of the disease, about how it spread and killed and where and why. Indeed, the fundamental question "What was the Black Death?"—presumably answered years ago: the bubonic plague spread by rats and fleas—has been reasked, and the competing answers are multiplying. When a major historian of the period opens his latest book with the bold declaration that the Black Death "was any disease other than the rat-based bubonic plague,"[2] one feels that the gauntlet has been slammed down as a challenge to orthodox thinking.

In this book I have attempted to outline both the orthodoxies and the current challenges to them that one finds in exploring research on the Black Death. While this approach may not make for neat conclusions, it does reflect the fact that our understanding of the disease and its myriad effects is evolving, and will continue to do so.

NOTES

1. J. Hirschleifer, *Disaster and Recovery: The Black Death in Western Europe* (Santa Monica: The Rand Corporation, 1966), p. 26.

2. Samuel K. Cohn, Jr., *The Black Death Transformed: Disease and Culture in Early Renaissance Europe* (Oxford: Oxford University Press, 2002), p. 1.

ACKNOWLEDGMENTS

I would like to express my gratitude to Marshall Poe and the National Endowment for the Humanities for providing me with the opportunity to utilize the resources of the libraries of Harvard University and to find stimulating fellowship in the 2002 Summer Institute. I would also like to thank Paige Carter and the library staff at Belmont University for their tireless assistance and encouragement in obtaining additional source materials. Special thanks to Maggie Monteverde, Patrick Gann, Jeff Williams, and Ray Wang for their contributions and to the seven members of the 2003 Belmont University Honors Seminar, who helped hammer out the shape and details of this book. Thanks also to Jane Chance and all who read, corrected, and commented upon the various stages of this book.

CHRONOLOGY

c. 460–377 B.C.E.	Life of Hippocrates, Greek physician who pioneered rational medicine and established practical rules for good health.
c. 130–201 C.E.	Life of Galen, Greco-Roman physician who wrote important works on humoral medicine and pestilence.
541–c. 760	The Plague of Justinian (First Pandemic); epidemic throughout Mediterranean—probably bubonic plague.
980–1037	Life of Avicenna, great Arab philosopher and medical writer (*Kanon*) who had great influence on Muslim and Christian medicine.
1260	Earliest organization of flagellants, in Perugia, Italy.
1330s	Probable outbreak of bubonic plague as epidemic in area of Gobi Desert or central Asia. "Triumph of Death" painted in Pisa's Camposanto cemetery.
1338–39	Gravestones at Issyk Kul testify to presence of pestilence near Lake Baikal in central Asia.
1347	Incident at Kaffa: warriors of Djanibeg's Golden Horde supposedly infect Genoese colony with pestilence; Genoese (and the Plague) escape to Constantinople.

Fall 1347	The Black Death (Second Pandemic) begins; Constantinople, Alexandria, and Messina on Sicily are struck by pestilence; it begins to move outward in Middle East, Africa, and Europe.
Winter 1348	Italian ports of Genoa, Pisa, and Venice struck, along with Ragusa, Marseille, and the French Riviera. Venice develops first board of sanitation.
Spring 1348	Naples, Florence, Siena, Perugia in Italy; Avignon in France; the Balearic Islands, Barcelona, and Valencia in Aragon; Damascus, Aleppo, Jerusalem, Cairo struck. First attacks on Jews in southern France and Aragon.
Summer 1348	Rome; Paris, Lyon, Bordeaux, Burgundy, Normandy, Brittany struck; pestilence first appears in England and Germany. Probable origins of flagellant movement. Pope Clement condemns anti-Semitic violence.
Fall 1348	London and Ireland struck; Italian and southern French cities begin recovery; anti-Semitic violence increases in Switzerland and upper Rhine, and Pope Clement condemns violence against Jews for second time; flagellant movement gains momentum. University of Paris medical faculty publishes its *consilium* on the pestilence.
Winter 1349	Pestilence moves northward through England; Switzerland struck.
Spring and summer 1349	Vienna and upper Rhine, Flanders, and Holland struck. Ordinance of Laborers promulgated.
Fall 1349	Bergen, Norway, Cologne, and middle Rhine region struck; Pope Clement condemns flagellant movement; last reported anti-Semitic pogrom, in Brussels; Black Death ends in Islamic regions.
1350	Scotland and Sweden struck; Roman Jubilee Year begins; flagellant movement fades away.

1351	Poland, Baltic region, and western Russia (Pskov) struck. England's Statute of Laborers reinforces Ordinance of Laborers.
1352	Russia (Novgorod) struck.
1355	Fall of The Nine, the government of Siena, due to tensions increased by the Plague.
1358	Boccaccio finishes the *Decameron*; French peasant uprising (*Jacquerie*).
1360–63	Second Epidemic: France, Catalonia, Italy, Britain, Sweden, Norway, Pskov, Egypt; later in Germany and Poland.
1370–74	Third Epidemic: France, Barcelona, northern Italy, Ireland and southern England, Germany, Hainaut.
1378	Ciompi Revolt in Florence.
1381	Peasants' Revolt in England.
1382–84	Epidemics in France, Catalonia, Seville, Portugal, northern Italy, London, Kent, Ireland, central Europe, the Baltic region, the Rhineland, Poland.
1390–91	Epidemics in Burgundy, Lorraine, northern England and Scotland, northern Italy.
1399–1400	General epidemic in Italy and northern Europe, Seville.
1410–12	General epidemic in western Europe, Silesia and Lithuania, Egypt.
1422–24	General epidemic in Italy, Flanders, Portugal.
1429–30	Widespread epidemic in Italy, Haute Auvergne.
1438–39	General epidemic in Italy, France, Portugal, northern Britain, Germany, Switzerland, Netherlands, Poland, Cairo, and Syria.

1448–50	General epidemic in northern Italy, France, northern and western Germany, Holland, Egypt.
1456–57	General epidemics in northern France, Barcelona, Italy.
1480–84	France, Portugal, central Italy, London, Germany, Poland.
1492	Expulsion of Jews from Spain by Ferdinand and Isabella.
1494–99	Epidemics in southern France, Italy, Aragon, Scotland, Luxembourg, central Germany, Austria, Bohemia, Poland.
1666	Great Fire in London and end of pestilence reports in England.
1722	Last pestilence in Marseille, France, and mainland western Europe said to have been imported from Syria.
1743	Last major Plague outbreak in Messina, Sicily.
1771–72	Last major pestilential outbreak in Russia, kills 100,000 in Moscow.
1894	Third Pandemic of bubonic plague begins in China, southeast Asia, and Hong Kong; Yersin and Kitasato conduct research, identifying Y. *pestis*; serum against the bubonic plague proven successful in following years.
1896–1914	Continued research identifies full epidemiology of bubonic plague bacillus.
June 2, 1899	Japanese ship carrying bubonic plague docks in San Francisco Bay, beginning American phase of Third Pandemic.
1998	Genetic link of Plague exposure to AIDS immunity identified.

CHAPTER 1

OVERVIEW: PLAGUE IN THE MIDDLE AGES

The Black Death is the name often given to what has usually been identified as a widespread outbreak of bubonic plague in Europe, the Near East, and North Africa from 1347 to 1352. It is commonly, but inaccurately, said that the term originated in the skin discoloration—dark blotches—that accompanies the disease. The unique appearance of the phrase *mors nigra* ("black death") at the time was in a Latin poem (1350) about the epidemic by Simon de Covinus, an astrologer from what is today Belgium.[1] More commonly the Latin *mors atra*, which can mean "black" or "terrible" death, appears in Swedish and Danish sources of the sixteenth and seventeenth centuries. Some claim that "Black Death" was used in English to designate the fourteenth-century outbreak only after the devastating outbreak of 1665, which most called the Great Plague.[2] In English literature, however, "Black Death" appears first in a historical work by a Mrs. Penrose in 1823, and a decade later (1833) in B. G. Babington's translation of the German physician J. F. Hecker's *Der Schwarze Tod* (*The Black Death*; 1832).[3] Common use of the term is thus fairly recent. In medieval sources the epidemic is called many things: pest, pestilence, sudden death, *epidemia*, malady, great death, or mortality, and usually with "the" in front of it. Many were the metaphors it spawned: among Muslims, for example, it was the cup of poison, an invading army, an arrow or sword, a predatory animal, a snake, fire, or a lightning bolt.[4] The word *plague* was traditionally used for any blow or strike, and might be a disease, or a "plague of locusts," so its specific meaning must be derived from its context.

But the terrible epidemic of 1347–52 was only the first of a long series of episodes that lasted over 350 years, and "Black Death" is often a label for the disease as it recurred time and again, down to the 1720s in France, and even later in North Africa and the Near East. Medical historians often refer to this string of occurrences as the Second Pandemic. An epidemic is a single but widespread outbreak of a disease over a fairly short period of time; *pandemic* refers to an outbreak on a huge scale, either or both geographically and over time, often recurring, with a very large number of victims. The Third Pandemic began in East Asia near the end of the 1800s and was cut short by modern medical research and developments that unlocked the Plague's secrets and provided a cure.

THE PLAGUE OF JUSTINIAN (541–c. 760)

The First Pandemic refers to a series of outbreaks of what was probably bubonic plague in the Mediterranean basin, and probably western Europe, from 541 to around 760. Because it broke out while Justinian I was the Byzantine emperor, and most famously ravaged his empire, his name is often linked to the First Pandemic. Contemporary sources agree that it began in Egypt, or further south in Abyssinia or the Sudan,[5] and spread by ship to Constantinople, the Near East, Italy, and Southern France. In the seventh century it may have also appeared in England and northern Europe west of the great German forests. Contemporaries observed that earthquakes, floods, fires, comets, and eclipses had preceded it. Following classical medical authorities, especially Hippocrates and Galen, the secular-minded blamed it on "corrupted air," perhaps caused by the comets, fires, or earthquakes. According to Isidore, the scholarly bishop of Seville, the corruption was caused by excessive dryness, heat, or rain. To the religious it was punishment by God for sin, an outbreak of divine wrath like the flood of Noah's time. Bede, the famed English monk and historian, split the difference, claiming that it was a "blow sent by the Creator," "sent from Heaven," and "by divine dispensation and will," but he makes no mention of human sinfulness as a reason. He does note, however, that people apostatizing, or leaving the Christian faith, was one result of the Plague in England.[6]

The diagnosis of specifically bubonic plague is based on the repeated mention in historical sources of swellings, or "buboes," on victims' bodies. In Constantinople the court historian Procopios (540s) mentions symptoms of swellings, delirium, and coma; later in the century Evagrius, a lawyer in Antioch, lists buboes, fever, diarrhea, carbuncles, and swollen and bloody eyes.[7] Gregory, bishop of Tours in France in the century's last decades, described what he saw: "Death was very sudden. A snakelike wound appeared in the groin or armpit and the poison affected the patients in such a way that they gave up the ghost on the second or third day. Furthermore, the power of the poison robbed people of their senses."[8] Swellings in the lymph nodes of the groin, armpit, or neck are common signs of bubonic plague. In northwestern Italy, historian Paul the Deacon wrote in the late 700s, "there began to appear in the groins of men and in other delicate places, a swelling of the glands, after the manner of a nut or date, presently followed by an unbearable fever, so that upon the third day, the man died. But if anyone should pass over the third day, he had a hope of living."[9]

The death tolls were unprecedented as far as observers were concerned, and the extreme measures taken were often unsettling. Gregory continues, "[s]ince soon no coffins or biers were left, six and even more persons were buried in the same grave. One Sunday, three hundred corpses were counted in St. Peter's basilica [at Clermont, France]."[10] The effects in and around Constantinople were clearly devastating: when leaving home people wore identification tags in case they died away from friends or family; people ceased working and crops went unharvested; Justinian had mass graves dug across the Golden Horn at Galata.[11] Paul records that in Italy, "Everywhere there was grief and everywhere tears. For as common report had it that those who fled would avoid the plague, the dwellings were left deserted by their inhabitants, and the dogs alone kept house. . . . Sons fled, leaving the corpses of their parents unburied; parents forgetful of their duty abandoned their children in raging fever."[12] Procopios claimed a death toll in Constantinople of half the population, and his contemporary John of Ephesus stated that at its peak the Plague took 16,000 lives per day, for a total of 300,000 victims.[13] John's figure is an extrapolation from official corpse counters, who, he said, had stopped at 230,000.[14] Modern historians are more conservative: Naphy and Spicer accept 200,000 dead, or a toll of about 40 percent of a population of 500,000, while Bratton agrees with the 40 percent, but Bratton believes it is out of a total population of only around 290,000 people, for about 115,320 dead in Constantinople.[15]

Clearly, arriving at a total population figure, even for a single city, is largely guesswork after a point, but deriving the percentages of those who died (mortality) is even trickier. Because medieval demographic records are either lacking, incomplete, or unreliable, modern reconstructions of population figures—including total populations, births, deaths, and migration—are going to be approximations at best. Even when a writer provides what appears to be a solid number, as does John of Ephesus, one must be careful: some numbers are merely symbolic or rhetorical, meant to imply "an unbelievable number"; others are necessarily partial, and some are merely being passed along from some unknown source of unknown reliability.

People dealt with the disease as best they could: they tried to purify the "corrupted air" with fire and aromatic smoke; they prayed and held processions; they used religious and magical amulets and incantations; Christians signed crosses on their houses and other objects; and they fled to avoid the bad air. But nothing they did could stop further outbreaks, which occurred some eighteen times in the East and eleven in the West, according to a very careful count done by French Plague historian Jean-Noël Biraben.[16] It stopped, however, in the Mediterranean and Europe as suddenly as it had started, and as mysteriously. Whether its sources metaphorically dried up, or its potential victims acquired immunity, or whether something else happened to disrupt the pattern, the West would not see its like for nearly 600 years.

Overall, the political effects of the First Pandemic on the Byzantine Empire were clear and historically momentous. The drop in population, economic decline, and blow to the Byzantine military facilitated the migration of the Slavs into the lightly defended Balkans and the Germanic Lombards into Italy. It also aided the eruption of new Muslim Arab armies that swept away Byzantine control of Egypt and North Africa, Syria, Palestine, and Armenia. In western Europe, before the First Pandemic was over Muslim armies found themselves in central France, having conquered Spain and the western Mediterranean. It may not be too much to say that the First Pandemic deeply wounded Byzantium and may well have retarded the social, political, and cultural growth of western Christendom.

OTHER MEDIEVAL "PLAGUES"

In major Plague years of the First Pandemic, early medieval Iraq shared the Mediterranean world's suffering, and may have shared it with

China as well. Chinese records are problematic because their vocabulary for diseases is very limited, and narrative sources like those of John, Paul, Gregory, and Procopios are lacking or unavailable. Nonetheless, Chinese historian Dennis Twitchett has correlated a series of Iraqi and Chinese outbreaks of disease, and the result is striking. The closest pairings show Plague, or at least epidemic, years in Iraq/China as 639–40/ 641–48, 684–85/682, 706/707, 763/762, 836/840, and 872/869.[17] While no narrative sources directly link Chinese and Western outbreaks, there is a clear suggestion here that through trade and other contacts disease was being passed in both directions.

Did bubonic plague appear in the West between the Pandemics? Most modern scholars agree that what struck the West in 1347 had not been seen for centuries. On the other hand, Michael Dols, a historian of the Plague in the Islamic world, has noted five limited outbreaks that might qualify: around Rome in 1167 and again in 1230, Florence in 1244, and southern France and Spain in 1320 and 1330.[18] Russian chronicles mention nine "plague" episodes between 1158 and 1344, though nothing indicates this was bubonic. Nevertheless, the report for 1230 is quite dramatic: in Smolensk four mass graves were dug in which 32,000 bodies were interred; in Novgorod a mass grave held 6,000 corpses and an accompanying famine caused people to sell their children for food, and eat grass, cats and dogs, and each other.[19] Recurring famine also killed off an enormous number of northwestern Europeans between 1317 and 1321, setting the stage for the demographic horrors of the mid-century.[20]

THE ORIGINS, ARRIVAL, AND SPREAD OF THE BLACK DEATH

The debate over what disease or diseases constituted the Black Death is properly part of Chapter 2. Suffice it for now to say that historians have long assumed that it was bubonic plague and its close relative, pneumonic plague (the same germ, settled in the lungs). In addition, historians have long assumed that this was also the disease of the First Pandemic. If the bubonic plague did not become epidemic anywhere in Europe or the Near East between the 760s and 1347, then where did it go, and why did it return? Neither question has a simple—or agreed upon—answer.

The bacillus that causes bubonic plague in humans exists naturally among wild rodent populations and their fleas. There are natural reservoirs in places such as the American Southwest and southern Russia that harbor the disease, and occasionally we hear of a fresh case. Because these are remote places, humans and disease rarely mix. Between the 760s and mid-1300s this appears to have been true of similar places in Asia, where the bubonic plague bacillus or germ may have been enzootic among the rodent population, living with it but not destroying it. Historians hypothesize that something happened to disturb this state of equilibrium, spreading the disease east, west, and possibly south, but *from* where is by no means certain.

Medieval Asian sources dealing with bubonic plague have yet to be found, and medieval Western sources on Asiatic bubonic plague cannot be trusted. Few who wrote them had any idea of Asian geography, and their personal sources of information are usually unknown. When discussing the Plague's origins some sources clearly claim "China," Russians claimed "India," and many merely "the east"; but none disagree that the Black Sea region was the doorway from Asia into the Mediterranean and Europe. Setting the tone for modern historians, William McNeill writes that bubonic plague probably originated in reservoirs in either Yunnan/Burma or the Manchurian/Mongolian steppe region, both of which areas became directly linked to China under the Mongolian Yüan dynasty (1260–1368).[21] For others, the Gobi Desert or the foothills of the Himalayas, in Garwhal or Kumaon, served as the reservoir. John Norris argues that any evidence for Chinese origins and Chinese bubonic plague is very slim and late, and he attacks the notion that bubonic plague could have been spread clear across central Eurasia. He places the reservoir of origin in southern Russia, from which it could have spread both east and west.[22]

How it spread is also open to speculation. Whether new human activity—an army passing through, pioneer villages being built—or natural occurrences such as floods or earthquakes in the reservoirs disturbed the rodents and caused them to migrate toward human settlements, people and the disease eventually mixed, and the disease spread. Most scholars claim that the Plague had to move with merchants, armies, and officials along the Silk Road from China to the West, with rats in grain sacks or fleas in cloth or on people. For others the migration of the disease had to take place from rodent colony to rodent colony until reaching urban areas in the western steppe. Written records provide little of use here, and the only archeological evidence found to date links three Christian gravestones from 1338/9 at Issyk Kul, south of Lake Balkhash, to pestilence of some sort.[23]

Once in the Black Sea region the Plague acquired "biographers," whose record is generally reliable on the course it took. The most famous and as yet unrefuted story has a colony of Italian merchants from Genoa coming under attack from Djanibeg, warrior lord of the Kipchak Khanate, a southern Russian nomadic state. By 1345 Djanibeg's people had contracted the Plague and two years later catapulted it into the besieged Black Sea port city of Kaffa in the form of diseased corpses. Horrified Genoese took ship, taking the disease with them. Gabriele de' Mussis, an Italian notary—or legal scribe—from Piacenza is our original source for this account, which seemed much more credible when scholars still believed that he was an eyewitness.[24] But the Byzantine emperor and his historian in Constantinople also relate that it arrived from southern Russia. Ships from the Black Sea made port in Constantinople, setting off the horrors that the emperor and Gregoras record in their separate accounts (see Document 1).[25]

Once it hit the water, the epidemic could spread at the speed of a ship. From Constantinople sailors, rats, cargoes, or all three carried it out into the Mediterranean Sea. Messina, Sicily, and Alexandria, Egypt, were hit at about the same time, early fall 1347. In North Africa and the Near East it may have traveled along the coast by boat or overland with soldiers, pilgrims, or merchants; most likely by both routes. In the western Mediterranean, tales were told of Plague ships from Messina being kept from Genoa by wary authorities, but at least one found port in Marseille, France, in January 1348. An anonymous chronicler has the same ship carry the disease westward to other French and Spanish ports, but this is unlikely. Other ships did, however, introduce the disease into the Adriatic Sea early on, infecting Venice and many of her colonies.

From northeastern Italy the Plague seems to have traversed the Alps and entered Austria and central Europe. This prompted an anonymous monk of Freisach Monastery to record, "And in this year [1348] a pestilence struck that was so great and universal that it stretched from sea to sea, causing many cities, towns and other places to become almost totally desolated of human beings."[26] Europe's great waterways such as the Rhône, Loire, Rhine, and Po Rivers allowed rapid movement into her interior. Recent research on later German outbreaks, however, shows that regularly traveled overland routes were just as effective.[27] French historian and physician Jean-Noël Biraben very carefully plotted the advance of the Plague through France, and concluded that it moved at an average speed of one to four kilometers per day in 1348–49.[28]

As our map shows, the epidemic flowed inland, reaching papal Avignon in early 1348 and Paris late in the same year. From the Atlantic coast of France, much of which was held by England as a result of the ongoing Hundred Years War, the disease made it to Britain, probably landing on the south coast at or near Melcombe-regis in August. England's tight network of commercial routes facilitated its spread, estimated to have been at a rate of about one mile per day,[29] though London was not hit until early 1349, when Ireland was struck as well. Pisa, Italy, was not as careful as Genoa and became the port of entry for the Plague into north-central Italy in January or February 1348. In places such as Florence and Siena the Plague raged from spring to fall. Coastal Aragon was hit both overland from southern France and through its seaports by maritime traffic from France and the Balearic Islands. Muslim Spain suffered badly as well, prompting some to wonder whose side God was really on: Christianity's or Islam's.

The year 1349 saw the Plague strike into Germany from the Rhineland and along the North Sea coast. Denmark, Sweden, Norway, and Prussia were visited late in the year, and the Baltic region's ports and rivers late the following spring. The year 1350 saw Europe's northwestern fringe depopulated: Scotland, the Orkneys, Shetland, and the Faeroes; Greenland was abandoned by its Danish and Norse colonists in 1350. For some reason, Russia was spared until 1349 and beyond, indicating that the Plague did not move northward along the region's river routes, but came eastward from Germany and eastern Europe. Polotsk, Pskov, Novgorod, Smolensk, and eventually Moscow—in 1353—tasted the bitter pill. The *Nikonian Chronicle* blames people's sins for God's anger and notes that many men in Pskov—where the Black Death was called the *mor zol*, or "evil plague"—fled to monasteries to pray for forgiveness and wait for death. Others gave away all they had to the Church in hopes of making things right with God. In Moscow the Metropolitan bishop died, as did Grand Prince Semen Ivanovich, two of his sons and heirs, and his brother, Andrei.[30]

From Greenland to Moscow, from the Norwegian fjords to Iraq's deserts, one of every three people died: suddenly, agonizingly, horrifically, and for reasons common people could hardly understand (and which, when formulated, were invariably incorrect). Saints and sinners, infants and the aged, Christians, Jews, and Muslims, rich and poor, nobles and peasants, all fell before the Great Death. Awed and terrified, the Egyptian historian al-Maqrizi wrote that the Plague "was without precedent, in the sense that it affected not only one region at the exclusion of another, but that it spread to all parts of the world, through the orient as well as the West, to the North as well as the South. Moreover, it engulfed not only all mankind but also the fishes in the sea, birds in the sky and wild beasts."[31]

But King Death had just mounted the throne. A boy born in Tuscany in the 1330s, such as Francesco Datini (see biography), could live to old age and witness five, maybe six more outbreaks. The great poet Francesco Petrarch (see biography) wrote in 1367 to his friend Guido da Sette, the bishop of Genoa,

> Plagues had been heard and read of in books, but no universal plague that would empty the world had ever been seen or heard of; this one has been invading all lands now for 20 years: sometimes it stops in some places, or lessens, but it is never really gone. Just when it seems to be over it returns and attacks once more those who were briefly happy. And this pattern, if I am not mistaken, is a sign of the divine anger at human crimes. If those crimes were to end, the divine punishments would grow less or milder.[32]

Historians agree that between 1353 and 1500 about eighteen major epidemics struck Europe on a broad geographic scale. Russia endured an outbreak about once every five or six years.[33] Dols counts fifty-eight Plague years out of 174 Islamic years from 1348 to 1517 in Egypt and Syria, for an average of once every five and a half years.[34] (Muslims use a lunar calendar and thus have a shorter year than the Common 365¼ days.) In western European cities the Plague was reported on average every six to twelve years, or two to four times a generation, down to about 1480, and every fifteen to twenty years thereafter.[35] But not all plagues were created equal. Papal physician Raymundus Chalmelli de Vivario reported that "In 1348, two thirds of the population were afflicted, and almost all died; in 1361 half contracted the disease, and very few survived; in 1371 only one-tenth were sick, and many survived; in 1382, only one-twentieth became sick, and almost all survived."[36] The picture was not really this rosy, but his point is important: over time, fewer fell ill and many fewer—in both percentage and absolute terms— died in a given episode. Why this might have been the case is unclear, but it warrants attention. Even if relatively lighter, however, these re- currences seem to have kept the overall population size depressed over much of the remaining medieval period.

IN THE WAKE OF THE BLACK DEATH

Chapter 4 of this book outlines what scholars believe to be the major demographic, economic, and political effects of the Black Death in Eu- rope, down to about 1500. Death on the scale that the Plague pre- sented—perhaps a third of the entire population—destroyed a good deal of the European human resource base. Knowledge, skills, experience, relationships, and raw person-power were all lost at a throw, in many ways crippling a generation and more. Despite some official efforts to increase birthrates, Europe did not achieve the earlier national levels of population for a century and a half. Some villages disappeared, some cities never recovered. Yet in general, with the fall in population, the average person had more goods, property, and money and, given the shortage of labor, could demand high wages to get even more. English historians have linked the Black Death to the final gasps of feudalism, to rationalization of markets, to increasing criticism of the Church and government, and even to changes in the roles of women in the work force. Recent scholarship continues to question older assumptions and conclusions and to create a more finely grained picture of the period and the changes it underwent. The better we understand the real effects of the Plague, the better we can understand people's responses to it; an ongoing process, to be sure.

People's reactions to the first and subsequent outbreaks of the Black Death varied widely, and many types of evidence remain to help us understand these reactions. Several factors could affect an individual's responses, including where a person lived; how well educated, deeply religious, wealthy, or mobile one was; and whether he or she lost close friends or relatives, trusted the Church or doctors, or was affected eco- nomically or socially by the epidemic. Many responded by doing something, such as praying, fleeing, helping the sick, following doctors' advice, joining processions or cults, or lashing out at scapegoats such as Jews, foreigners, or beggars. Government documents outline official responses to the need for new burial grounds, for tax relief, and for protection of orphans, as well as attempts to avoid the Plague. Medical books provided explanations, advice, cures, and hope. Official records of court cases display the range of criminal activity the Plague unleashed, from robbery and assault to fraud and the stealing of inheritances. Some, who were literate, recorded their reactions and chronicled the events around them in journals, diaries, letters, and family or community histories. These are filled with observations, anecdotes, and expressions of anxieties, disbelief, and vain attempts to make sense of the omnipresence of suffering and death. Fears, faith, hopes, and resignation were set down in last wills; poets captured their own feelings of sorrow, anger, revulsion, and even penitence in their verses. We have paintings, drawings, and sculptures that reflect the raw realities of human mortality and death in the streets, as well as the believer's prayers and thanks for protection or healing. These survive not only from the mid-fourteenth century, but also from the remainder of the Middle Ages and beyond, as generation after generation coped with the fears and the horrors the Plague brought.

Chapter 5 of this book is concerned with how the Black Death affected social and psychological patterns of life over the course of the late Middle Ages. Chapter 6 focuses on art and ritual as cultural expressions that reflect the impact of the era's uncertainty. In Chapter 7 Florence, Italy, and Cairo, Egypt, undergo scrutiny as urban centers— one European and Christian, one African and Muslim—whose responses on all levels will provide a case study in cross-cultural responses. Finally, Chapter 8 outlines modern theories of why the Plague disappeared from Europe, and why modern society is still so intrigued with the Black Death.

NOTES

1. Jón Steffensen, "Plague in Iceland," *Nordisk medicinhistorisk årsbok* (1974): pp. 41–42.

2. Tom B. James, *The Black Death in Hampshire* (Winchester, England: Hampshire County Council, 1999), p. 1.

3. J. F. Shrewsbury, *History of Bubonic Plague in the British Isles* (New York: Cambridge University Press, 1970), p. 37.

4. Michael Dols, *The Black Death in the Middle East* (Princeton: Princeton University Press, 1977), p. 236, n. 2.

5. Christopher Wills, *Plagues: Their Origin, History, and Future* (London: HarperCollins, 1996), pp. 57–58.

6. John R. Maddicott, "Plague in Seventh-century England," *Past and Present* no. 156 (1997): pp. 18, 37.

7. Pauline Allen, "The Justinianic Plague," *Byzantion* 49 (1979): p. 7.

8. Quoted in Jean-Noël Biraben and Jacques LeGoff, "The Plague in the Early Middle Ages," in *The Biology of Man in History*, ed. and trans. Elborg Forster and P. M. Ranum (Baltimore: Johns Hopkins University Press, 1975), p. 57.

9. Paul the Deacon, *History of the Lombards*, trans. W. D. Foulke (Philadelphia: University of Pennsylvania Press, 1974), p. 57.

10. Biraben and LeGoff, "Plague," p. 57.

11. Allen, "Justinianic Plague," p. 12.

12. Paul the Deacon, *History*, p. 57.

13. T. L. Bratton, "The Identity of the Plague of Justinian," *Transactions and Studies of the College of Physicians of Philadelphia* (1981): p. 174.

14. Allen, "Justinianic Plague," p. 10.

15. William G. Naphy and Andrew Spicer, *The Black Death* (Charleston: Tempus, 2001), p. 22; Bratton, "Identity," p. 178.

16. Jean-Noël Biraben, "Les routes maritimes des grandes épidémies au moyen âge," in *L'Homme, la santé et la mer*, ed. Christian Buchet (Paris: Champion, 1997), p. 23.

17. Dennis Twitchett, "Population and Pestilence in T'ang China," in *Studia Sino-Mongolica* (Wiesbaden: Franz Steiner Verlag, 1979), p. 59.

18. Dols, *Black Death*, pp. 31–32 n. 57.

19. Lawrence N. Langer, "The Black Death in Russia," *Russian History/Histoire Russe* 2 (1975): pp. 54–55.

20. In general see William C. Jordan, *The Great Famine: Northern Europe in the Early Fourteenth Century* (Princeton: Princeton University Press, 1996).

21. William H. McNeill, *Plagues and Peoples* (Garden City, NY: Anchor Press, 1975), p. 145.

22. See John Norris, "East or West? The Geographic Origin of the Black Death," *Bulletin of the History of Medicine* 51 (1977): pp. 1–24.

23. See T. W. Thacker, "A Nestorian Gravestone from Central Asia in the Gulbenkian Museum, Durham University," *Durham University Journal* 59

(1967): pp. 94–107; David Herlihy, *The Black Death and the Transformation of the West* (Cambridge, MA: Harvard University Press, 1997), p. 23; Naphy and Spicer, *Black Death*, p. 31.

24. For his account in translation see Rosemary Horrox, *The Black Death* (New York: Manchester University Press, 1994), pp. 14–26. That he was not an eyewitness was proven through a study of his record books for the period which show him remaining in Italy.

25. Christos Bartsocas, "Two Fourteenth Century Greek Descriptions of the 'Black Death,' " *Journal of the History of Medicine* 21 (1966): pp. 394–400.

26. Quoted in Samuel K. Cohn, Jr., *The Black Death Transformed: Disease and Culture in Early Renaissance Europe* (Oxford: Oxford University Press, 2002), p. 100.

27. Edward Eckert, *Structure of Plague and Pestilence in Early Modern Europe* (New York: Karger, 1996), passim.

28. Jean-Noël Biraben, *Les hommes et la peste en France et dans les pays européens et méditeranéens* vol. 1 (Paris: Mouton, 1975), p. 90. Biraben is the most complete and most widely accepted source on the Plague's spread in Europe in any language; on Islamic areas see Dols. Both, however, have been updated by publications on specific areas since the mid-1970s.

29. Graham Twigg, "The Black Death in England: An Epidemiological Dilemma," in *Maladies et société (XIIe–XVIIIe siècles), Actes du Colloque de Bielefeld, novembre 1986,* ed. Neithard Bulst and Robert Delort (Paris: Editions du C.N.R.S., 1989), p. 77.

30. Langer, "Black Death in Russia," pp. 55–56; see also Serge A. Zenkovsky, *The Nikonian Chronicle* vols. 4 and 5 (Princeton: The Darwin Press, 1989), passim.

31. Quoted in Cohn, *Black Death*, p. 100.

32. From his "Letters of Old Age," X, 2, quoted in Renee Neu Watkins, "Petrarch and the Black Death," *Studies in the Renaissance* 19 (1972): p. 218.

33. Langer, "Black Death in Russia," pp. 61–62.

34. Dols, *Black Death*, p. 223.

35. Naphy and Spicer, *Black Death*, p. 81.

36. Quoted in Cohn, *Black Death*, p. 191.

CHAPTER 2

THE BLACK DEATH AND MODERN MEDICINE

According to most modern scientists and historians, the Black Death was bubonic plague and its variations, pneumonic and septicemic plague (settled in the lungs or blood, respectively). Since the last decades of the twentieth century, however, this conclusion has been challenged by historians and scientists alike. In broad terms, there are now three models of what caused the Black Death.

The Black Death was the bubonic plague. In the late 1890s and early twentieth century, scientists unraveled the secrets of the cause and nature of bubonic plague as it raged in Asia during the Third Pandemic. They concluded that what they were witnessing and studying was the same disease that they knew as the Black Death, which had disappeared from Europe 180 years earlier. The swellings, or buboes, in the human lymph nodes gave it away, as did the swiftness of death. As researchers linked the buboes to the germ and the germ to the rat and the rat to the flea and the germ to the flea to the human victim, the picture seemed even clearer. Certainly medieval people lived in primitive conditions, if not squalor, not unlike the Indians, Chinese, and Vietnamese natives they were treating. Rats and fleas must have been very common, merely background noise that never made it into the medieval chronicles or medical works, and germs were fairly recent discoveries, invisible to the medieval eye. The medieval folk blamed God and planets and bad air, and sometimes Jews, but never the rats or fleas or germs. Modern students of the Black Death read every medieval account of its origins, movement, duration, symptoms, and death tolls through the lens of this new paradigm: bubonic plague as experienced in the twentieth century.

The Black Death certainly was not the bubonic plague. Since about 1980, however, more and more studies have discussed the bubonic plague and its characteristics in order to demonstrate how and why the Black Death does not resemble the Third Pandemic. Such researchers, including historians and scientists, no longer use the modern bubonic plague as a lens through which to interpret the historical record, and instead set the modern picture of the Plague beside the medieval one and compare them carefully. These people find far too many disturbing differences, and seek an alternative explanation of the Black Death. If the resemblance is so dim, then either bubonic plague has changed radically or some other disease or diseases have to account for the death tolls.

The Black Death was the bubonic plague plus some variety of other diseases. Something of a middle position has emerged in this debate, one also based upon the medieval record. Quite simply, bubonic plague played its role, but so did any number of other diseases. Distinguishing pneumonic and septicemic forms of rat-borne plague, caused by the same germ but without the buboes, was the first step. We are now well up the staircase, as the list of alternatives continues to lengthen.

THE BUBONIC PLAGUE

In the 1830s the German physician J. F. Hecker wrote that the Black Death was caused by poisoned air released by earthquakes. Over the next sixty years people such as Louis Pasteur and Robert Koch developed germ theory, and germs replaced poison as the cause of the pestilence. In 1891 English medical historian Charles Creighton attributed the Plague to a "typhus of the soil" that was more malignant than other types "just because of underground fermentation of the putrescible animal matters"; it was "a leaven which had passed into the ground, spreading hither and thither therein as if by polarizing the adjacent particles of the soil."[1] Three years later, when bubonic plague broke out in Hong Kong, eastern China, and Viet Nam, French, English, and Japanese scientists quickly began correcting the picture again. Working independently in Hong Kong, the Swiss-born student of Pasteur, Alexandre Yersin (see biography), and Koch's best Japanese student, Shibasaburo Kitasato, isolated the specific bacillus (germ) responsible for the Plague, which came to be named *Pasteurella pestis*. In 1971, in part to honor Yersin, the scientific community renamed it *Yersinia pestis*, or simply *Y. pestis*. Yersin and others quickly developed successful serums for treating victims. Between 1896 and 1905 Masanori Ogata and Paul Simond, laboring in Taiwan and Bombay, India, respectively, made the connection of the bacillus to the rat, *Rattus rattus* (*R. rattus*), and one of its fleas, *Xenopsylla cheopis* (*X. cheopis*). Simond discovered the flea's role as "inoculator" of the bacillus into people in 1898. Experiments in British India in 1908 confirmed the rat's role, and research published in 1914 by A. W. Bacot and C. J. Martin outlined how the flea contracted the bacillus and passed it on to people.[2] Despite this new knowledge and the development of serums to fight the disease, this Third Pandemic claimed 50,000 victims in Manchuria in 1910–11 and more than twelve million in India from 1898 to 1948.[3]

Around 1925 Ricardo Jorge introduced the idea that rat or rodent populations that were selvatic, or living isolated in the wild, could host the fleas and bacillus in an enzootic fashion, all three living underground in relative harmony, undisturbed by people.[4] In such a permanent "reservoir" or "focus" either the rats had natural immunity or strong resistance to the effects of the bacillus, or the amount of the microorganism was too small to harm the animals. Such foci continue to exist, usually involving rodents such as prairie dogs and squirrels, in places such as the American Southwest. Between 1947 and 1996 there were 390 cases of bubonic plague reported in the United States.[5]

It is generally accepted that the black or house rat, *Rattus rattus*, of which the flea *X. cheopis* is very fond, was the rodent-culprit in the Second Pandemic. Its strong tendency is to live among people, nesting in high places such as rafters—especially in houses with thatched roofs—and inside walls and other sheltered areas. They reproduce throughout the year, with females bearing between twenty and thirty pups per year. These rats are commensal rather than selvatic: they "share the table" with people, so to speak. They are territorial and not prone to move very far at all. A 1951 study showed that most never venture farther than fifty yards from their nest.[6] To cover large distances, they need to be carried, unwittingly, one would presume. Because they feed predominantly on grain, the standard model of medieval pestilence has them moving in and with grain shipments by boat or cart or even saddlebag. But how do commensal rats contract a disease of selvatic rodents? This is purely a matter of speculation. People and their rat companions may move into a selvatic plague focus, and commensal rats and selvatic rodents intermingle and exchange fleas. Conversely, displaced diseased selvatic rodents may migrate to an area near human habitations, mixing with the local rodent population.

The disease-carrying fleas bite and suck blood from the commensal rats, passing the bacillus along. The commensal rats, having no natural immunity or resistance to the bacillus, grow ill and die. As the body of the dead rat cools, its fleas seek a live host on which to feed. A healthy rat will have around seven fleas in its coat, but as it weakens with the sickness and stops grooming itself, the number can rise to between fifty and one hundred.[7] Scientists have identified about thirty species of flea as potential carriers, or vectors, of the disease. The most efficient and effective is the *Xenopsylla cheopis*, a wingless parasite that ranges from 1.5 to 4 millimeters in length and lives no longer than a year. When the weather turns frosty, *X. cheopis* hibernates. Reproduction takes place only in moderate to warm weather. Flea eggs fall to the floor of the nest, or to the ground, and young fleas feed on organic bits. Older fleas can also live away from a blood host for up to eighty days, sustaining themselves on organic matter such as grain dust.[8] Some scholars, however, have concluded that the human flea, *Pulex irritans* (*P. irritans*), was the main culprit. This removes the need for rats and a serious outbreak of plague among them. This type of flea, however, is universally considered a poor transmitter of the bacillus: as medical researcher Thomas Butler wrote, "*P. irritans* is not an efficient vector and rarely, if ever, has transmitted plague from man to man."[9]

X. cheopis displays an important characteristic known as "blocking." Unlike other rat fleas or *P. irritans*, *X. cheopis* has a fore-stomach, or proventriculus, in which the bacilli from the infected rat's blood collect and multiply. This essentially blocks the flea's digestive tract, making it impossible for its stomach to receive new food. Such fleas, perhaps 12 percent of those feeding on infected blood, become exceptionally hungry and will bite a host many times, or move from host to host trying to feed successfully. Some blood will enter the flea's esophagus and mix with the infected mass in the proventriculus. This mix—containing from 11,000 to 24,000 bacillus cells—is then spat back into the host, infecting him or her.[10] A blocked flea can live up to six weeks, but remains infectious for only about two weeks on average.[11] Though fleas prefer rats, they will hop onto people if enough of their animal hosts are dead. Even if there is no blocking, an infected flea's excrement can contain the bacillus. If left on the skin, this can enter a person's body if the skin is torn by scratching. In feces the bacillus can live up to five weeks. An intense case of disease among animals—in this case the rats—is called an epizootic, and is generally accepted as necessary before bubonic plague can break out among people on a large scale.

Yersinia pestis is an oval-shaped bacillus-type bacterium that does not move under its own power (nonmotile). There are three recognized types or biovars of *Y. pestis*: *antiqua*, found in Africa; *mediaevalia*, found in central Asia, and *orientalis*, found in east Asia and elsewhere in the world. Its optimum growing temperature is 20 to 25°C, typically found inside the *X. cheopis* flea, but it becomes far more active and virulent at higher temperatures, as in rat or human internal organs. It can enter an animal or person through damaged or perforated skin, or through a mucous membrane, as in the eye, mouth, or nose. The bacillus can remain alive inside a host or even suitable soil for years. This is the case in large part because it can encase itself in a gel-like capsule that protects it from the environment, including the human body's normal defenses called phagocytes ("cell-eaters"). It moves through the body, but it does not invade cells as other bacilli or viruses do. It reproduces, however, in the body at a rate that doubles its numbers every two hours, and so the problem for the human, as for the flea, is the effect of huge numbers of these microorganisms: "it is the sheer numbers of these bacteria that kill their hosts, by inducing toxic shock syndrome."[12]

At the site of the bite, cells die (necrosis), the skin turns dark, and a small bump or pustule develops. The body cannot effectively kill off the invading bacilli, but its lymphatic system ushers them and other debris to the nearest lymph node, where normally an antibody would be developed to fight the intruder. Here, however, the bacilli overwhelm the node through their unhampered reproduction. Phagocytes continue to die off as the encapsulated bacilli that are "swallowed" actually use their organic material to reproduce. The dead cellular material and, as Yersin found, the hordes of bacilli, collect in these nodes and create the characteristic swellings or "buboes" in the groin and armpits and behind the ear. These appear four to six days after the initial infection and can be very hard and very uncomfortable as the tissue around them grows very tender. If the lymphatic system drains the bacilli and other material to an interior lymph node, there may appear to be no bubo, nor is external swelling apparent when the bacilli multiply very rapidly in the bloodstream, creating a type of bubonic plague known as septicemic.

This causes a collapse of the circulatory system, hemorrhaging, and direct damage to the heart, lungs, and kidneys. This happens in a few percent of cases, and is virtually always fatal.

In about 5 to 15 percent of modern cases of bubonic plague, the bacilli overwhelm the lungs in a form of the disease known as pulmonary or pneumonic plague. Death is so swift that buboes generally have no time to form. There are two ways to contract pneumonic plague: one is through a flea bite whose bacilli travel rapidly to the lungs, and the other is by breathing in the bacillus directly from the air. The first type is called secondary pneumonic plague and clearly requires at least fleas, if not rats and fleas. The second type is called primary pneumonic plague and is spread from one person to another, as an infected person sprays bacilli encased in water droplets into the air around him or her. Normal speech sprays these about two yards out; sneezing or coughing extends this range to three or four yards. These droplets do not remain in the air indefinitely; if the air temperature is cold enough it can freeze and preserve them. New victims may inhale these infected droplets, or the droplets may land on mucous membranes and enter the body. In the lungs the *Y. pestis* bacilli collect in abscesses or pockets that easily burst, spewing the bacilli around inside, depositing blood in the lungs, and creating open sores and further points of infection. Victims naturally cough this material up and spit it out as long as they are able. High fever, delirium, and asphyxia result as the lungs fail to take in enough oxygen, and the bacilli may spread to other parts of the body. From the point of infection victims live about five days; from the onset of obvious symptoms, perhaps a day or two.[13] Biologist Chester Rail states that pneumonic plague is "considered the deadliest bacterial disease known to mankind" with a death rate near 100 percent in modern times.[14] Studies of modern pneumonic plague, however, seem to indicate that it is not terribly contagious: people who shared rail cars with victims did not even contract it. In addition, outbreaks recognized as pneumonic plague have been geographically very restricted: presumably, those who have it are bedridden so soon that the bacilli do not travel far.[15]

Are certain people more susceptible to bubonic plague than others? Though some have reservations, modern students generally agree: "True bubonic plague tends to affect all members of a population equally ... if all are equally likely to be infected." Mary Matossian, however, suggests that poisonous microfungi, known as mycotoxins, that grow on most types of grain, especially under very damp conditions, may well have been ingested by rats or people over large parts of the West. Many of these mycotoxins suppress the immune system, and they may have made many more susceptible to bubonic plague and the death tolls higher.[16]

WAS THE SECOND PANDEMIC BUBONIC PLAGUE?

Unless Y. *pestis* changed radically between the Second and Third Pandemics, the essential epidemiology of the two outbreaks of the disease should be very similar if the Black Death was indeed bubonic plague. The information that survives about the medieval Plague is far more limited and far less informed than what researchers have developed during the modern era. Apart from some archeological evidence, all that survive are written descriptions of the Plague and its effects and some pictorial evidence of symptoms. From these can be drawn a reasonable picture of the various symptoms that people noticed, their observations on whether and how it spread within a community, while evidence from diaries, chronicles, and official records shows how quickly it moved from one locale to another and how long it persisted locally. Insofar as this picture matches the modern pattern of these same matters, the medieval outbreaks can be confidently labeled bubonic plague. Insofar as they differ, other diseases—or a very different strain of Y. *pestis*—were at work.

It is said the disease takes three forms. In the first people suffer an infection of the lungs, which leads to breathing difficulties. Whoever has this corruption or contamination to any extent cannot escape but will die within two days. . . . There is another form which exists alongside the first one in which boils erupt suddenly in the armpits, and men are killed by these without delay. And there is also a third form, which again co-exists with the other two, but takes its own course, and in this people of both sexes are attacked in the groin and killed suddenly.

(Louis Heyligen, priest visiting Avignon, 1348)

They felt a tingling sensation, as if they were being pricked by the points of arrows. The next stage was a fearsome attack which took the form of an extremely hard, solid boil. In some people this developed under the armpit and in others in the groin between the scrotum and the body. As it grew more solid, its burning heat caused the patients to fall into an acute and putrid fever, with severe headaches. In some cases it gave rise to an intolerable stench. In others it brought vomiting of blood, or swellings from near the place from which the corrupt humor arose . . . the majority [died] between the third and fifth day.

(Gabriele de' Mussis, notary of Piacenza, Italy, 1348)

Most who fell ill lasted little more than two or three days, but died suddenly, as if in the midst of health—for someone who was healthy one day could be dead and buried the next. Lumps suddenly erupted in their armpits or groin, and their appearance was an infallible sign of death.

(Jean de Venette, Carmelite friar, Paris, c. 1360)

First of all it would hit one as if with a lance, choking, and then swelling would appear, or spitting of blood with shivering, and fire would burn one in all the joints of the body; and then the illness would overwhelm one; and many after lying in that illness died.

(*Novgorod Chronicle*, Russia, 1417)

The disease was such that men did not live for more than a day or two with sharp pangs of pain, then they began to vomit blood, and then they expired.

(*Lawman's Annal*, Iceland, early 1400s)

At God's command, moreover, the damage was done by an extraordinary and novel form of death. Those who fell sick of a kind of gross swelling of the flesh lasted for barely two days.

(John of Fordun, monk of Aberdeen, Scotland,
between 1350 and 1383)

At the start, the disease settles in the groin, a symptom that appears more or less clearly.[17]

(Critoboulos, chronicler, Constantinople, 1467)

"Ulcers broke out in the groin and the armpit, which tortured the dying for three days," wrote the monk John of Reading in the 1360s. Physicians Meister Bernhard of Frankfurt and Johannes of Tornamira both wrote that the buboes distinguished the pestilence from all other fevers.[18]

Mirko Grmek writes that chroniclers from Dalmatia (along coastal Croatia) described the symptoms of the pest as setting in quickly and including high and continuous fever, buboes, terrible headaches, delirium, spitting up of blood, and rapid and frequent death. He also says that the chroniclers distinguished between bubonic and pneumonic plague.[19]

Most writers were not physicians, but monks and priests and lawyers; their descriptions were not clinical, but part of their narratives. Even so, they do seem to be describing a disease whose symptoms match bubonic plague in most if not all particulars. Admittedly other accounts list different visible marks, such as scabs, small pustules, rashes, blisters, blotches, or carbuncles. These may have been preexisting or the result of necrosis, scratching, or infection at the flea-bite site. The claim that the Second Pandemic was in fact bubonic plague seems well founded on the symptoms as listed by chroniclers of the Black Death. Historical demographer Ole Benedictow writes, "These clinical and demographic descriptions of the Great Pestilence correspond closely to modern medical descriptions of plague."[20] Proponents also point out that pictorial images of Plague victims usually show them with arms outstretched and legs apart, positions that would relieve additional pressure on swollen groins and armpits.

In the pages of several issues of the British medical journal *Lancet: Infectious Diseases* in 2002 and 2003, scientists argued over whether the Black Death was bubonic plague. By then the debate was a quarter of a century old. Among those who think it was not bubonic plague are the historians Koenraad Bleukx and Samuel Cohn, anthropologist James Wood, and the scientists Graham Twigg, Susan Scott, and Christopher Duncan. Bleukx, Twigg, and Scott and Duncan all write about England, Cohn and Wood more broadly: "Both clinical pathological and historical facts simply do not square with the [bubonic] plague syndrome" (Bleukx). "It is a biological impossibility that bubonic plague had any role in the Great Pestilence" (Scott and Duncan; they go on to list twenty distinct differences). It "was any disease other than the rat-based bubonic plague" (Cohn).[21] From the works of these and other scholars emerge seven main lines of criticism.

First, these critics agree that the medieval descriptions of symptoms do not necessarily add up to bubonic plague. Bleukx suggests that typhus, cholera, smallpox, and anthrax could all fit the same basic profile. Cohn claims that scrub typhus, filarial orchitis, relapsing fever, malaria, typhoid, and glandular fever all can produce buboes. Medical researcher Stephen Ell lists eighteen diseases that he says can mimic bubonic plague's symptoms, and he reminds his readers that only careful clinical descriptions can be the basis of a sound diagnosis. Another medical researcher, Thomas Butler, mentions that tularemia is characterized by fever and buboes and that staphylococcus aureus, streptococcus pyrogenes, infectious mononucleosis, and some venereal diseases can also cause intense lymphatic swelling.[22] Biologist Twigg finds anthrax to be a good fit. On the other hand, Ann Carmichael, who holds doctorates in both medicine and history, counters that "there is no other disease [than bubonic plague] that characteristically produces acute enlargement of the regional lymph nodes, visible in the groin, under the arms, in the neck or behind the ears." Nonetheless, she wrote a decade earlier, "It seems more reasonable to consider the full range of probable infections than to search for a possible explanation which would preserve a retrospective diagnosis of plague."[23]

Second, the Black Death seems to have been far more contagious than the Third Pandemic's bubonic plague. Even at the height of modern outbreaks, the rates of infection in a locale are far below the numbers reported during the era of the Black Death. Twigg points out the discrepancy between estimated medieval mortality rates of 20 to 50 percent and modern "overall mortality rates of under 1 percent."[24] Even allowing for medieval exaggeration, to such critics the numbers seem all out of proportion.

Third, movement of the medieval pestilence from one locale to another seems far too swift. Anthropologist Wood summed it up: "This disease appears to spread too rapidly among humans to be something that first must be established in wild rodent populations, like bubonic plague," and he added, "it was clearly spread by person-to-person transmission." J. F. Shrewsbury, who accepted bubonic plague as the Black Death, nonetheless argued that population densities of both humans and rats in England were far too low for spread of the disease to have been as fast or thorough as described and the human infection rate as high as reported.[25] Few scholars accept that the movement of rats or other rodents across the countryside could have occurred at speeds necessary to account for the spread. Could infected people have brought the fleas from one village or city to the next before the symptoms set in? Could enough diseased rats and fleas have been transported across Europe,

North Africa, and the Near East to account for this rapidity? Critics doubt it.

Fourth, were enough commensal rats present in any one area to sustain the necessary epizootic? Critics point to the need for rats and fleas to produce bubonic plague, including septicemic and secondary pneumonic. But they also point to the lack of any evidence of large rat populations, especially in far northern Europe, and to the utter lack of any evidence—written or archeological—of large-scale rat die-offs in any part of the Western world. As rat expert David Davis points out, there has always been the assumption that the rat played its role in the Plague, but it remains just that: an assumption. He also points out, however, that in modern India only 20 percent of local outbreaks were accompanied by obvious mortality among *R. rattus*.[26]

Fifth, medieval evidence points to year-round occurrence of the Plague, whereas rat fleas hibernate when the temperature drops. One should expect Plague-free winters in much of Europe, with perhaps some evidence of pneumonic plague, and resurgence during later spring and summer. Yet winter outbreaks were common. Davis goes so far as to assert that "[m]ost cases during the Black Death were of pneumonic plague and its spread was rapid." He also claims that buboes can occur with pneumonic plague, and that pneumonic plague does not require rats. Few agree with him, however. Shrewsbury points out that rats are necessary to sustain an epidemic of pneumonic plague; Twigg states that pneumonic plague does not normally produce buboes: it moves too quickly through the body. Benedictow cites modern figures that show the low rates of death from pneumonic plague: in Manchuria in 1910–11 only 0.4 percent of the population in the affected area died.[27] But should wintertime plague be necessarily labeled "pneumonic"? Would not human or rat body heat be enough to keep fleas active? Might not fires and wool or fur clothing and bedding provide enough protection from the cold? The likelihood is that people washed and changed clothes even less often during cold weather, thus disturbing the fleas even more infrequently, perhaps helping sustain the Plague.

Sixth, modern bubonic plague outbreaks last locally for years, becoming enzootic, but the Black Death swept through areas far more rapidly, usually lasting four to nine months, and then disappearing with no cases of pestilence for several years.

Seventh, critics point out that over time the lethality of the medieval pestilence dropped for no clear reason linked to modern understanding of bubonic plague. Unlike modern medicine, medieval medicine did nothing effective to prevent or cure cases of bubonic plague. A logical reply is that people became immune or resistant to bubonic plague by previous exposure in nonlethal doses: the body was able to develop the antibodies necessary to fight off the bacillus. Ell claims "survivors of plague infection have a potent immunity," but Biraben, Carmichael, and Benedictow disagree, or at least they would qualify the claim by saying that immunity is short-lived: depending on the individual "from some months to several years." Cohn flatly denies the possibility, stating that modern "human hosts have no natural or acquired immunity."[28] Ell, however, also states that typhus and at least one form of leprosy confer immunity to bubonic plague, as do various species of salmonella, a cause of food poisoning that, he notes, "may safely be assumed to have been ubiquitous" in medieval Europe. An earlier outbreak of typhus may have immunized many Milanese in 1348, for indeed the city of Milan was barely touched by the pestilence.[29] Critics of "Black Death as bubonic plague," however, dismiss any notion of large-scale immunization. They also traditionally disbelieved the idea that the bubonic plague bacillus mutated on a huge scale, so that its lethality and virulence would have dropped over time. The picture, however, is changing.

Completed research on and mapping of the Y. *pestis* genome sequence was reported in 2001 and showed that genetically it is very dynamic and fluid and subject to change. Scott and Duncan claim that only a slight mutation in Y. *pestis* can cause hypervirulence and potential epidemic by triggering the blocking mechanism in the flea's proventriculus. They echo microbiologist Richard Lenski, who points out that high virulence kills off hosts, which can thus isolate the mutation. Virulence thus drops as the number of potential hosts drops. Less virulent forms are favored naturally, since they do not kill off their host population to the same degree. This might explain why recurrences of the pestilence tended to have lower mortality rates than the first outbreak. Scott and Duncan do not believe that any plague caused by Y. *pestis* appeared in England, but they do accept its presence on the continent. In November 2000 Didier Raoult and his team of French microbiologists published their findings from a study of the tooth pulp of corpses found in a Plague cemetery in Montpellier, France. One child's tooth and nineteen of nineteen adult teeth from three victims showed the presence of Y. *pestis*. For many this is definitive evidence, but for James Wood the study's value is very limited until it is replicated by other researchers.[30]

To historian Samuel Cohn the evidence against bubonic plague as the cause of the Black Death is so strong that it amounts to "the end of a paradigm." To summarize, those who agree base their case on seven main points: the medieval descriptions of the pestilence may be of something other than bubonic plague; the Black Death spread far more rapidly both locally and across the countryside than did modern bubonic plague; there is too little evidence of the presence of the necessary rats in medieval Europe, and no evidence of epizootic die-offs; the presence of pestilence in wintertime suggests a disease or diseases other than bubonic plague; medieval pestilence moved through an area far too quickly to be rat-borne bubonic plague; for no reason directly connected to known characteristics of Y. *pestis* the cause of the pestilence became less virulent over time and across large distances.

COULD THE BLACK DEATH HAVE BEEN PLAGUE PLUS . . . ?

In 1922 W. Rees, an English medical researcher, wrote, "The plague of 1348 . . . is usually regarded as the bubonic plague in a particularly virulent form, but this hardly explains all the symptoms as may be gathered from the accounts of experienced observers." He went on to suggest "that there was more than one disease raging at the time." Scott and Duncan, also with reference to the pestilence in England, contradicted him in 2001: "nor is there any evidence to suggest that more than one lethal disease was raging during the Black Death."[31] Many modern scholars, however, accept that the lethality of the Black Death stemmed from the combination of bubonic and pneumonic plague with other diseases, and warn that every historical mention of "pest" was not necessarily bubonic plague. For Shrewsbury, summer deaths were from bubonic plague, but winter deaths were due to typhus, smallpox, or respiratory infections. Twigg believes that even summer mortalities were a mix of bubonic plague and other insect-borne and intestinal diseases. In her study of fifteenth-century outbreaks, Ann Carmichael states that worms, the pox, fevers, and dysentery clearly accompanied bubonic plague.[32] While this middle position between "Y. *pestis*-caused plague" and "not Y. *pestis*-caused plague" does not address all of the critics' issues, it does provide a sounder basis for discussion of the Black Death, if only because of its implied complexity.

Nonetheless, Scott and Duncan contend there was no medieval bubonic plague in England. They concede that there may have been simultaneous bubonic plague in the Mediterranean and elsewhere. They are convinced, however, that in England it was a viral (rather than bacterial) agent that caused an as-yet unidentified hemorrhagic fever, not unlike Ebola, which was the English Black Death. Infection would have been person-to-person, and people could be carriers—having and passing on the virus—for a long period before the symptoms hit. No rats, no fleas, no problems with seasons, and, at least theoretically, the symptoms fit. In fact, medieval English sources tend to be rather vague on specific symptoms.

Exposure to the hypothetical virus could have induced immunity, and the drop in lethality of the Black Death over time can be explained by a growth in resistance due to mutations in cells' CCR5 receptors. These are features of the cell that are like doorways that allow foreign microorganisms to get inside the cell. Once in, viruses use the cellular material to copy themselves. A mutation might have closed the "door" and blocked access of the virus to the interior of the cell, denying the virus the material with which to copy itself.

These scientists go further still and claim that this same hypothesized causative agent (virus) accounted for all outbreaks of the pestilence in England from 1348 to 1666.[33] This theory may also account for recently discovered natural resistance in some people to Human Immunodeficiency Virus (HIV). Molecular biologist Stephen O'Brien reported that "a historic strong selective event" created a mutation in cells that benefits about 15 percent of the modern Caucasian population. In these descendents of Europeans the CCR5 receptors on cells are different from the norm, in that they do not allow the HIV to enter the cell and begin copying itself. O'Brien's team dated the event that sparked the mutation to about "700 years ago," and thus it may well have been the Black Death and its recurrences.[34]

The fields of modern medical science and history are carefully reconsidering the cause and nature of the greatest natural catastrophe to befall humankind. Evidence ranging from a monk's scribbles to mutations of a single gene is undergoing close study, but students of bubonic plague and the Black Death are far from reaching a clear consensus. Research—and the debate—will continue.

NOTES

1. Charles Creighton, *A History of Epidemics in Britain*, 2nd ed. (London: Cass, 1965), 1: pp. 171–75.

2. L. F. Hirst, *The Conquest of Plague* (Oxford: Oxford University Press, 1953), pp. 108, 173, 185.

3. Henri H. Mollaret, "Introduzione," in *Venezia e la peste, 1348/1797* (Venice: Marsilio Editori, 1979), p. 12.

4. Jean-Noël Biraben, *Les hommes et la peste en France et dans les pays européens et méditeranéens*, Vol. 1 (Paris: Mouton, 1975), p. 16.

5. Susan Scott and Christopher Duncan, *Biology of Plagues: Evidence from Historical Populations* (New York: Cambridge University Press, 2001), p. 50.

6. David Davis, "Characteristics of Rat Populations," *Quarterly Review of Biology* 28 (1953): pp. 380, 391.

7. Ole Benedictow, *Plague in the Late Medieval Nordic Countries: Epidemiological Studies* (Oslo: Middelalderforlaget, 1992), p. 181.

8. Graham Twigg, *The Black Death: A Biological Reappraisal* (New York: Schocken Books, 1985), p. 21; Scott and Duncan, *Biology of Plagues*, p. 113; Rosemary Horrox, *The Black Death* (Manchester, England: Manchester University Press, 1994), p. 7; Hirst, *Conquest*, pp. 307–16.

9. Thomas C. Butler, *Plague and Other Yersinia Infections* (New York: Plenum Medical Book Co., 1983), p. 51.

10. Scott and Duncan, *Biology of Plagues*, pp. 57–58; Chester David Rail, *Plague Eco-toxicology* (London: Charles C. Thomas Publishing, Ltd., 1985), pp. 105–6.

11. Twigg, *Black Death*, p. 60.

12. Scott and Duncan, *Biology of Plagues*, pp. 51–53; Butler, *Plague*, pp. 48, 112; quote from Christopher Wills, *Plagues: Their Origin, History, and Future* (London: HarperCollins, 1996), pp. 85–86.

13. Scott and Duncan, *Biology of Plagues*, p. 66; Jean-Noël Biraben, "Current Medical and Epidemiological Views on Plague," in *Plague Reconsidered* (Matlock, Derbyshire, England: Local Population Studies, 1977), p. 28.

14. Rail, *Plague Eco-toxicology*, p. xv.

15. Samuel Cohn, Jr., *The Black Death Transformed: Disease and Culture in Early Renaissance Europe* (Oxford: Oxford University Press, 2002), p. 23; Benedictow, *Nordic Countries*, p. 26.

16. Ann G. Carmichael, *Plague and the Poor in Renaissance Florence* (New York: Cambridge University Press, 1986), p. 91; M. K. Matossian, "Did mycotoxins play a role in bubonic plague epidemics?" *Perspectives on Biological Medicine* 29 (1986): pp. 244–56.

17. Horrox, *Black Death*, pp. 24–25, 42–43, 55, 84; quoted in John T. Alexander, *Bubonic Plague in Early Modern Russia* (Baltimore: Johns Hopkins University Press, 1980), p. 15; Benedictow, *Nordic Countries*, p. 71; Pierre Villard, "Constantinople et la peste (1467) (Critoboulos, V, 17)," in *Histoire et société: Mélanges offerts à Georges Duby* (Aix-en-Provence: Publications de l'Université de Provence, 1992), 4: p. 144.

18. Horrox, *Black Death*, p. 74; quoted in Stephen R. Ell, "The Interhuman Transmission of Medieval Plague," *Bulletin of the History of Medicine* 54 (1980): p. 504.

19. Mirko Grmek, "Les débuts de la quarantine maritime," in *L'Homme, la santé et la mer*, ed. Christian Buchet (Paris: Honoré Champion, 1997), p. 47.

20. Benedictow, *Nordic Countries*, p. 125.

21. Koenraad Bleukx, "Was the Black Death (1348–49) a Real Plague Epidemic? England as a Case-study," in *Serta devota in memoriam Guillelmi Lourdaux, II: Cultura mediaevalis*, ed. Werner Verbeke et al. (Leuven: Leuven University Press, 1995), p. 66; Scott and Duncan, *Biology of Plagues*, pp. 101, 356–62; Cohn, *Black Death*, p. 1.

22. Bleukx, "Real Plague," p. 66; Cohn, *Black Death*, p. 58; Stephen R. Ell, "Immunity as a Factor in the Epidemiology of Medieval Plague," *Review of Infectious Diseases* 6 (1984): p. 870; Butler, *Plague*, p. 91.

23. Ann Carmichael, "Bubonic Plague: The Black Death," in *Plague, Pox and Pestilence: Disease in History*, ed. Kenneth Kiple et al. (New York: Marboro Books, 1997), p. 61; and "Plague Legislation in the Italian Renaissance," *Bulletin of the History of Medicine* 57 (1983): p. 517.

24. Graham Twigg, "The Black Death and DNA," *Lancet: I.D.* 3 (2003): p. 11.

25. Wood quoted in online *BBC Health News*, April 12, 2002, and in "Yersinia seeks pardon for Black Death," *Lancet: I.D.* 2 (2002): p. 323; J. F. Shrewsbury, *History of Bubonic Plague in the British Isles* (New York: Cambridge University Press, 1970), e.g., p. 24.

26. David Davis, "The Scarcity of Rats and the Black Death: An Ecological History," *Journal of Interdisciplinary History* 16 (1986): pp. 455–56, 467.

27. Davis, "Scarcity," p. 461; Shrewsbury, *History*, p. 2; Graham Twigg, "The Black Death in England: An Epidemiological Dilemma," in *Maladies et société, (XIIe-XVIIIe siecles). Actes du Colloque de Bielefeld, novembre 1986*, ed. Neithard

Bulst and Robert Delort (Paris: Editions du C.N.R.S., 1989), p. 97; Benedictow, *Nordic Countries*, pp. 26–27.

28. Ell, "Immunity," p. 875; Carmichael, *Plague and the Poor*, p. 94; Benedictow, *Nordic Countries*, pp. 130–31; quote from Biraben, "Current Medical," p. 29; Cohn, *Black Death*, p. 238.

29. Ell, "Immunity," pp. 875–76; "Interhuman Transmission," p. 500.

30. Scott and Duncan, *Biology of Plagues*, pp. 63–65; R. E. Lenski, "Evolution of Plague Virulence," *Nature* 334 (11 August 1988): pp. 473–74; Didier Raoult et al., "Molecular Identification of 'Suicide PCR' of *yersinia pestis* as the Agent of the Black Death," *Proceedings of the National Academy of Science* 97:23 (Nov. 7, 2000): 12, p. 800; James Wood, "Was the Black Death yersinial plague?" *Lancet: I.D.* 3 (2003): p. 327.

31. W. Rees, "The Black Death in England and Wales," *Proceedings of the Royal Society of Medicine* (History of Medicine Section) 16 (1922–23): p. 33; Scott and Duncan, *Biology of Plagues*, p. 101.

32. Leslie Bradley, "Some Medical Aspects of Plague," in *Plague Reconsidered* (Matlock, Derbyshire, England: Local Population Studies, 1977), pp. 18–19; Shrewsbury, *History*, p. 50; Twigg, "Dilemma," p. 95; Carmichael, "Plague Legislation," pp. 515–16.

33. Scott and Duncan, *Biology of Plagues*, pp. 107–8, 355, 384–86, 389.

34. Scott and Duncan, *Biology of Plagues*, pp. 352–54; Norman Cantor, *In the Wake of the Plague: The Black Death and the World It Made* (New York: Harper, 2000), pp. 20–21.

CHAPTER 3

THE BLACK DEATH AND MEDIEVAL MEDICINE

When the Plague struck the West in the middle years of the fourteenth century, no one really knew how to prevent or treat the disease. Many thought they did, but no diet or bloodletting or prayers or concoctions proved successful. The culture's intellectual framework for dealing with illness was deeply flawed, and therefore the various guesses people made based upon it were flawed. From 1348 to 1500 many physicians, Muslim and Christian, wrote treatises on the Plague, and scores of these survive. They contain clear evidence of this flawed framework and the largely useless advice that emerged from it. The failure of medieval medicine stems from stubborn adherence to ancient authorities and reluctance to change the model of human physiology and disease that they presented. The discoveries and inventions that did finally effect this change, however, took place over hundreds of years. Around 1700, a century after development of the microscope and telescope, scholars and physicians were still offering astrological explanations for the Plague and ignoring the tiny animals the human eye could now detect. A century after that they were still blaming the noxious "exhalations" of earthquakes for poisoning the air and causing the Plague. The accurate model of bubonic plague and its successful treatment are only a century old, while the Black Death began 550 years ago.

THE MEDIEVAL PHYSICIAN

The fourteenth-century physician found himself ill prepared in theory and practice to confront the Black Death. Medical theory and practice relied heavily upon the imperfectly understood ideas of the fourth-

century B.C.E. Greek physician Hippocrates and philosopher Aristotle
and the second-century Greco-Roman physician Galen (see biography).
Each of these men in turn had moved human understanding of illness
beyond the mythological "the gods did it" to a rationally structured, if
often incorrect, series of purely physical explanations. The ninth-century
Muslim medical scholar Hunayn bin Ishaq al-Ibadi and his colleagues
in Baghdad translated into Arabic the important works of these men
and their Byzantine commentators. Later generations of Muslim physicians and writers such as the tenth-century Persians Abu Bakr ar-Razi
and Avicenna and twelfth-century Avenzoar and Averroes of Cordoba,
Spain, built upon these foundations by further study and, most importantly, the experience of treating patients. They also tied the theory and
practice of astrology much more closely to practical medicine than had
been done before. Modern medicine ascribes great influence to one's
genes, and similarly medieval physicians ascribed great influence to the
celestial bodies: sun, moon, planets, and stars. Muslim doctors ration-
alized the impacts of these bodies on the four fluids—or humors—that
the Greeks had declared were inside the human body: blood, phlegm,
and black and yellow bile. A proper balance among these fluids—humoral balance—was vital for good health, and the heavens played their
role in maintaining or disrupting this. But the Greeks had taught that
other factors, such as diet, environment, and even mood also played
their roles, and the Muslims worked with these ideas as well, not least
because they could be modified far more easily than the stars or a person's horoscope. Islamic medicine, then, was an amalgam of Greek mis-
information and rationalism, Near Eastern astrology, and personal
experience interpreted through these filters.

The Christian West had its first medical school at Salerno in southern
Italy. As it developed in the eleventh and twelfth centuries, it received
the evolving Muslim medical doctrine in the form of translations by the
monk Constantine the African and by Jewish scholars at Toledo, Spain.
In 1180, Count William VII of Montpellier chartered the medical school
at Montpellier, France; Paris and Avignon received theirs in 1253 and
1303, respectively. In the Catholic university, education was heavily
philosophical and only mildly practical. The Christian religion had little
to say about the nature of the human body, so the absorption of Muslim
and pagan Greek medical science—with all of its flaws—presented few
problems. Western medicine thus began with the interrelationships of

the four elements that constitute all natural things, including the body (earth, air, fire, and water), the four qualities that define them (hot, cold, moist, and dry), the four humors, and the planetary and zodiacal influences on the earth and on individuals. Since astronomy, which was indistinguishable from astrology in many ways, was a standard subject in the basic university arts curriculum, medical students had easy access to experts on the stars. University of Bologna medical students were formally students of *physica & astrologica*, and from 1405 underwent a full curriculum of mathematics and astrology. This was also true of central and eastern European universities, as at Erfurt, Vienna, Krakow, and Leipzig; at Paris medicine and astrology were divorced as late as 1537.[1]

As for anatomy and physiology, physicians still labored under much of the nonsense found in the fourth-century B.C.E. Greek philosopher Plato's *Timaeus*, verbal descriptions drawn from the Roman Galen's work, and simplistic and misleading schematics in medical textbooks. As students they witnessed only the occasional dissection, if any. Here Church authorities were responsible for preventing or limiting the routine practice of autopsy, which seemed to violate prohibitions against willfully destroying a human body—even a dead one. The earliest public dissection in the Latin West apparently took place in Bologna in 1281, but students had to wait thirty years for their first female corpse. In 1316 the earliest known dissecting manual appeared, the *Anathomia* by Mondino de'Luzzi, but it could not have sold well, since the only medical school to add regular dissections before the Black Death was at the University of Padua in northern Italy.[2] Many Muslims, on the other hand, believed with Averroes that "whosoever becomes fully familiar with human anatomy and physiology, his faith in God will increase."[3] At the time of the Black Death the Spanish-Arab Abi Gafar Ahmed ibn Khatimah defined medicine itself as "an art which through research and experiment has arisen with the object of maintaining the natural temperament, and of restoring it to him who has lost it."[4] Despite this advanced approach, however, Muslim doctors were no better able to treat the Plague successfully than Christian. Medieval medical ignorance and impotence cannot simply be laid at the Catholic Church's door, as some scholars do.

Of Christian European regions Italy tended to be best served by physicians, who were available both in cities and the countryside.[5] At the time of the Plague France had around 1,700 doctors, about 100 of whom resided in Paris. Roughly half of these were connected to the university there. This was about three times the number found in the previous century.[6] But many of the French physicians directly served noble families and not the general public, while Italian doctors in cities were organized in guilds, partaking heartily of civic life and treating all. English physicians, whose training often included study at Padua or Paris, were more like their French cousins, and organized for only a brief time in the 1420s.[7] Guilds policed the performance of their members and judged disputes that stemmed from claims of malpractice. Where physicians were guildsmen, as in Italy, this contributed to the solidarity of the profession and the uniformity of practice. In most countries people distinguished between medical men who had had university training and barber-surgeons, who were educated through apprenticeship and carried out most medical procedures, from bonesetting to minor surgery. Both utilized the services of pharmacists, or apothecaries, who prepared and provided various herbs, minerals, pills, and concoctions as the doctor ordered. Though not university trained, pharmacists were respected and powerful professionals on whom physicians relied for their own success. In most places people had access to folk-healers and midwives and other nonprofessional health care providers. In many ways the physicians were least competent among all these, due to the very education that gave them high status.

THE MEDIEVAL PLAGUE TRACT OR *CONSILIUM*

The medical *consilium* was a formal written communication, usually in the form of explanation and advice, sent by a physician to someone who requested it. It could be short and to the point or long and complex, but it was written for a specific nonacademic audience to address a specific, therapeutic purpose. The Black Death elicited many of these, and they are important windows into medieval medical theory and practice.

Between 1910 and 1925 the German medical historian Karl Sudhoff collected and published the original texts of over 200 different *consilia* written by late medieval physicians on the plague, its prevention, and its treatment. He mentions or prints a total of 288, but more recently historian Samuel Cohn has estimated that there were perhaps as many as 1,000 written between 1348 and 1500.[8] This was clearly a major literary genre, and it remained important. Many of these works, usually written in Latin, were translated into various vernacular languages, and after 1454 they were printed for more general distribution. Eighteen of those known and confidently dated were written during the initial outbreak of the disease; some, such as those of the University of Paris medical faculty and that of Pierre de Damouzy, a physician from Reims, France, were written before their authors had even witnessed a single case.

The Damouzy *consilium*, titled *Treatise on epidemic*, suggests remedies he had used on other illnesses, and he boldly declared "none who uses this [remedy] dies from plague."[9] In fact, the remedy came directly from the Persian ar-Razi. Damouzy's tract is replete with quotations from and citations to the works of Aristotle, Galen, Avicenna, and the Arab Ali-Abbas, and others, among whom only Galen had ever witnessed the Plague. As the Black Death advanced through southern France, the French king Philip VI demanded a *consilium* on the disease from the medical faculty at the University of Paris. Their *Compendium de epidemia* was the medical school's first major scholarly work. The *Compendium* was written by committee and presented in October 1348 as the Plague ravaged Paris. Like Damouzy's work, it is filled with references to Greco-Muslim medical authorities and their ideas. It became immensely popular in France, where it was quickly translated and abridged and even appeared in a poetic version by Olivier de la Haye in 1425.

But manuscripts of the *Compendium* circulated even more widely, influencing authors in Spain, Italy, the Holy Roman Empire, and even Poland; it was still being copied for use in the seventeenth century. In Prague the imperial physician Master Gallus wrote a *consilium* for Holy Roman Emperor Charles IV (see biography) and a less complex "Preventives and measures against the disease" for the margrave of Moravia, both based on the Paris *Compendium*.[10] At Montpellier, an anonymous "practitioner," probably connected to the rival university there, wrote a critical response to the Paris tract dated May 19, 1349. Assuming he was in Montpellier as the Plague struck the city, killing the entire medical faculty in the process, his analysis and recommendations should have reflected his experience and trumped the mere conjectures of the Paris faculty. In fact, his work is every bit as reliant on medical tradition and ancient authorities as any other, though he cites Aristotle, the astrologer Ptolemy, the mathematician Euclid, and Pope Gregory the Great more than medical writers. In Italy the earliest *consilium* was written by Gentile of Foligno, a member of the University of Perugia's faculty (see biography). He wrote "for the common benefit of all" and "to preserve and honor this university, moved by affection as much as by the praise of many citizens."[11] Christian Spanish physicians such as Alfonso de Cordoba, Jacme d'Agramont of Lérida, and Juan de Aviñon of Seville wrote in the vernacular for their fellow citizens, relying on classical authorities as well as contemporary physicians such as Gentile and the Muslim Ibn Khatimah.

EXPLAINING THE PLAGUE'S CAUSE(S)

Christian and Muslim physicians alike shared the same basic notions of what caused the Plague and how to deal with it for two reasons: the circulation of the Plague tracts and the common inheritance of Greco-Muslim medical thought. One of Aristotle's most important contributions to medieval science—or "natural philosophy"—was his notion of causation. For example, for a chair to exist there must be four "causes" at work: a maker, a plan or blueprint of the form, some material, and a reason for making it. One could explain anything that existed, God excepted, in these four terms, and all four were really needed for a full explanation. Most *consilia* opened with a discussion of the Plague's causes, and these discussions tended to treat causation in a similar manner, at least implicitly. The "maker" was ultimately God, though some went out on a limb and identified it as Satan or the Anti-Christ. The reason for the Plague was clear for Christians: punishment for sin. As for formal and material causes—the "how" and "what"—theologians stepped back and physicians stepped up. For the physician, acceptance of metaphysical causes in addition to natural causes was not merely a matter of religious belief or adherence; it was a matter of accepting the philosophical framework that united the entire Western intellectual enterprise.[12] Multiple causes were expected and not considered a matter of confusion—a point modern scholars sometimes miss.

The idea that God would use pestilence to punish the wicked or his enemies is firmly rooted in the Bible. In the Book of Exodus, Pharaoh's Egypt received seven "plagues" before he released Moses and the Hebrews from their slavery; in 2 Samuel 24 David chose a plague on his people as punishment for his having carried out a divinely forbidden census of the Hebrews; in 1 Samuel 5 those who had stolen the Hebrews'

Ark of the Covenant were struck by painful swellings, not unlike buboes. Sin brought on punishment in this life or the next. Physical pain could be spiritually beneficial, however: at Vienne, France, "unclean" lepers, who later became a cultural prototype for Plague victims, were separated from healthy society in a religious ceremony that included the words "our Lord gives you a great gift when he wishes to punish you for the evil you have done in this world. Wherefore, have patience in your illness."[13] Punishment in this world reduced punishment in the next, so leprosy was—in this case at least—interpreted as a divine kindness. Regarding the Plague, devout Muslims considered those victims who were righteous and holy as martyrs, whose deaths took them directly to Paradise. But sinners were God's main target, most taught, as in the time of Noah and the flood. And, as the author of the Bible's Book of Psalms wrote: "God judges the righteous and God is angry with the wicked every day. If he turn not, he will whet his sword; he has bent his bow, and made it ready. He has also prepared for him the instruments of death; he ordains his arrows against the persecutors" (7:11–13). It is not an accident that the arrow became the principal metaphor for the disease.

Catholic theology taught that all people are sinners and deserving of suffering. They are saved only by God's mercy. Clergy often made that position clear: in an open letter to his diocese in the summer of 1349 Archbishop Zouche of York wrote, "There can be no one who does not know, since it is now public knowledge, how great a mortality, pestilence, and infection of the air are now threatening various parts of the world, and especially England; and this is surely caused by the sins of men who, while enjoying good times, forget that such things are the gifts of the most high giver." But what of the children who were struck down in great numbers? A preacher's sermon had an answer for that, too: "and it may be that it is in vengeance of this sin of dishonoring and despising of fathers and mothers that God is slaying children by pestilence, as you see daily. For in the old [Hebrew] law children who were rebellious and disobedient to their fathers and mothers were punished by death." One expects such sentiments from bishops and preachers, but lay Christians were just as adamant. In his *Historia de morbo* the Italian Gabriele de' Mussis of Piacenza described the divine Judge who observed "the entire human race wallowing in the mire of manifold wickedness, enmeshed in wrongdoing, pursuing numberless vices, drowning in a sea of depravity because of a limitless capacity for evil, bereft of all goodness, not fearing the judgments of God, and chasing after every evil regardless of how hateful and loathsome it was." In his righteous wrath God thundered out: "I pronounce these judgments: may your joys be turned to mourning, your prosperity be shaken by adversity, the course of your life be passed in never-ending terror. Behold the image of death. Behold I open the infernal floodgates."[14] The great legal scholar Bartolus of Sassoferrato agreed that the Plague was divine retribution, and even Magnus II, king of Sweden, wrote, "God for the sins of men has struck this great punishment of sudden death. By it most of our countrymen are dead."[15]

Physicians, too, recognized the hand of God in the Plague: the Paris *Compendium* gives the Lord his due, but notes that it was also he who gave man medicine and doctors to cure people. This underlines a fundamental problem for some physicians: were they trying to thwart God's will by treating the wicked victims; or was medicine simply ineffective on the evildoer? The Italian friar and physician Giovanni da Rupescissa considered the Plague a divine but imprecise tool for punishing the wicked, who would not recover in any case. Innocent people, he wrote, could be harmed as "collateral damage": for them prevention and treatment were vital. Since physicians could not distinguish the two, everyone had to be treated.[16] Both Muslims and Christians seemed resigned to the notion that God would take whom he would, a convenient answer to those who asked why some became ill and recovered and some never suffered at all. For German physician Heinrich Lamme writing in 1411, "it is better to say that the epidemic comes from God than to repeat all the opinions one hears." He did, however, go on to question whether God or the Devil was the true instigator. The great French Renaissance medical writer Ambroise Paré stated in 1582, "The plague is a malady come from God: furious, tempestuous, swift, monstrous, and frightful, contagious, terrible, fierce, treacherous, deceptive, mortal enemy of human life and that of many animals and plants." As late as 1668 physicians in Rouen, France, were still claiming that God's anger was the root of the Plague.[17] Anything so deadly and so parallel to the pangs of Judgment Day had to have an unearthly cause.

But unearthly could mean merely celestial rather than Heavenly, and that meant astrological. Since astrology played such an important part in medieval medicine, the impulse to look to the stars was compelling. For churchmen like Thomas Brinton, archbishop of Rochester, to do so without acknowledging the anger of their Maker and human responsibility was wrong:

> Today the corruption of lechery and the imagining of evil are greater than in the days of Noah, for a thousand ways of sinning which were unknown then have been discovered now, and the sin of the Sodomites prevails beyond measure, and today the cruelty of lords is greater than in the time of [Hebrew King] David. And therefore, let us not blame the flails of God on the planets or the elements but rather on our sins, saying, as in [the biblical book of] Genesis, "We deserve to suffer these things because we have sinned."[18]

This was no refutation of astrology itself, but of those who would ignore the more fundamental theological cause. The great Spanish Muslim physicians avoided discussion of astrological causation for two different reasons: Lisad-ad Din ibn al-Khatib (see biography), who often went against the grain, claimed the stars were simply outside the realm of medicine, and Ibn Khatimah held that people understood too little about them, whatever their role. Many Christian physicians liked to start with celestial causes, probably because they were thereby working at the level of the natural rather than the supernatural, and here they could exercise their theories.

The ninth-century Arab Albumasar laid the groundwork for Plague theory by explaining that Great Conjunctions in the heavens—when major planets appear to line up with the earth with specific zodiacal constellations behind them—cause extreme natural and political events on earth. Albert the Great, a thirteenth-century natural philosopher at the University of Paris, accepted this and wrote in "On the Causes and Properties of Elements" that a "conjunction of Mars and Jupiter provokes a great pestilence in the air, particularly when it happens in a warm and humid sign of the zodiac." Jupiter is a "moist" planet that attracts earthly vapors, essentially drawing them heavenward. Mars, being "warm and dry" by nature, "ignites the elevated vapors, thus causing the multiplication in the air of lightnings, sparks, pestiferous vapors and fires."[19] This was a physical, mechanistic explanation that clearly linked the forces of the heavens to atmospheric events. The Paris masters repeated this almost perfectly, as did those whose *consilia* were dependent on theirs. In

1350 Simon Couvin, a clergyman in Liège, wrote *On the Judgment of Sol at the Feasts of Saturn*, an allegorical poem that put mankind on trial. The god/planet Saturn prosecutes humanity for familiar moral failings, while Jupiter defends the human race. Sol—the sun—is the agent of God who makes the judgment against humanity and actively unleashes the pestilence as punishment. Juno, Jupiter's wife, tries to intervene, but, like well-intentioned physicians, she fails and humanity suffers.[20] Besides Great Conjunctions—one of which did occur at 1:00 P.M. on March 20, 1345, according to the Paris masters—other celestial phenomena such as eclipses, comets, and meteor showers may have played their parts as well, at least as signs of coming doom.

Theories of astrological causation (see Document 2) were long-lived because they were considered scientific and not mystical or religious. The Lutheran pioneer Melanchthon accepted them, as did the personal physician of Marguerite of Austria (1599). The French Royal Physician wrote in 1629 that the Plague outbreak of 1628 was due to the "bad [mauvaises] constellations and celestial conjunctions [and] the eclipse of the moon" of that year. In 1679 the Austrian court physician Dr. Sorbait attributed an outbreak to the conjunction of Saturn and Mars, and scientists in France blamed the moon as recently as 1785.[21]

Yet this type of explanation had its critics. Some pointed out that conjunctions had occurred before but had not been attended by similar horrific outcomes. The German Konrad von Megenberg attacked the theory by pointing out that a conjunction lasts but one or two years, while the Plague raged for five. He also noted that the stars follow strict courses in the heavens, while the Plague seemed to wander aimlessly over the countryside. Ironically, in another work, the *Book of Nature*, he admitted that the conjuncture of Mars, Jupiter, and Saturn had influenced an accumulation of underground gases that was released into the air, causing the great mortality of the Plague.[22]

Whatever the relationship of mankind to God to celestial bodies, most medical theorists agreed that people directly suffered from bad air, or *miasma*, which was thus the immediate cause of the Plague. For both Hippocrates and Galen bad air caused pestilences; more correctly, bad air was the pestilence. Galen had directly connected the bad air to human illness, which resulted from this air's effect on the balance of humors in the body. The Greeks had spoken, the Arabs and Persians accepted it, and this was the orthodox model available to the medieval

Western physician (see Document 3). Regarding what caused bad air, many explanations circulated, no two of which were considered mutually exclusive. Some theorists followed Albert the Great and blamed the planets for "igniting" the air; others agreed with Konrad and blamed them for stirring up earthly gases. The Paris masters and others attributed the Plague at least in part to the release by earthquake of poisonous gases trapped inside the earth. Chroniclers often mentioned earthquakes in Europe or Asia in connection with the origins of the Plague, and modern historian Jean-Noël Biraben notes that earthquakes did precede outbreaks in Barcelona in 1410, 1413, and 1448 and in Angers in 1485. As mentioned in Chapter 1, earthquakes may in fact have disrupted rodent plague reservoirs, unleashing the disease on people.

Southern winds, against which both Hippocrates and Aristotle warned, were considered unhealthy, as were "exhalations" from swamps and marshes, decaying plants, dung heaps, cesspools, sewers, and decaying animal carcasses. Human corpses in large numbers, as after a battle, putrefied and created unhealthy vapors, as attested to by the French nobleman Jean de Joinville a full century before the Black Death. Battles were common in the mid-fourteenth-century West, and who knew what great campaigns might have left huge piles of dead Mongols or Chinese or Indians on Asia's vast plains? Gentile of Foligno thought that poisonous air might be imported on southern winds, but probably was released locally by opening up long-sealed caverns, wells, or even rooms or houses. When elemental air or the clean air that constitutes our atmosphere becomes corrupted or putrefied or poisoned by "igniting" or mixing with poisonous vapors, whatever the source, it can kill.

THE PLAGUE AND THE HUMAN BODY

In Book IV of his *Canon*, Avicenna described how, specifically, the bad air affected the human body: "When the air that has undergone such putrefaction arrives at the heart, it rots the complexion of its spirit and then, after surrounding the heart, rots it. An unnatural warmth then spreads all around the body, as a result of which a pestilential fever will appear. It will spread to any human who is susceptible to it."[23] Gentile noted that the bad air enters the body through the lungs or skin pores. By its effects on the humors it generates poisonous material around the heart and lungs; the poison around the heart can kill, and if the poison gets into the lungs, it can be exhaled and enter and infect other people. Physicians saw the buboes as additional collection points for the poisonous material. Ibn Khatimah noted that buboes formed in the neck, armpit, and/or groin. He explained that the thickness of the corrupted blood determined where it would collect, the lightest near the ears, and the heaviest "hurled to the groin." Al-Khatib agreed, identifying the three areas with Galen's three "emunctories," or organs that are the seats of the three human souls and that eject from the body "subtle matter"— such as this poison—as opposed to matter such as sweat, urine, or feces. The emunctories are the brain (neck), heart (armpit), and liver (groin), from which the body tries to eject the poison that collects in the bubo. If the matter in the buboes does not harden it might be discharged naturally or by lancing, and the patient might survive.

That some people contracted the disease and lived while others died, and that some did not contract it at all, should have been a problem for any general theory of a poisoned atmosphere. But Galen provided the answer, or at least the seeds of an answer: susceptibility to any disease depended on the condition of one's body, and this meant the balance of humors. In part because of the "moist" nature of the Great Conjunction and in part because the vapors that poisoned the air were considered "moist," this quality was the most dangerous among the four. When moist poison met moist person, the person's "vital principle" was weakened greatly, and death was likely. This meant that women and children, who were considered naturally "moist"—"replete with humors," as the Paris masters put it—were at greatest risk, while "dry" men could stave off disease better, all things being equal. Warm and moist was the worst combination, and this meant younger, chubbier, or "highly sensual" women were the most susceptible. But the quality of one's humoral balance was affected by his or her behavior and emotional state as well: diet, drinking habits, fighting in battle, exercise, chosen environment, mood, and even sexual activity contributed to one's "warmness or coldness," as well as one's "humidity."

The spread of the disease from person to person, however, threw a wedge between theory and observation regarding poisonous air. As the Plague took its toll, it became clear that humoral balance seemed to play only a small role in personal susceptibility to bad air. People seemed to catch it from one another or even from things. Muslim physicians were especially troubled by these patterns. Their religious authorities, following teachings of the Qur'an, denied the possibility of transmitting of the disease outside of the will of Allah. Ibn Khatimah, like others, therefore denied the possibility of contagion; al-Khatib, apparently unique among Muslims, relied on his experience and observation: whatever the Qur'an said, the Plague was infectious. His distant Christian neighbor in Lerida, Master Jacme d'Agramont, listed the diseases "that can thus be transferred from one person to another": leprosy, phthisis, ophthalmia, pestilential fever, smallpox, measles, and skin diseases, "[a]nd, in general, all maladies that come from pestilential air."[24] Like other Christians, he clearly saw no contradiction. The Florentine Mariano di Ser Jacopo noted "it happens often that men die of plague in healthy air simply through contagion." Gentile of Foligno explained interpersonal infection as occurring through "continuity," whereby the victim passed along the poison through breath, or exhalation through skin pores: "communication of the disease happens principally from contagious conversation with other people who have been infected."[25] The Irish friar John Clynn, who succumbed to the disease, noted that it was so contagious that anyone who merely touched the dead died himself, and the Florentine chronicler Matteo Villani wrote, "It seems that this pestiferous infection is caught by the sight and by the touch."[26] The great papal physician Guy de Chauliac also believed in contagion through sight, as did the anonymous practitioner of Montpellier, who wrote, "However, the most virulent moment of this epidemic, which causes an almost instant death, is when the air spirit emitted from the sick person's eyes, particularly when he is dying, strikes the eye of a healthy man nearby who looks closely at him; then the poisonous nature of [the eye] passes from one to another, killing the healthy individual."[27] When people decided that the Plague could be caught even from touching inanimate goods belonging to a victim or coming from a Plague-infested place, then theory and reality truly parted company. Surprisingly, this did not undermine the basic model of the disease.

PREVENTION AND TREATMENT IN THE *CONSILIA*

Despite their continued reliance on an incorrect model, the physicians of fourteenth-century Europe and the Mediterranean were rational men who sought to link prevention and treatment with the causes and nature of the disease. They believed in the accuracy of their analysis, and were truly overwhelmed by their failures. However odd, most of their preventive and curative recipes and suggestions were founded on this analysis, though some reflected the logic of the disease itself as they observed it. There was some movement away from their authorities, but it was limited.

"What a wonder! Everything was tried for the sake of health," observed Dionysius Colle. Jacme d'Agramont of Lerida recognized the value of knowing the Plague's source in order to treat it properly:

> one must consider whether [the air's] corruption or putrefaction was sent for our desserts in chastisement for our sins, or whether it came through the infection of the air, or of the water, or of allied things, or whether it came from higher or superior causes such as the influence of the conjunction or appositions of planets. Because if [it] has come because of our sins the remedies of the medical arts are of little value.[28]

All Christian medical *consilia* begin their recommendations for prevention and cure with some combination of pious calls to prayer, repentance for sin, reception of the sacraments, and acts of piety.[29] Many people hoped that God would lend a gracious ear to specific Plague prayers such as this one, found in the *Hausbuch* (Housebook) of Michael de Leone of Würzburg, Germany, from about 1350:

> Ever almighty God, who because of the prayer of your most glorious martyr, St. Sebastian, called back a universal and lethal epidemic of plague, grant those asking you, that those who thus pray and bear this prayer about with them, and seek refuge in you because of their confidence that a wholly similar epidemic of plague would be recalled [that] through his prayers and merits, they will be liberated from the plague or disease as well as from every danger and tribulation.[30]

Jacme first recommended acknowledging "our sins and our failings by hearty repentance and oral confession by works and acts [since] thus is given satisfaction to God by a true penance."[31] To avoid celestial influences he suggested shunning sun- and starlight, even to the point of moving underground (which is quite atypical). Once past the divine and celestial agents, the physicians generally addressed the matters of bad air, the poison itself, and humoral imbalance.

Jacme and many others agreed that bad air was a localized and not universal problem: it came to a place, stayed, and left. Today scholars agree that the most useful and nearly universal advice was to flee a Plague-ridden area. *Consilia* often suggest avoidance of marshy or swampy areas, or places with natural stench; Ibn Khatimah recommended moving to the mountains. Keeping bad air out appealed to many, such as Damouzy, who said to seal all windows and doors tightly. From Hippocrates' time south winds were considered dangerous and to be blocked; perhaps they were thought to be too damp with sea air, or overheated by the tropics. Many suggested free ventilation with windows open to healthier northern winds. Holding one's breath when around the ill or filtering it through cloth could keep the bad air out. Burning aromatic things, such as wood from ash, pine, or juniper, to create smoke that would fumigate an enclosed area was supposed to keep the corrupted air away or alter its character, and could cleanse an area already affected. The heat would dry the "moistness" and the aroma would counteract the "putrefaction" of the air. Gentile suggested burning wood of aloes, marjoram, mint, savory, amber, and musk; Damouzy recommended ambergris burnt with camphor or aloe wood. Alfonso de Cordoba presented a complicated recipe for a pungent powder to be burnt or left out to treat the air: among other things it contained powder of red roses, spikenard, mastic, sandal, ladanum, saffron, rind of colocynth ("bitter apple"), liquid storax, pepper, cardamom, camphor, and barley. If nothing else, it probably served as a mild stimulant and made people feel better.[32]

Similar combinations of aromatics were bound together into what are generically called "amber apples," which were to be worn or kept near the mouth and nose. Thirteen recipes survive, and most include ambergris or amber, camphor, aloes, musk, and rose water. Gentile suggested simpler herbs for poor folk. Eau de Cologne—"water from Cologne"—and perfume have their European origins with the Plague as personal fumigants, but some physicians preferred the effects of vile odors, such as that from human feces or urine: to be breathed in deeply (see Document 4).

To counteract the poison directly, gold, in some drinkable form, was commonly prescribed. According to the author Solemnis Medicus, gold contained the power of the incorrupt sun itself, and could purify any poison, which by nature was corrupted. Gentile suggested rose water or barley water (for the poor) with gold soaked in it, or cordials with ground pearls or gold; Friar Giovanni da Rupescissa advocated strong distilled alcohol with gold in it. Gems, too, were thought to be capable of counteracting Plague poison. These could be ground up and swallowed in a potion, or worn on the body, especially the ring finger of the left hand, the one nearest the heart.

The logic of humoral medicine dictated avoiding that which would "moisten" or "heat" the body. Hot baths could open pores to let corrupted matter out, but they could also let bad air enter the body, and so on balance were to be avoided. Excessive exercise could lead one to inhale too much bad air and overheat the body. Sexual activity overheated the body and so was to be avoided. The connection of "humoral balance" to one's mood—called an "accident of the soul"—was well established, and negative feelings negatively affected this balance, as well as one's spirit. As the German physician Jobus Lincelius of Zwickau wrote, "All physical exertions and emotions of the mind should be avoided, such as running, jumping, jealousy, anger, hatred, sadness, horror or fear, licentiousness and the like, and those who, by the grace of God, are in a position to do so, may spend their time in relating tales and stories and with good music to delight their hearts, as music was given to man by God."[33] Such pleasures literally strengthened the heart against the poison. Some also understood what we would call autosuggestion to be a cause of the Plague that needed to be addressed: Jacme wrote "from imagination alone can come any malady. . . . Thus, it is evidently very dangerous and perilous in times of pestilence to imagine death and to have fear."[34]

As for diet, physicians naturally suggested moderation in eating and drinking, and avoidance of "moist" foods such as fish and milk, and heavily spiced "hot" foods. Foods should be easily digestible and lead to little putrefaction in the body. Foods that were acidic, bitter, lean, and roasted, not boiled or fried, were acceptable. There is a lot of variation among the authors, especially over fruits and vegetables, which were considered warm and moist but were also good purgatives. Wine heated the body but was acceptable if heavily diluted or very light. Physicians also recommended various pharmaceuticals such as distilled fresh water and pills made of aloe, myrrh, or saffron. This type of advice was also passed along in popular forms, such as John Lydgate's fifteenth-century "A Diet and Doctrine for the Pestilence" (see Document 5).

Removal from the body of superfluous humors meant keeping up the normal functions of sweating, urinating, and defecating. It could also mean extraordinary methods such as the use of laxatives, diuretics, suppositories, and even enemas. Bloodletting (phlebotomy, venesection) had supposedly saved Galen's life during a plague and was quite popular in the fourteenth and fifteenth centuries. No humor was easier to get to than blood. Astrological considerations dictated the best times of year or season for a phlebotomy—generally spring during a waning moon in a zodiac sign that was good for the person. Jacme advocated the third lunar quarter, while avoiding bad signs such as Leo, Gemini, Virgo, Capricorn, "and others."[35] Different doctors applied the procedure as they saw fit. Avicenna suggested only bleeding sick people; Dionysius Colle related, "With the young I abstained from venesection, because all those who were abundant in blood who used this practice [and] who died displayed burnt black blood, flowing thickly with some greenness, and very watery with some yellow color, and waxy."[36]

After the first outbreak in 1347–52, accurate diagnosis of the Plague was very important, as a false diagnosis could lead to unnecessary panic in the community on the one hand or a lack of action on the other. The signs or symptoms of the Plague were many, and lists of these varied (see Document 6). Fever and buboes in the groin or armpit are most often mentioned: occurrence together seemed a sure sign of the Plague. But many *consilia* mention other changes in the skin such as blotches, spots, pustules, and carbuncles. An erratic pulse, cramps, and chills that alternate with fever are commonly listed, less commonly a blackening of the tongue. Most *consilia* discuss humoral changes that could be noted by examining urine, feces, and blood, as Dionysius Colle suggested above. Changes in the mind or soul, such as lethargy, agitation, hallucination, or delirium, were also associated with the Plague. Hemorrhaging and spitting up blood, taken by modern scholars to be symptoms of pneumonic plague, were seen even then as inevitably fatal. Some physicians and even laymen noticed at least two different types of disease at work. Papal physician Guy de Chauliac noted that the Plague killed more rapidly, with fewer noticeable buboes and more spitting up of blood, during January 1348 than during the spring season, when the presence of buboes became more obvious and the illness longer lasting and somewhat less lethal. In 1382 another papal physician, Raymundus Chalmelli de Vivario, discussed in his *Three Books on the Plague* the different levels of lethality of Plague types that seem to parallel the modern division of bubonic, pneumonic, and septicemic. Sometime before 1402 Jacopo di Coluccino da Lucca wrote in his diary about treating a woman "who died of the worst and most contagious kind of plague, that with blood spitting."[37] However poor their theoretical model, these physicians did catalog a wide range of observations, continuing the Hippocratic tradition and setting important precedents for the advance of medicine.

For the physician confronted with a Plague case, an anonymous tract of 1411 recommends five clear steps: use the symptoms to determine whether it is the Plague; tell the patient to make his or her peace with God; monitor the course of the disease by examining the patient's pulse, feces, and urine, and watch for the crisis point, which usually leads to death, but may not; simply leave the patient, if incurable, to die without further treatment; but if curable, begin treatment.[38] Courses of treatment followed the same logic and general forms as preventives. The patient should pray both for recovery and for divine mercy in the next life. Some suggested fumigation; "dry, cool" diets were more important than ever, as were maintenance of a peaceful mind and soul. Bloodletting and other surgical techniques were now to be employed against the buboes themselves, which were believed to contain the poison. Some suggested lancing the bubo, but Gentile advocated an indirect approach: "If the bubo is located on the neck or head, then open in succession the cephalic vein in the two thumbs. If under the armpit or in the right arm, then open the pulmonary vein, which one can find in the middle and ring fingers of the right hand." "Cupping" was another method recommended for drawing out the poison. Simply, a cup would be placed over the bubo and heated, creating suction. Jacme mentions how "some pluck the rump of a cock or a hen and hold it on the swelling to draw out the poisonous matter." Many formulas survive for pastes or "plasters" that also supposedly pull out the poison when smeared on the bubo. A fifteenth-century English "Leechbook," or popular medical manual, recommends an ointment made of honey, duck grease, turpentine, soot, treacle, egg yolks, and scorpion oil.[39]

Potions brewed with gold could help to expel the poison, as could theriac, a concoction that contained chopped up snake and up to sixty other ingredients. It was sold "over the counter" by most pharmacists. Antidotes were many and varied, and might contain animal horns, hooves, flesh, brains, lungs, liver, urine, or dung. In Portugal, Dr. Diogo Afonso provided his king with this recipe for "badger powder," "the best possible thing against the pestilence": get a badger drunk on wine mixed with ground gold, seed pearls, and coral; decapitate and drain the blood from the animal; mix the blood with a powder made of many specific spices and heat; mix this with a paste made of the badger's heart, liver, skin, and/or teeth; mix this with wine or vinegar and let it "sweat." Use within one year; Diogo's wife accidentally consumed some that was six years old, and she died.[40]

THE MEDIEVAL PHYSICIAN AND THE PLAGUE

The Black Death played havoc with the medieval medical profession. While some, like Gentile, died at his post, probably of exhaustion, many others were criticized for following their own best advice and fleeing. Critics charged physicians with cowardice and greed and, of course, the inability to prevent or cure the Plague. The Florentine Marchionne di Coppo Stefani wrote of the doctors of 1348: "Those available wanted an exorbitant sum in hand before entering the patient's house, and once inside they felt his pulse with their faces turned away and inspected his urine from afar, holding strong-smelling substances to their noses." From the other side Dr. Johannes Jacobi stated in 1373: "I was not able to avoid contact because I went from home to home in order to treat the ill for the sake of my poverty and then I kept in my hand a piece of bread, or a sponge or a cloth dipped in vinegar and held it to my mouth and nose and thus escaped such pestilence; though my friends did not believe I would survive."[41] Death rates among physicians attest to their engagement with the ill and the real risks they ran: Ann Campbell noted that five of twelve papal physicians died and three of ten known in Muslim Granada, for example.[42] The continued popular demand for plague *consilia* and medical services, which lasted for centuries despite no major breakthroughs in prevention or treatment, suggests an oddly high level of credibility and popular confidence. One thing that undermined this faith, however, was the presence of charlatans, quacks, and newcomers with questionable credentials. The Florentine Physicians

Guild's statutes complain that even people "who previously worked as smiths or in other mechanical trades, have begun to practice medicine."[43]

But some critics, such as the poet Francesco Petrarch, had little use for the entire profession. Petrarch considered them "madmen" who carry on "a battle with God": "the secrets of nature, and the most profound mysteries of God, that we accept with the humility of faith, they seek to penetrate." He saw medicine at its root as a challenge to God, who blesses one person with health and tests another with illness. For Petrarch the whole matter of causation with its conjunctions and hot winds and corrupt air was "madness," and all remedies, including fleeing the area, useless in the face of God's will. Overall, "the art of medicine, if it plays any part in maintaining health and curing minor ailments, when it comes up against serious illness is of no value whatsoever."[44]

Modern students of the Black Death cannot credit medieval doctors with much success. We can examine, however, whether there was any real movement away from slavish reliance on ancient authorities and toward greater trust in one's own observation and experience. This, after all, would be the heart of the later Scientific Revolution. French historian Danielle Jacquart studied three fifteenth-century physicians from France and Italy, one of whom served the duke of Savoy, another the Este court in Ferrara, Italy, and all of whom taught at Padua or Paris. She concludes that these distinguished healers and teachers were trapped in the medical world of 1348. Others, however, detect some progress. Melissa Chase studied twenty-five Plague treatises or parts of them dating from 1348 to 1420 and concluded that physicians were increasingly capable of and interested in distinguishing the Plague from other diseases, and eventually distinguishing among pestilential diseases. She credits their own experiences and roles as teachers for their search for deeper, if still misguided, understanding. Samuel Cohn, who read scores of *consilia*, agrees, and he finds increasing confidence and optimism among writers beginning with the outbreak of the early 1360s. They took credit for cures and trumpeted their own experience, leaving their other authorities behind, he claims. "Medicine became the first field of secular endeavor in which late-medieval moderns claimed to have surpassed the ancients."[45] But even if Chase and Cohn are correct, the confidence was unfounded and the road to any real success remained very long indeed.

NOTES

1. R. Lemay, "The Teaching of Astronomy at the Medieval University of Paris," *Manuscripta* 20 (1976): pp. 198–99.

2. Arturo Castiglioni, *A History of Medicine*, trans. E. B. Krumbhaar (New York: Knopf, 1958), pp. 340, 342.

3. Quoted in Sami K. Hamarneh, "The Life Sciences," in *The Genius of Arab Civilization* (Cambridge, MA: M.I.T. Press, 1983), p. 183.

4. Quoted in Anna M. Campbell, *The Black Death and Men of Learning* (New York: Columbia University Press, 1931), p. 78 n. 44.

5. R. Palmer, "The Church, Leprosy and Plague," in *The Church and Healing (Studies in Church History)* 19 (1982): p. 79.

6. Jean-Noël Biraben, "L'hygeine, la maladie, la mort," in *Histoire de la population français*, ed. Jacques Dupâquier (Paris: Presses universitaires de France, 1988), 1: p. 433.

7. Robert S. Gottfried, "Plague, Public Health and Medicine in Late Medieval England," in *Maladies et société (XIIe–XVIIIe siècles)*, ed. Neithard Bulst and Robert Delort (Paris: Editions du C.N.R.S., 1989), p. 360.

8. Samuel Cohn, *The Black Death Transformed: Disease and Culture in Early Renaissance Europe* (Oxford: Oxford University Press, 2002), p. 66.

9. Alfred Coville, "Ecrits contemporaines sur la peste de 1348 a 1350," in *Histoire litteraire de la France* (Paris: Imprimerie Nationale, 1938), 37: p. 329.

10. William C. McDonald, "Death in the Stars: Heinrich von Mügeln on the Black Plague," *Mediaevalia* 5 (1979): p. 92.

11. Quoted in Jon Arrizabalaga, "Facing the Black Death: Perceptions and Reactions of University Medical Practitioners," in *Practical Medicine from Salerno to the Black Death*, ed. Luis Garcia-Ballester et al. (New York: Cambridge University Press, 1994), p. 269.

12. Roger French, *Canonical Medicine: Gentile da Foligno and Scholasticism* (Boston: Brill, 2001), p. 30.

13. Palmer, "Church," p. 84.

14. Quoted in Rosemary Horrox, *The Black Death* (New York: Manchester University Press, 1994), pp. 11, 111, 134.

15. Piero Morpurgo, "La peste: dinamiche di interpretazione storiografica," in *The Regulation of Evil*, ed. Agostino Paravicini Bagliani and Francesco Santi (Florence: Sismel, 1998), p. 41; Magnus quoted in William Naphy and Andrew Spicer, *The Black Death and the History of Plagues, 1345–1730* (Stroud, Gloucestershire, England: Tempus, 2001), p. 32.

16. Chiara Crisciani, "Black Death and Golden Remedies," in *The Regulation of Evil*, op. cit., p. 14.

17. Lamme quoted in Sèraphine Guerchberg, "The Controversy over the Alleged Sowers of the Black Death in the Contemporary Treatises on Plague," in *Change in Medieval Society: Europe North of the Alps, 1050–1500*, ed. Sylvia Thrupp (New York: Appleton-Century-Crofts, 1965), p. 213; Paré quoted in Raymonde Elise Doise, *La Peste en Bretagne*, (La Poiré-sur-Vie: Sol'air, 1998), pp. 31–32; Jean-Noël Biraben, *Les hommes et la peste en France et dans les pays européens et méditerranéens* (Paris: Mouton, 1975), 2: p. 8.

18. Horrox, *Black Death*, p. 146.

19. Quoted in Arrizabalaga, "Facing the Black Death," p. 253.

20. Horrox provides a translation of the prose prologue that summarizes the poem, *Black Death*, pp. 163–67.

21. Biraben, *Les hommes*, 2: pp. 10–11; Doise, *Peste en Bretagne*, pp. 32–33.

22. Guerchberg, "Controversy," p. 211.

23. Quoted in Arrizabalaga, "Facing the Black Death," p. 251.

24. M. L. Duran-Reynals and C.-E. A. Winslow, "Jacme d'Agramont: 'Regiment de preservacio a epidemia o pestilencia e mortaldats,' " *Bulletin of the History of Medicine* 23 (1949): p. 69.

25. Both quoted in John Henderson, "The Black Death in Florence: Medical and Communal Responses," in *Death in Towns*, ed. Steven Bassett (New York: Leicester University Press, 1992), p. 140.

26. Clynn quoted in Maria Kelly, *A History of the Black Death in Ireland* (Stroud, Gloucestershire, England: Tempus, 2001), p. 22; Villani in Henderson, "Black Death in Florence," p. 141.

27. Quoted in Arrizabalaga, "Facing the Black Death," p. 263.

28. Duran-Reynal and Winslow, "Jacme d'Agramont," p. 78.

29. Biraben, *Les hommes*, 2: p. 83; see Chapter 5 of this book for further discussion of religious responses to the Plague.

30. Quoted in Stuart Jenks, "The Black Death and Würzburg: Michael de Leone's Reaction in Context" (Ph.D. dissertation, Yale University, 1977), p. 215.

31. Duran-Reynal and Winslow, "Jacme d'Agramont," pp. 78–79.

32. Dominick Palazzotto, "The Black Death and Medicine: A Report and Analysis of the Tractates Written between 1348 and 1350" (Ph.D. dissertation, University of Kansas, 1974), pp. 180–81.

33. Quoted in Johannes Nohl, *The Black Death: A Chronicle of the Plague*, trans. C. H. Clarke (New York: Ballantine Books, 1960), p. 91.

34. Duran-Reynal and Winslow, "Jacme d'Agramont," p. 84.

35. Ibid., p. 85.

36. Palazzotto, "Black Death and Medicine," p. 218.

37. Carlo Cipolla, *Public Health and the Medical Profession in Renaissance Florence* (Cambridge, England: Cambridge University Press, 1976), p. 24.

38. D. W. Amundsen, "Medical Deontology and Pestilential Disease in the Late Middle Ages," *Journal of the History of Medicine* 23 (1977): pp. 416–17.

39. Gentile quoted in Palazzotto, "Black Death and Medicine," p. 221; Jacme quoted in Duran-Reynal and Winslow, "Jacme d'Agramont," p. 82; on the Leechbook see Robert S. Gottfried, *Epidemic Disease in Fifteenth-Century England: The Medical Response and the Demographic Consequences* (New Brunswick, NJ: Rutgers University Press, 1978), p. 74.

40. On antidote ingredients Palazzotto, p. 203; on badger powder A. H. Oliveira Marques, *Daily Life in Portugal in the Late Middle Ages*, trans. S. S. Wyatt (Madison: University of Wisconsin Press, 1971), pp. 143–44.

41. Marchionne quoted in Katherine Park, *Doctors and Medicine in Early Renaissance Florence* (Princeton: Princeton University Press, 1985), p. 35; Johannes in Amundsen, "Medical Deontology," pp. 411–12.

42. Campbell, *Black Death*, p. 94.

43. Park, *Doctors and Medicine*, p. 36.

44. Francesco Gianni, "Per una storia letteraria della pesta," in *The Regulation of Evil*, op. cit., pp. 67–71.

45. On Jacquart and Chase see bibliography; Cohn, *Black Death*, p. 240.

CHAPTER 4

EFFECTS OF THE BLACK DEATH ON EUROPEAN SOCIETY

The Black Death and its recurrences during the later fourteenth and fifteenth centuries shook but did not shatter medieval Western societies. The most obvious effect was the tremendous and sudden drop in population. Of course this affected families and loved ones, but it also shocked the economic and social patterns that Europeans had been developing for over 300 years. The balance between those who supplied goods and services and those who required them was upset and took decades to readjust. Swings in wages and prices reflected this, as did quickening changes in the relationships between landowners and agricultural laborers. In northern Italy, sharecropping became more common, and many believe that English feudalism saw its last days due to the landlords' desperate need for willing laborers. Some poor became rich, and the rich got richer as wealth was redistributed through inheritances and new economic opportunities.

Governments had to adjust their methods of gathering revenue, while intervening in sometimes revolutionary ways to retain the traditional balance between the haves and the have-nots. The scourging by the pestilence of the clergy right alongside their parishioners altered many people's ideas of the Church and its role in keeping humanity in God's good graces. Men and women entered the religious life without the care previously taken to screen, prepare, and educate them, and critics remarked on the disappointing result. It is not too much to say that the seeds of Protestantism were sown in the wake of the great epidemic. European culture changed in other ways, too, as vernacular literacy and literature made headway against the governments' and Church's Latin. Not only were there greatly increased demand and new opportunities for farmers, craftsmen, and priests, but also for educated lawyers, notaries, physicians, and teachers. New schools and universities appeared to fill the demand, and some of these helped usher in changes that brought the medieval world to a close.

THE EFFECTS ON POPULATION

"We are faced with the evidence of an almost unimaginable catastrophe. The Black Death on a global scale exceeded in mortality any other known disaster."[1] At the end of the first epidemic Pope Clement VI (see biography) was informed that 28,840,000 people had died, or about 31 percent of the population of 75 million.[2] All three of these numbers are fictions, however. No one will ever know with any certainty how many people died of pestilence in Europe from 1347 to 1352. No one knows how many people lived in Europe in 1346, or 1330, or 1300, so that deriving an exact percentage is impossible. Scholars argue over the size of well-documented cities such as London, Florence, and Paris and defend very different numbers for even a compact society such as England's. By now, most shy away from declaring any gross figures to be accurate. Many medieval authors were not so cautious and boldly claimed that barely one in ten survived (Burgundian chronicler), or half the population of the world succumbed, or the biblical one-third (Rev 9:18) were swept away as a warning to the survivors (Jean Froissart). One must discount any such numbers as mere guesses, or as the equivalent of "very high numbers," or as symbolic figures. Even on a local level a counting of the dead was never carried out over the duration of the epidemic anywhere in Europe, yet many chroniclers satisfied the desires of an increasingly number-conscious urban audience for a satisfying accounting. The poet Boccaccio claimed 100,000 dead in Florence, and a Paduan chronicler used the same number for Venice. Robert of Avesbury said over 200 died each day in London, Jean Venette stated that 500 died each day in Paris, and one chronicler counted 500 funerals on a single day in Vienna. Agnolo di Tura claimed 52,000 dead in Siena; Friar John Clynn reported 14,000 dead in Dublin; and a Flemish chronicler wrote that 62,000 died in Avignon in just three months. All told, 97 of the 407 European chronicles studied by historian Samuel Cohn provide some estimate of the death toll, but none of them may be considered reliable as exact figures.[3]

Modern historians have turned to sources of data other than narratives to provide numbers or percentages on a small, local scale, such as the English manor, parish, or village. But at even this level few consistent records were kept, gaps in these appear, and accuracy of the source is always debatable. In all of fourteenth-century Europe only three parishes preserved burial records for both normal and Plague periods. In England "inquisitions post-mortem," which presented information about a deceased landholder and his heirs, exist, but only for the knightly class and higher. Courts that tried cases on manors recorded the deaths of those who owed rents on land, but only the head of the household, not family members. Heriots were death taxes owed by serfs to landlords, but records of these no doubt undercount those who were not holders of property. Some scholars have used bishops' registers to determine the death rates among priests and extrapolated from these across the whole population; others have used wills, and still others burial sites to get some sense of death counts or rates. In France and elsewhere governments levied taxes by "head" or by "hearth," roughly a count of individuals or families (occupied house). Hearths were far easier to count, but a modern researcher needs a firm sense of how many people lived around a "hearth." The multiplier one uses to represent average family size is crucial, but always controversial. Also, during Plague times, the abandonment of a hearth can mean many things: the whole family lived but fled, the husband died but all others went to live with relatives, or all died.[4]

Just for the record, some scholars have made estimates of mortality. Ann Carmichael estimates that across western Eurasia, out of a population of 100 million, perhaps 20 percent died, with local percentages in Europe as high as 40 to 50 percent. Naphy and Spicer posit a population of western Europe in 1290 of 75 to 80 million, and a mid-Plague estimate in 1430 of 20 to 40 million, for a maximum population drop of 75 percent. Of course the pestilence by no means accounts for this entire drop—famine, war, and other diseases did their dirty jobs—but if their estimates are anywhere near accurate, the demographic effect was horrendous. One trend is clear in recent scholarship: no one is reducing the generic percentage loss. Several decades ago it was "a quarter to a third" of the population; more recently "a third to a half"; for

England, historian John Aberth suggests 40 to 60 percent is warranted by local studies.[5] In 2002 historian Christopher Dyer summed up the view of many: "it would be reasonable to estimate the death rate in 1348–49 at about half of the English population. Its effects were universal, and no village, town nor region for which records exist escaped. If the total population stood at about 5 or 6 million, there were 2.5 or 3 million casualties."[6]

But England—and Europe—did not merely take the midcentury hit and recover. Local records show modest recovery in the 1350s, but some combination of lower birth rates and high death rates, due in part to recurrences of pestilence, kept populations low and shrinking until at least the mid-fifteenth century. Of course women of childbearing age and younger died in great numbers, but after the Plague some, perhaps many, English women entered the wage-earning work force, especially in towns, thus delaying marriage and childbearing. In his classic study, population historian John Hatcher suggested that adults were financially and materially better off in the wake of the Plague, and may have chosen to keep their families smaller than before, the better to enjoy this higher standard of living. But he also concluded what most scholars today agree: the high mortality from pestilence was the main factor in keeping population low. Plague returned across England some fifteen times after 1370: in 1379–83, 1389–93, 1400, 1405–7, 1413, 1420, 1427, 1433–34, 1438–39, 1457–58, 1463–64, 1467, 1471, 1479–80, and 1485.[7] Death tolls were far lower than in 1348–49, perhaps generally in the range of 8 to 15 percent, but the cumulative effect was to keep England's population low or even declining until sometime during the second half of the fifteenth century, when the country began to experience a sustained period of growth that laid the foundation for her growth under the Tudors.

Elsewhere in Europe the pattern was similar: a very heavy drop in population at the mid-fourteenth century, followed by a mild recovery, which in turn was followed by a continual slide well into the fifteenth century. Using tax rolls for hearths, regional French historians have noted the heavy blows caused by the pestilence. For example, between 1343 and 1357 the city of Albi's hearth count was halved, her population supposedly dropping from around 10,000 to about 5,000. At nearby Millau, between 1346 and 1353 the hearth count dropped from 1,541 to 918. But the lag in Albi's count was fourteen years, and that in

Millau's only seven. One should have more confidence in attributing epidemic deaths as the main factor in Millau's drop than in Albi's case. In both cases other diseases, famine, local warfare, and, of course, flight account for some unknown percentage of lost hearths. In a study of eight parishes near Montmelian in France, the number of hearths was counted in 1347, 1348, and 1349/50 for tax purposes. With this tight a series of observations, one can be quite confident that the Black Death was responsible for much in the drops from 303 to 260 to 142, or a decline of 53 percent over about two years' time.[8]

Much, but not all: what happened to the members of these households is not at all clear. Many people did die, but others fled and families mixed members. A close study of the changes inside Albi after 1343 demonstrates how movements of people as well as deaths affect these figures. In 1343 in the Vigan Quarter of Albi there were 638 taxpayers' (heads of households) names listed on the roll. In 1357 the number had dropped to 242 names. Of the original 638, seventy-four remained on the list; sixty-eight moved to another quarter of town (presumably to better lodgings); and 496 names disappeared from the area. On the new list of taxpayers, 124 were from Albi, but 118 (49 percent) were new to the area, or at least were new taxpayers. The pestilence not only killed people, but also mixed up the remaining population. People fled the Plague, rural folk moved into town looking for work, orphans moved in with others, widows returned to their birth families, widowers remarried, poorer branches of families took over the houses of wealthier ones or took inherited wealth and moved away.[9]

Between 1345 and 1355, in ten French localities studied by historian Emmanuel Ladurie, the number of hearths dropped from 8,511 to 3,839, or nearly 60 percent. Henri Dubois found similar numbers for Aix-en-Provence (45 percent), Moustiers (67 percent), Apt (52 percent).[10] These records rarely show any recovery: the French population continued to slide. In the Lyonnais region of France pestilence returned in 1361, during much of the 1370s, in 1382, 1387, 1391, 1397, 1401, 1403–6, 1410–14, 1420, 1457 (very hard), 1471, and 1493. In each case death rates were said to be six to seven times normal rates.[11] Ladurie estimates the population of France at about seventeen million in 1330; by the mid-fifteenth century it had dropped and hovered around ten million, beginning its ascent only after 1470. By 1700 France had about nineteen million people. In Catalonia one finds a similar pattern: 1365, 104,000 hearths; 1378, 83,000 hearths; and 1497, 61,000 hearths. Demographer Ole Benedictow estimates that Norway reached its low point in the last half of the fifteenth century, having shrunk from around 350,000 people in 1300 to 125,000 in 1450–1500, a drop of some 64 percent. Norway would reach its pre–Black Death population about 1650. In Russia, where the Plague hit somewhere once every five or six years from 1350 to 1490, pre-Plague populations seem to have been reached as early as 1500. Of course, as elsewhere, other trends and events played their parts, complicating any analysis of the specific role of pestilence: Mongol control disintegrated, three-field crop rotation spread, urban life developed more completely and new settlements appeared, and the Muscovites unified northeastern and northwestern Russia.[12]

ECONOMIC EFFECTS OF THE BLACK DEATH

Economics is essentially the study of how people create, trade, and use goods and services. People need certain things and to have certain things done, and others provide these through their labor, at a price. Those who demand, or need, these goods and services are willing to pay for them, and they pay more for them when their need or desire for them is great or when the supply of them is small. The Black Death killed both those who demanded goods and services and those who supplied them, but in general it did not affect the supply of things—including money—available in a given place. Over the longer run, however, it affected all of these: supply, demand, prices, labor wages, even the amount of money and things available.

During the epidemic the people who needed and bought many types of goods and services died, and thus demand for many of these dropped, and prices dropped in the short run. There was an increase, however, in demand for other things, such as coffins, candle wax, medicines and herbs, cloth for shrouds, and the services of physicians, barber-surgeons, notaries, gravediggers, and priests. Prices or fees for these rose as they became scarcer, or as the professionals died off.

Gravediggers aside, the other professionals had a wealth of training and experience that disappeared when they died, and replacing them would not be easy or inexpensive. The same was true of people with other desired skills, such as carpenters, stonemasons, brewers (good ones), artists, teachers, shoemakers, and metalworkers. Not only were they not there to carry on their own work, they were also not there to teach a new generation their craft. Survivors could command high fees, prices, or wages. Cities, where such people tended to congregate, often made special efforts to bring survivors with these skills to their towns under very advantageous conditions, such as quick licensing for professionals, tax exemptions for certain types of merchants, or free lodging.

But this was only one type of "human capital." In cities unskilled laborers also died and were in short supply, and they came to command rather higher wages than before the Plague. Some of these came from other towns or cities, but many moved in from the countryside around the city, leaving fields and crops behind and unattended. This certainly accounts for some of the rural-urban migration found throughout Europe from Dublin to Novgorod. This, of course, hurt the landlords, whose land and crops lay abandoned or underattended. In some places there was an excess of labor to begin with, or the death rates were minimal, and all of the jobs that needed doing were filled by the previously underemployed. In such places wages did not rise appreciably, nor did the prices of the produce or other goods supplied. But in most places labor became scarce and employers had to pay more for it, either by raising wages or lowering rents or by eliminating traditional services that landbound peasants owed. Prices for grain and other food, which initially dropped as people died and demand fell, rose again as the supply fell (people ate it up) and the cost of supplying it rose. The tenants and laborers, rather than the landlords, however, were the ones to benefit from this situation.

Agricultural workers who were free to move about—and many who by law were not—followed the market incentives. In Italy landlords both old and new made sharecropping contracts with farmers, providing capital (land, seed, tools, housing) in exchange for their labor. In this *mezzadria* system the tenant received a fixed percentage of the crop, and thus had a real incentive to work hard and produce as much as possible. In England peasant holdings tended to increase in size as there were fewer workers to tend to the same amount of cultivated land. Landlords had to make better deals with their tenant-farmers to convince them to stay. On large Church-controlled estates that were still essentially manorial, the religious landlords often reduced or eliminated the extra work or payments traditionally expected of peasants. Some even leased out to tenants their demesne land, which had traditionally been worked by peasants for the exclusive benefit of the landlord. In short, as long as labor was in relatively short supply, wages and other conditions for the laborer would be relatively good. Laborers also tended to profit from the redistribution of wealth that followed the initial drop in population. In villages poorer folks married slightly richer ones, and people combined their families and belongings and even landholdings; some moved into better housing, or acquired money, tools, or furnishings through inheritance or theft. On average, across Europe, the agricultural worker was better off financially and materially after the epidemic of 1348–50.

The landlord, however, lost by every concession. Higher prices for grain and other produce reflected their scarcity and higher cost of production, not greater demand, and certainly not higher profits for the landlord. Owners took less productive land out of production, and they shifted away from grain production. Especially in England and the Central Meseta in Spain landowners began to raise sheep, which were quite useful for both their wool and flesh, and which were also far less labor-intensive than agriculture. The revenue from sheep grazing was not as high as that for most agricultural crops, but there was a profit to be had. At Merdon in Hampshire, England, sheep pasture acreage more than doubled from before the Plague to the mid-1370s: 1347–48, 513 acres; 1353–54, 791 acres; and 1376–77, 1,232 acres. This trend in turn aided the burgeoning English wool cloth industry; annual cloth exports increased tenfold from 1350 to 1362 (1,115 to 10,812 bolts of cloth).[13] Abandoned farmsteads, village houses, and even entire villages soon fell into disrepair and then ruin, meaning either their loss to the landlord or high costs for repair or replacement. In locales close to an urban area that was growing or thriving the demand for food might remain high, or even grow, but then another wave of death killed laborer and customer alike, and the landlord—if he survived—absorbed the losses in revenues. In central Italy some rural landowners became so poor that they turned to banditry or rented out their services as military mercenaries.[14]

In England and Aragon the royal governments took steps to dampen these effects by restricting what an employer or landlord could offer in wages and benefits and forcing workers to accept the wages offered. Even the Church did this to regulate clerical incomes, amid claims that priests were charging excessively for their services. Edward III of England issued the Ordinance of Laborers in June 1349 in the immediate wake of the pestilence. "Employees" were choosing not to work, or to work for only "outrageous wages." The Royal Government established 1346, "or five or six years earlier," as the benchmark for appropriate wage levels. As historian R. C. Palmer summarized it, these were mechanisms to "force people to work, to diminish competition, and to moderate demands for higher wages."[15] Those who refused to work for such wages were to be imprisoned. Enforcement of the Ordinance was left to the landlords and employers, who apparently did a poor job.

Two years later, in 1351, a more official Statute of Laborers was is-sued, which tightened some of the restrictions: hiring had to be done in the open with no secret agreements, and "without food or other bonus being asked, given, or taken." Enforcement was taken out of the hands of the landowners themselves and placed in those of public officials, specifically "stewards, bailiffs, and constables," who were responsible to the court of the Justice of the Peace. All who charged a fee for goods or services were to take an oath to charge as they had before the Plague. Oath-breakers were referred to as "rebels," and prison terms were in-creased with subsequent breaches of the law—and their oaths.[16] The charges brought could be as simple as the following: "they present that John Loue of High Easter is a common reaper and moves from place to place for excessive wages, and gets others to act in the same way against the statute." It may not have been enforced vigorously everywhere, as some claim, but in Essex County in 1352, courts fined 7,556 people, of whom 20 percent were women, for breach of the Statute. As late as thirty-seven years later (1389), 791 fines were levied for such breaches in Essex.[17]

This kind of economic legislation by the English royal government was really new in two ways. First, it forced the king's will right into the wallets of Englishmen, from the poorest laborers to wealthy merchants, for something other than taxes. It interfered in both guild and free-market wage-setting. What the Ordinance and Statute really intruded on was the freedom of contract, and the intrusion was radical. Second, this is indicative of the slowly growing royal power and authority; the Crown would use the law to control society directly, not merely through the rapidly expiring feudal system. In so doing, the Crown allied itself not with local nobles, but with the lower, knightly class whose members increasingly served as sheriffs, bailiffs, and other Crown officers at the local level. This group emerged as the new gentry class, who became, in the words of one historian, "the self-interested architects of good order." Landowners big and small tended to cease squabbling among themselves and found common cause against laborers and the new legal weapon with which to oppress them.[18] To some—often disputed—extent, this led to the Peasants' Revolt of 1381. Despite the changes in the role and even structure of government, the Crown's efforts were strictly conservative, and their purpose to preserve the social and economic status quo. Sumptuary laws restricting certain behaviors and styles of dress were issued in 1363 and meant to prevent lower classes from dressing or acting like their social betters. Though not well enforced, these did reinforce the line between classes and kept down the demand for—and price of—expensive cloth. Even beggars were soon to be regulated: the Statute of Cambridge (1388) sought to keep them from wandering and licensed those who needed to travel seeking work.[19]

But was all this repression a sign of an English "second serfdom," or was feudalism in fact disintegrating and disappearing under these pressures? English historians have long argued the role of the Black Death in ending English feudalism. For our purposes this was defined by the fourteenth century as the manorial relationship of landlord and unfree serf who is due protection, justice, and a share of the crop in return for labor in the lord's demesne fields and on roads and such, customary payments, and the obligation not to run away. Landlords had always used both free and serf labor, but the percentage of land worked by free peasants seems to have been steadily growing for a couple of centuries prior to 1348. Studies of local conditions appear to indicate that the nonagricultural burdens on serf labor were also lightening before the Black Death in many places. As in other aspects of social and cultural change, feudalism's decline seems to have been accelerated by the Black Death and its recurrences; the Black Death was a crisis in the history of feudalism. The weakness of the landlords' position, despite the Statute of Laborers, and the failure of the English population to regenerate itself inevitably meant that negotiation rather than coercion would become the norm. The fifteenth century saw the withering away of most obligations and restrictions on peasant labor, though serfdom on a limited scale survived into the sixteenth century.

THE EFFECTS OF THE BLACK DEATH ON THE CHURCH AND EDUCATION

The economic forces of supply and demand unleashed by the pestilence affected the Church and clergy as well as everyone else. Priests supplied the necessary sacraments and religious ceremony during Plague-time, and people were willing and able to bid prices up by offering more and more in fees as the clergy itself fell to the pestilence. Clerical death tolls tended to be at least as high as among the rest of society: during the first epidemic over half of the Dominicans in Florence died (77 of 150); at least 40 percent of the clergy in Barcelona died; in the Diocese of Coventry and Lichfield, England, about one-third of the priests died; and in Winchester Diocese almost 49 percent died between 1348 and 1350.[20] The problem was so bad that the English bishop of Bath and Wells issued the following ruling to his flock in January 1349: "The contagious pestilence of the present day, which is spreading far and wide, has left many parish churches without parson or priest. . . . Since no priest can be found . . . many people are dying without the sacrament of penance (confession). . . . Persuade all men . . . that if they are on the point of death to make confession to each other . . . or [even] to a woman."[21] This was truly a sign of desperation, though the pope himself allowed the practice. But priests were disappearing from their rectories for reasons other than death.

The clergy everywhere was organized in a hierarchy, and the pestilence opened up new opportunities for the ambitious to advance. As pastors died, bishops moved priests from small parishes to bigger ones—from poorer to richer—in a frenzy of ad hoc personnel management. Some clergy merely abandoned their poorly paid positions to grab the higher fees offered by individuals and groups who needed chaplains or private priests. Furthermore, the wills of guilt-ridden victims often demanded that hundreds and even thousands of Masses be celebrated for the spiritual benefit of their souls, and the will-makers set money aside for this purpose. On May 28, 1350, England's chief bishop, the archbishop of Canterbury Simon Islip, issued the constitution *Effrenata*. Its title derives from the document's first word in Latin, "unbridled," as in "unbridled greed of the human race." He stated that the laity had been complaining to him of the priests' flight from their duties and "unreasonable appetites" for better-paying positions and exorbitant fees. In fact, the initiative was as much the king's as anyone's. To stem this tide, Islip fixed the fees allowed and urged his fellow bishops in the House of Lords to do the same. The effort's success was very limited, and the constitution was reissued following further complaints in October 1362, during the next epidemic, with no changes. The amount allowed for fees was raised in November 1378 by Archbishop Sudbury.[22]

Sudbury's remarks in reinvoking the salary cap reflect the fact that among the strongest critics of clerical abuses were the Church leaders themselves. Sudbury wrote that his clergy were "so tainted with the vice of cupidity that they are not content with reasonable stipends, but demand and receive excessive wages. These greedy and fastidious priests vomit from the excess of their salaries, they run wild and wallow, and some of them, after sating the gluttony of their bellies, break forth into a pit of evils."[23] When others in society enumerated clerical abuses or attack the clergy for such abuses they are often labeled as anticlerical. Though anticlerical satires and attacks date back to at least 1100, after the first epidemic they appear more frequently and from widely different corners of society.[24] Anticlericalism shapes characters and stories created by Geoffrey Chaucer, Giovanni Boccaccio, and William Langland. In her study of Ireland during the Plague, Maria Kelly lists the most common charges leveled on that island: fornication, adultery, clerical marriage, nepotism (unfairly helping relatives), drunkenness, gluttony, hypocrisy, greed, lack of spiritual motivation, and ignorance.[25] Part of this dissatisfaction stems from actual clerical behavior, but part must also be a matter of lay disappointment and dismay with the Church's inability to please God and stop the pestilence. In light of what appeared to be the price paid by society for immoral behavior, people may have become far less tolerant of what had been dismissed previously as minor offenses.

Another factor, often remarked upon, was the fact that bishops and religious orders raced men through the preparation for preaching, teaching, or the priesthood in order to fill the many vacancies. They had to recruit very actively and lower standards such as age and basic literacy. Looking back to forty years earlier, the English Augustinian canon Henry Knighton wrote of the 1350s, "in a very short time there came crowding into orders a great multitude whose wives had died in the pestilence. As might be expected of laymen many of these were illiterate, and those who knew how to read could not understand what it was they read."[26] Knighton had little use for many of those in the generation who had died off, but others lamented the loss of so many pastors, teachers, preachers, and role-models. Many thought that the good, dedicated men had disappeared, leaving the shirkers and vice-ridden and the new and unprepared. This loss of valuable human capital affected lay as well as religious education. Men who taught local primary schools often died or assumed better jobs, and few remained to take their places. By the 1360s this lack of preparation was telling in the university classrooms, and academic standards began to decline.[27]

Civic-minded will-makers sometimes included scholarships or even the foundations of new colleges in their wills. At Cambridge the bishop of Norwich, William Bateman, founded Trinity Hall in 1350, and supported Gonville Hall, whose founder died in 1350. When Elizabeth de Clare took over as patron of University Hall in 1359, she noted the large number of men who served God and the state who had died in the pestilence a decade earlier. William of Wykeham founded Winchester College (1382) to provide an educated clergy and to ensure prayers for his and his parents' souls. Corpus Christi College was founded in the wake of the first epidemic, and at Oxford, Canterbury College was established in 1362 and New College in the 1370s. Emperor Charles IV not only established the first central European university in his capital at Prague in 1348, but he also founded five more between 1355 and 1369. In each of the five cases, the school's charter specifically mentions the pestilence as part of the reason for the foundation.[28] The initiatives worked, as enrollments in theology schools increased significantly after 1350. Historian William Courtenay attributes this to three factors: society's general need for new and educated clergy, with opportunities for good incomes; the rising need for so-called chantry priests who served people's private spiritual needs; and the fact that the newly rich wanted their sons to pursue lucrative clerical careers.

Though Latin would remain entrenched in universities and the Church and its study would preoccupy Renaissance humanists, it seems clear that vernacular literacy and literature emerged rapidly and strongly after the Black Death. Prayers, poetry, short stories, Plague tracts, even the Bible: all began to circulate more widely in vernacular languages than ever before. Charles IV encouraged German and Czech literature in his empire, and Old Irish (Gaelic) literature replaced Anglo-Irish after the pestilence in Ireland. In England, French all but disappeared as a common language: Latin texts were increasingly translated into English instead of French; between 1362 and 1364 three parliaments were opened in English; and in 1362 French was banned from the law courts.[29] While some of this was due to a rising sense of nationalism—England was in the midst of the Hundred Years War—it is hard to avoid the conclusion that English speakers in Ireland, French speakers in England, and Latin speakers everywhere were declining in numbers absolutely and in relation to native speakers. This trend helped ensure that the Italian of Machiavelli, the French of Montaigne, the Spanish of Cervantes, the German of Luther, and the English of Shakespeare would develop alongside the revival of Cicero's Latin and Homer's Greek as expressions of the cultural Renaissance of the fifteenth and sixteenth centuries.

NOTES

1. Christopher Dyer, *Making a Living in the Middle Ages* (New Haven: Yale University Press, 2002), p. 233.

2. William G. Naphy and Andrew Spicer, *The Black Death and the History of Plagues, 1345–1730* (Stroud, Gloucestershire, England: Tempus, 2001), p. 34.

3. Yves Renouard, "Conséquences et intérêt démographiques de la peste noire de 1348," in his *Etudes d'histoire médiévale* (Paris: SEVPEN, 1968), p. 158; Samuel K. Cohn, Jr., *The Black Death Transformed: Disease and Culture in Early Renaissance Europe* (Oxford: Oxford University Press, 2002), pp. 106–7.

4. Ole J. Benedictow, *Plague in the Late Medieval Nordic Countries: Epidemiological Studies* (Oslo: Middelalderforlaget, 1992), p. 64; S. L. Waugh, *England in the Reign of Edward III* (Cambridge, England: Cambridge University Press, 1991), pp. 87–88; John Aberth, *From the Brink of the Apocalypse: Crisis and Recovery in Late Medieval England* (New York: Routledge, 2000), p. 127; Elisabeth Carpentier and Jean Glénisson, "Bilans et méthodes: La demographie Française au XIVe siècle," *Annales: E.S.C.* 17 (1962): p. 128.

5. Ann Carmichael, "Bubonic Plague: The Black Death," in *Plague, Pox and Pestilence: Disease in History*, ed. Kenneth Kiple et al. (New York: Marboro Books, 1997), p. 61; Naphy and Spicer, *Black Death*, p. 41; Aberth, *Brink*, p. 128.

6. Dyer, *Making a Living*, p. 233.

7. Mark Bailey, "Demographic Decline in Late Medieval England," *Eco-*

nomic History Review 49 (1996): pp. 4–5; John Hatcher, *Plague, Population, and the English Economy, 1348–1530* (London: Macmillan, 1977), pp. 55–60.

8. Carpentier and Glénisson, "Bilans," 117–18; Henri Dubois, "La dépression: XIVe et XVe siècles," *Histoire de la population française*, Vol. 1, ed. Jacques Dupaquier et al. (Paris: Presses Universitaires de France, 1988), p. 322.

9. Genevieve Prat, "Albi et la peste noire," *Annales du Midi* 64 (1952): p. 18.

10. Emmanuel Ladurie, "A Concept: The Unification of the Globe by Disease (14th to 17th centuries)," in *The Mind and Method of the Historian*, trans. Siân and Ben Reynolds (Chicago: University of Chicago, 1981), p. 44; Dubois, "Dépression," p. 322.

11. Jean Canard, *Les Pestes en Beaujolais—Forez—Jarez—Lyonnais du XIV-ème au XVIIIème siècle* (Régny: Abbaye de Pradines, 1979), pp. 9–10.

12. Paul Freedman, *Origins of Peasant Servitude in Medieval Catalonia* (New York: Cambridge University Press, 1991), p. 163; Benedictow, *Plague*, p. 104; Lawrence Langer, "The Black Death in Russia: Its Effect upon Urban Labor," *Russian History/Histoire Russe* 2 (1975): pp. 61–62.

13. Colin Platt, *King Death: The Black Death and Its Aftermath in Late-medieval England* (Toronto: University of Toronto Press, 1996), p. 43; Tom Beaumont James, *The Black Death in Hampshire* (Winchester, England: Hampshire County Council, 1999), p. 10; R. H. Britnell, "The Black Death in English Towns," *Urban History* 21 (1994): p. 209.

14. Elisabeth Carpentier, *Une ville devant la peste* (Paris: SEVPEN, 1962), p. 236.

15. R. C. Palmer, *English Law in the Age of the Black Death, 1348–1381: A Transformation of Governance and Law* (Chapel Hill: University of North Carolina Press, 1993), p. 139.

16. Rosemary Horrox, ed., *The Black Death* (New York: Manchester University Press, 1994), pp. 240, 312–16 (where the statute is printed in translation).

17. Quoted in David Aers, "Justice and Wage-labor after the Black Death," in *The Work of Work: Servitude, Slavery, and Labor in Medieval England*, ed. Allen Frantzen and Douglas Moffat (Glasgow: Cruithne Press, 1994), p. 175; Larry Poos, *A Rural Society after the Black Death: Essex, 1350–1525* (New York: Cambridge University Press, 1991), pp. 220–21.

18. Platt, *King Death*, pp. 133–34.

19. Dyer, *Making a Living*, pp. 282–83.

20. Renouard, "Consequences," p. 160; Richard Gyug, "The Effects and Extent of the Black Death of 1348: New Evidence for Clerical Mortality in Bar-

celona," *Mediaeval Studies* 45 (1983): p. 395; R. H. Davies, "The Effect of the Black Death on the Parish Priests of the Medieval Diocese of Coventry and Lichfield," *Bulletin of the Institute of Historical Research* 62 (1989): p. 87; James, *Hampshire*, p. 3.

21. Quoted in Naphy and Spicer, *Black Death*, p. 39; full text printed in translation in Horrox, *Black Death*, p. 271–73.

22. *Effrenata* printed in translation in Horrox, *Black Death*, pp. 306–9; William Dohar, *The Black Death and Pastoral Leadership: The Diocese of Hereford in the Fourteenth Century* (Philadelphia: University of Pennsylvania Press, 1995), pp. 104–5; Bertha Putnam, "Maximum Wage Laws for Priests after the Black Death, 1348–1381," *American Historical Review* 21 (1915): pp. 19–20.

23. Quoted in Christopher Harper-Bill, "The English Church and English Religion after the Black Death," in *The Black Death in England*, ed. W. M. Ormrod and P. G. Lindley (Stamford, Lincolnshire, England: Paul Watkins, 1996), p. 91; full text printed in translation in Horrox, *Black Death*, pp. 311–12.

24. Caroline Bynum, "Disease and Death in the Middle Ages," *Culture, Medicine and Psychiatry* 9 (1985): p. 99.

25. Maria Kelly, *A History of the Black Death in Ireland* (Stroud, Gloucestershire, England: Tempus, 2001), pp. 125–26.

26. Quoted in Dohar, *Black Death*, p. 118; full text translated in Horrox, *Black Death*, pp. 75–80.

27. William Courtenay, "The Effects of the Black Death on English Higher Education," *Speculum* 55 (1980): pp. 706–7.

28. Raymond Williamson, "The Plague in Cambridge," *Medical History* 1 (1957): pp. 51–52; Anna Campbell, *The Black Death and Men of Learning* (New York: Columbia University Press, 1931), pp. 149, 152–54.

29. Cohn, *Black Death*, p. 68; Kelly, *History*, p. 65; Phillip Lindley, "The Black Death and English Art: A Debate and Some Assumptions," in *The Black Death in England*, ed. W. M. Ormrod and P. G. Lindley (Stamford, Lincolnshire, England: Paul Watkins, 1996), p. 131.

CHAPTER 5

PSYCHOSOCIAL REACTIONS TO THE BLACK DEATH

The mortality swept away so vast a multitude of both sexes that none could be found to carry the corpses to the grave. Men and women bore their own offspring on their shoulders to the church and cast them into a common pit. From these came such a stench that hardly anyone dared to cross the cemeteries.

(England, William of Dene in *Rochester Chronicle*, 1349)

And it was necessary to send corpses to be buried at San Giorgio d'Alega, San Marco Boccalame, San Lionardo di Fossaruola, and Sant'Erasmo; and such was the number of the dead that they were buried on top of one another in the cemeteries and scarcely covered. And thus the cemeteries became filled. And many died without doing penance, and without being seen. And all remained in hiding for fear of one of the other. And it was provided to send about barges [with men] shouting "Corpi morti!" [Dead bodies!] and whoever had such dead in his house had to throw them down into the barges [or suffer a] heavy penalty.

(Venice, Marino Sanudo in his *Ricordi* [diary], 1348)

. . . at the time of the first great pestilence the servants [of whom he, John Palfryman, was one] of William Wyngrave, then rector, went with a cart to Templeton to bring back the bodies of the dead by night for burial at Witheridge; and at Belbyford, so full was the cart, one body fell off; and William atte Henne was given a penny to go and fetch it next day.

(England, reminiscence of 72-year-old John Palfryman in bishop's register of events fifty-seven years earlier, c. 1387)

In this plague the mortality was so great that no one remembered or had heard of anything like it; because many farms were devastated, and on most farms only three or two survived, sometimes children, usually two or mostly three, and some of them yearlings, and some sucking on their dead mothers. Of these I saw one, who was called Tungfell's-Manga. . . . Where there had been nine children, two or three were left alive.

(Iceland, Jón Egilsson, *Bishop's Annals*, on the Plague of 1494–95)[1]

Those who lived through the Black Death and in a few pen-strokes recorded the death tolls mentioned in Chapter 4 actually experienced the pestilence day by day and week by week. Historian Rosemary Horrox reminds us that "if the figures are exaggerated, they are not meaningless. The chroniclers resort to them as a measure of their horror and disbelief at the number of deaths they saw around them."[2] The dead, however, were not only many, but dear: those who died and were dying were their neighbors, friends, children, lovers, and sisters; those piled on Wyngrave's cart or dumped in the Venetian barges were loved ones and playmates and parents. What so horrified were the number of loved ones who died, and the suddenness, and that their corpses were treated so barbarously. And who would be next?

For the individual living through this, the emotions piled on: fear, grief, anger, guilt, fatigue. The Italian poet and author Giovanni Boccaccio catalogued many human responses in the Introduction to his *Decameron*, which was set in the midst of the first epidemic in Florence. Some fled to avoid the horrors and preserve their health; some repented, prayed, and tried to help as best they could; still others lost their inhibitions and drowned their fear in merry-making and immoral excess. In certain places people openly blamed others in their midst for the pestilence and deaths: the immoral, the poor, foreigners, or Jews. People sometimes joined together to take what they considered positive actions in the face of the threat of epidemic. When groups within a society take actions that reflect what are normally individual psychological responses to events (fear, hope, hatred, blame-placing), then one may call them psychosocial responses. From an outsider's viewpoint these might be very positive, or benign or harmless, or quite negative and harmful. The remainder of this chapter is concerned with three, interrelated types of response: "acceptable" religious activity, suspicious activity of the flagellants, and the destruction of Jewish communities in Spain, France, and Germany.

THE CHURCH'S PRESCRIPTIONS AND POPULAR PRACTICES

The Catholic Church had long sought to harness the individual's conscience, and by extension his or her behavior, in order to bring it in line with the divine will. This would ensure both an individual's salvation from damnation to Hell and the well-being of the community. Sins, and the penances—specific acts such as prayer, charity, or pilgrimage that reflected a contrite spirit—that were necessary to reconcile oneself with God were defined in great detail and with an authoritative clarity by the Church. The clergy saw to it that people feared unrepented-for sin and the damnation it brought more than anything, including death itself. The "good death" was one accompanied by taking of communion, confession of sin, and prayer that was meant to preserve one from hellfire, if not gain one entrance into Paradise immediately after death. When Sanudo (above) mentions that many died without "doing penance" or "being seen" by a priest, he is describing a Catholic's spiritual nightmare. A "good death" was also a sign of divine favor: Florentine aristocrat Alessandra Strozzi wrote to one of her sons concerning the death of his brother in Naples, "I am certain he was provided with doctors and medicine, and that everything possible was done for his health, and that nothing was spared. Yet, it was all to no avail; such was God's will. I have also been comforted by the knowledge that when he was dying, God granted him the opportunity to confess, to receive communion and extreme unction [last anointing]. . . . God has prepared a good place for him."[3] As mentioned in Chapter 4, the willingness of some bishops to allow extraordinary deathbed confession to be made to anyone, "even a woman," was one way by which the Church could alleviate this. But the pope went even further: as successor of St. Peter, who "holds the keys" to the Kingdom of Heaven, he declared that a full, or plenary, indulgence was granted to all who died "in the true faith," whether or not the last sacraments had been taken.

But death was still to be feared, and dying "in the true faith" meant living in it as well. Christians taught that death itself was the result of sin: Adam and Eve became mortal through their disobedience in Eden;

St. Paul taught that "the wages of sin is death" (Romans 6:23). Death was not merely a neutral fact of nature, but the result of evil and sin in the world. It had a moral dimension to it that was sometimes reflected in the art of the era. Death was depicted as frightening and ugly. In an age that regularly witnessed dead bodies, it took depictions of rotting and worm-ridden corpses to make an impression. Tombs were decorated with such images, and poetry such as the anonymous Middle English "Disputation Betwixt the Body and Worms" (see Document 10) portrayed in graphic language the fate of the carcass as ordained by God. A powerful strain in Christianity had long taught the need to discipline and even mortify (literally, to treat as if dead) the body while one lived as a way of avoiding sinful excesses. Monks, whose predecessors had pioneered purposefully harsh lifestyles, had left this ascetic path long before the fourteenth century. St. Francis of Assisi and his followers, however, had long championed the simple life, and tried by example and preaching to bring increasingly materialistic Europeans back to a more spiritual way of living. In the wake of the first epidemic Franciscan spirituality became quite popular. In Prato, Italy, the very wealthy—and spiritually anxious—Francesco Datini was chief patron of the local Franciscans, as were many like him elsewhere. While people might not have denied themselves much during their lives, in their wills many went against the grain of large funerals and fancy memorials. Some insisted on dying on the ground, as St. Francis had; some wanted burial in a simple cloth sack; others asked to be buried under the floor at the church entrance so that all would walk over them upon entering.[4] Such demonstrations of humility had spiritual benefits, or so it was believed, but they also were object lessons to those who were left behind to alter their lives by denying the body and thus feeding the spirit. This was one way to give meaning to one's own death.[5]

The Church on earth was considered only a part of what St. Augustine had called the City of God. The living prayed to God for the souls of those who had died and gone to Purgatory, a spiritual "place" where, through suffering, the soul that died while tainted by sin could be purged and prepared for Paradise. Those already in Paradise, the saints, could likewise pray to God on behalf of those still living. The living could ask the saints for their prayers, and, as examined more carefully in Chapter 6, this "cult of the saints" was extremely important in preserving some degree of hope. If God was sending the Plague, and sinful humanity was justifiably at fault, who but the saints could intervene on humanity's behalf? Throughout the era of the Black Death people built churches, wrote prayers, painted portraits, and venerated relics in the hope that the merits and prayers of the Virgin Mary and saints such as Sebastian and Roch would temper God's just punishment and lift the scourge. Prayers, then, went to God and to the saints; they went in sorrow, repentance, fear, and hope; they requested healing for the sick, a lifting of the pestilence from the community, preservation of oneself from disease, shortened time in Purgatory for the dead, and a good death for the living; they thanked God for his mercy and saints for their prayers. Priests celebrated Masses in churches every day for these intentions and bishops organized processions of the praying faithful, which wound their way through the towns and cities in hopes of demonstrating the community's faith in and love of God. Pope Clement himself (see biography) wrote a special Mass "for turning away the plague":

> And he granted 260 days of indulgence ["time off" in Purgatory] to all penitents, being truly contrite and confessed, who heard the following Mass. And all those hearing the following Mass should hold a burning candle while they hear Mass on the five following days and keep it in their hand throughout the entire Mass, while kneeling; and sudden death shall not be able to harm them. And this is certain and proved in Avignon and neighboring regions.

The prescribed prayer for after Communion reads: "Hear us O God our salvation, and at the intercession of Mary, blessed Mother of God, free your people from the terrors of your anger and in your mercy let them be secure in your bounty."[6]

THE FLAGELLANTS

In the course of the High Middle Ages, in towns and cities across western Europe, lay men, and sometimes women, from all walks of life organized themselves into religious confraternities, or brotherhoods. In some ways these echoed the earlier Crusaders' combining of the secular life with religious duties and purpose. By the later fourteenth century confraternities tended to be associated with specific parishes or churches, and had chaplains drawn from the local clergy. They tended to be of one of three types: the charitable, who helped the poor, or during the Plague buried the dead; the *lauds*-singers, who gathered regularly to sing and pray; and the *disciplinati*, named for the whip they used to beat themselves and each other as a form of individual and collective penance for sin. In each case the lay "brothers" established and followed their own constitution that dictated proper behavior. This generally included regular participation in the sacraments and following the Church's teachings about living the good life. Members marched together in religious processions, and often attended Sunday Mass together as a group. Participation in these groups was voluntary and did not replace the religious duties expected of one, but augmented them, making the "brothers" participants in and not merely observers or supporters of the life of the Church.

Those who chose to be *disciplinati*, or flagellants (*flagellum* = whip), took the practice of penal flagellation and made it both an individual and group exercise. Jesus had been whipped by Roman soldiers before his crucifixion, and the early Church used whipping as punishment for disobedient monks and clergy. Monks themselves often chose self-flagellation as a form of penance that mortified the body, demonstrated sorrow for sin, and joined one with Christ in his Passion. In Perugia, Italy, in 1260 a group of laymen adopted the practice and performed it publicly, their heads covered for anonymity. A group would travel from town to town, disseminating the call for personal and communal penitence. This spread in Italy and into central and eastern Europe before Church authorities, who had little or no control over participants, stopped and disbanded the traveling groups. In northern Italy, southern France, and Germany they became associated with parishes and were absorbed by the religious landscape. In Orvieto, Italy, the Franciscan *disciplinati* confraternity gained about six or seven new members per year before the Black Death. In 1348 they accepted 106; by the end of the year 109 had died.[7]

With the advent of the Black Death people flocked to the confraternities, which offered organized prayer, camaraderie, and guaranteed burial. Because of the culture's emphasis on sin and the need for repentance to alleviate the pestilence, numerous new *disciplinati* groups were formed in cities and towns, and most were under clerical direction: even the pope participated in one procession in Avignon in 1348. Others were not. Some scholars trace the origins of the itinerant flagellant movement—as distinct from the confraternities—to Sicily, in the months following the introduction of the pestilence. They detect the unorganized groups moving northward in waves through Venice in August 1348, and across the Alps into Carinthia and Styria (Austria) by September.[8] Most scholars, however, place the origins of the 1348–49 movement in Austria itself, specifically Zwettl, about fifty miles from Vienna, on September 29, 1348. There had been communal fasting, Mass, and a procession, and then "twenty went from church to church naked all the way to the waist, whipping themselves, throwing themselves to the ground and singing a hymn."[9]

Known in German-speaking lands as the Brethren of the Cross, imitators of these men, in groups ranging from twenty to two hundred, moved through central Europe and Poland, spawning new groups at each stop. Any given town on their route might be visited as many as five times by five groups. They wore white robes, and sometimes white capes, both decorated with crosses, and hats or hoods, also with crosses on them. Their personal journeys were to last thirty-three and a third days, one day for each year of Jesus' life. They would not wash, shave, change their clothes, or sleep in a bed. One member carried a cross or banner as they traveled or processed into a town, and the movement developed a number of vernacular songs or hymns. Having entered a town they would proceed to the central square, strip to the waist, and begin the ritual. Henry of Herford, who provides the most complete witness account of the ritual, called them "a race without a head," openly alluding to a lack of both leadership and sense. But they were canny performers and people responded enthusiastically, sometimes hysterically, at least to the first few waves.

Henry says that they entered the town's main church, stripped, and came out one by one, clearly hoping to associate themselves with the official Church in some way. They threw themselves to the ground in a pose that reflected their own main sin: on their side meant adultery, on their back meant murder. A leader would strike each in turn with his flagellum—a whip of three thongs, each tipped with a bent nail—and wish him the mercy of God. One by one the group rose and formed a procession that sang a hymn, but at the mention of Christ's Passion all fell to the ground "like logs," stretched their arms out like a cross, and prayed. After two repetitions they returned to the church and accepted any offerings, but asked for nothing.[10] Other accounts of their ritual highlight the whipping, and one mentions that their blood was collected and revered as a holy relic.

And herein lay the problem: they were not saints, and the popular adulation made certain among them arrogant. Some leaders went so far as to preach, hear confessions, and impose penances, all prerogatives of the clergy. Some groups became violently anticlerical, even stoning priests in public. Some interrupted church services, openly denying the presence of Christ in the Eucharist; others claimed direct revelation from God. As they moved westward into the Rhineland they appear to have lost the social leaders—nobles and upper bourgeoisie—they had had earlier, and found themselves led by renegade friars and monks. In the eyes of many, they became a dangerous rabble. Historian Richard Kieckhefer concluded that they were most radical and strongest in their effect on communities that were fearfully awaiting the pestilence, and far less so when visiting Plague-stricken areas.[11] Either way, they took on a messianic fervor: their spilled blood could save the world, as Christ's blood had.[12]

By the summer of 1349 their behavior was at least arguably heretical, and local Church and secular leaders began to condemn them and/or forbid them entry into their territories or cities. In western Germany flagellants were said to have spawned anti-Semitic riots. Come autumn, the University of Paris' Theology Faculty sent to the pope the Benedictine monk Jean de Fayt, who had witnessed the flagellants' behavior in Flanders. Under additional pressure from Emperor Charles IV, Clement almost immediately condemned the movement in a bull of October 20, 1349.[13] He cited their independence in choosing clothing, prayers, and ritual and their disobedience of authority. He denounced those who "cruelly extending their hands to works of impiety under the color of piety, seem not in the least afraid to shed the blood of Jews, whom Christian piety accepts and sustains."[14] He recognized that the majority were simple folk who were misled by vile heretics, but nonetheless insisted that bishops and secular rulers alike shut down the processions. Many did, including the king of France, who issued a royal interdict on February 15, 1350, according to which all flagellants would be arrested. Charles IV banned them from the empire, and Manfred of Sicily forbade their activities on pain of death.[15] Those who defied these authorities were automatically excommunicated from the Church, and brutal reprisals were conducted by secular rulers, such as public beheadings in

Westphalia. Many of the impulses bound up in the flagellant move-ment—such as the itch for novelty and travel, the desire to do penance and gain spiritual indulgences—were cleverly harnessed by the pope in his declaration of the Jubilee or Holy Year of 1350. Those who visited Rome as pilgrims during the year and followed a strict itinerary would have the penalty for their sins removed. Many went in fulfillment of vows they had made during the Plague ("If I survive I will . . .") and others in thanksgiving for their own survival or that of loved ones.

The flagellant movement appeared again and again in fifteenth-century Germany. In 1414, between eighty and ninety were burned to death; two years later in Sangershausen, 300 were executed on one day. In Nordhausen in 1446 even those flagellants who recanted or re-nounced their previous practices were burned, and in the 1480s the last trials and executions took place.[16] The failure of the Catholic Church to harness these spiritual energies testifies both to its own disarray within the empire and to the deep-seated nature of the social and spiritual anxiety that drove people to participate either as flagellants or as wit-nesses in the rapt crowds that attended them. The pestilence itself both undermined people's faith in the Church and gave form to the fears and frustrations with which people lived on a daily basis even in normal times. The apparent suffering and sacrifice of the flagellants were inter-preted as positive repentance, and thus in those towns not yet touched by pestilence, it was hoped that the flagellants would provide a powerful spiritual prophylaxis. By practicing—in an extreme and public way—what the Church itself preached, the flagellants gave themselves legiti-macy and angered the clergy who had lost control of penance and thus of the means of salvation itself. In pre-Reformation Germany this was intolerable.

THE ATTACKS ON JEWISH COMMUNITIES

Jews constituted about 1 percent of late medieval Europe's population and lived among the Christian majority of Europe in an often tense state of toleration. Officially, the Church protected them and sanctioned their communities, but just under the surface popular Christianity stig-matized Jews as "Christ-killers," those who refused to see the truth of the Gospel, and allies of Christianity's enemies, especially Islam. During the First Crusade dozens of Jewish communities in Germany were attacked by members of the People's Army who decided that Europe should be cleansed of nonbelievers. At various times Jews were accused of and/or punished for ritual murders of children (in 1235 thirty-four were burned at Fulda, Germany, and in 1255 nineteen were executed at Lincoln, England), mistreatment or desecration of the Eucharist (in 1298 Jews in 417 localities were beaten or killed by mobs), and the poisoning of wells (Bohemia in 1161, Vienna in 1267, and southern France in 1321).[17] This last false claim, or libel, resurfaced in southern France in the immediate wake of the Black Death.

The mysterious nature of the pestilence led many to accept as fact the various "causes" discussed earlier in Chapter 3; it led others to believe in accusations of deliberate poisoning. Early on, eleven "paupers and beggars" in the French region around Carcassonne were caught with "packets of poison" meant for water wells and executed by dismemberment and burning as enemies of France. As the Plague spread, the fear spread, as did the need to place blame. In Provence blame fell on English spies, nobles, lepers, and Jews. In Aragon, a royal official reported "widespread rumors that the water is being poisoned by such as they," by which he meant pilgrims who moved through the area. At Huesca local authorities were told to protect the Muslim communities because they lay under a cloud of popular suspicion.[18]

Soon Jews were linked with the "poison," and the old libel was broadcast again, among the simple and the powerful. The physician Alfonso de Cordoba wrote from Montpellier in 1349 that the third wave of pestilence that hit the city was not natural, but of "human artifice." He conjectured that unidentified men filled glass jars with gaseous poison and dashed them against rocks to unleash the corrupting vapors. Jacme d'Agramont echoed these thoughts in his *consilium*, labeling the supposed perpetrators "evil men, sons of the Devil," in the popular mind a designation of the Jews.[19] The earliest "confession," that of a "Jew of Savoy" working under orders of a rabbi, was extracted in Geneva in September 1348. But by then, hundreds if not thousands of Jews in southern France and Aragon had already been massacred. And few, it seems, questioned the relationship of poisoned water and "corrupted air." The libel, however, carried great weight: as the German Franciscan Hermann Gigas wrote in 1349, "Some say [the pestilence] was brought about by the corruption of the air; others that the Jews planned to wipe out all the Christians with poison and had poisoned wells and springs everywhere. And many Jews confessed as much under torture: that they had bred spiders and toads in pots and pans, and had obtained poison from overseas."[20]

But irrational accusations of well poisoning constituted only one strand in the web in which European Jews found themselves trapped. In these early stages people cast about for likely enemies of Christian society. Jews and Muslims fit the bill, and their religion made them enemies of God as well: perhaps all were suffering for God's anger at them and their sins. While some hotheads formulated and spread this notion, for many others anti-Jewish sentiment was a simpler matter. In Aragon educated Jews held prominent places at court, and many Spaniards resented these men and their power. Other Jews served as financiers and tax-farmers, collecting revenues due to the Crown from a very grudging populace.[21] Jews had been officially expelled from England (1290) and much of France (1306), but elsewhere they were often successful merchants and shopkeepers, extending credit to their poorer Christian neighbors or serving as moneylenders outright. But debtors often resent their debts and those who hold them. Though the mix differed no doubt among communities and regions, the combination of religious bigotry, economic resentment and debt, and the poisoning libel drove the anti-Semitic violence that broke out in a line snaking from Barcelona to Belgium via Switzerland and the Rhine Valley. The horrors of the pestilence, and even the fear generated by mere word of its approach, unleashed humanity's darkest impulses.

In the wake of the pestilence, on Palm Sunday of 1348, the day on which the Passion of Christ is recounted in Catholic churches, forty sleeping Jews in Toulon, France, were killed in their beds; their bodies were dragged into the street and set upon by the bloodthirsty mob. In May, the Jews of Carcassonne and Narbonne were exterminated, and all the Jews of La Baume were killed and their goods plundered. On May 17 a mob attacked and plundered the Jewish Quarter of Barcelona; they destroyed documents relating to local debtors, and killed twenty Jews. Soon after and farther inland, 300 were slaughtered in Tàrrega, and in Cervera eighteen died and all Jewish houses were sacked. Though King Pedro IV tried to protect "his" Jews, local authorities defied his commands. In June, Queen Jeanne, who ruled part of modern southern France, also tried to protect local Jews, but a mob drove her representatives out of Apt and killed whom they would. She denounced them as "sons of Satan."[22] The pattern extended along lines of communication, as did the pestilence, into the Dauphiné and eastward into Swiss territory by September. Zurich banned all Jews forever, and in January 1349 Basle's 200 Jews were herded into a large barn and burned to death. Emperor Charles IV forbade the mistreatment of Jews in imperial territories, but there were persecutions in November in Stuttgart and Augsburg, and in December in Esslingen, Lindau, Landsberg, Buchen, and Meiningen. "[A]nd on 20 December in Horw they were burnt in a pit. And when the wood and straw had been consumed, some Jews, both young and old, still remained half alive. The stronger of [the bystanders] picked up cudgels and stones and dashed out the brains of those trying to creep out of the fire, and thus compelled those who wanted to escape the fire to descend to hell."[23] In July, September, and October 1348 Pope Clement VI had extended the Church's protection to the Jews, and he ordered clergy to stop or punish anti-Semitic actions.[24]

In January 1349 Jews were massacred at Freiburg im Breisgau and Ulm, while Speyer's Jews locked themselves in their synagogue and burned themselves up—or so we are told. At Strassburg the bishop met with town leaders and local noblemen in essence to try the Jews for poisoning, but the popular will won out. Of the city's 1,884 Jews, 900 were burned alive (see Document 11), and the rest were expelled (though they could conduct business from sunrise to sundown). As the Plague moved through the Rhineland, cities farther east carried out their dreadful prophylaxis. In March, Jews arrested in January in Constance, Baden, Worms, and Erfurt were executed for their "crimes." Until the very end of the year Jews were executed or slaughtered in northern Germany, Silesia, and Poland. Jacob Twinger of Königshofen summed up what many—including the pope—saw and still see as the impetus behind the carnage: "Money was the reason the Jews were killed, for had they been poor, and had not the lords of the land been indebted to them, they would not have been killed."[25] But the "lords" were not the only debtors: the working class and underclass apparently owed a great deal, and these violent pogroms gave them the opportunity to destroy records of debt as well as the creditors themselves.

Europe's upper classes at court and in cities had several reasons to want to curb this violence, and at times they succeeded. The Jews were a major source of credit for them in a society that forbade Christians charging realistic interest on loans; Jews as a community were easily and efficiently taxed when funds were needed; and mob violence, like the flagellants, could not easily be controlled. One tactic was to hold official show trials and executions in hopes of satisfying the bloodlust. Another was to defy the mobs: at Regensburg a group of 237 city fathers swore to protect the Jews in their midst. The bishop, nobles, and patricians at Strassburg closely studied the charges of poisonings brought by nine cities and concluded they were false. For his integrity the patrician leader Peter Swarber was stripped of all his property by the bloodthirsty guild government.[26] Charles IV managed to save many Jewish communities in his personal, Bohemian territories, as did Duke Albert II of Austria; Prussian authorities not only stopped major violence, but also brought troublemakers to justice. The pope's condemnation of anti-Semitic acts may have saved some Jews, but the Church clearly bore responsibility for having long fostered anti-Semitic sensibilities if not for condoning anti-Semitic violence. As we know today, the line is a thin one indeed. Henry Gigas completed his thought on the "well-poisoning" Jews: "God, the Lord of vengeance, has not suffered the malice of the Jews to go unpunished. Throughout Germany, in all but a few places, they were burnt." Many German Jews migrated eastward, quadrupling Hungary's Jewish population by 1490 and quintupling Poland's. Despite renewed anti-Semitic violence and unhappy conversions in Spain in the 1390s, her Jewish population expanded from 150,000 to 250,000 during the fifteenth century.[27] King Ferdinand and Queen Isabella ushered in the modern age in 1492 by expelling all Jews who would not convert to Christianity.

The sociopsychological effects of the Black Death were complex. In the short run the Black Death both intensified Christian observance and opened the door to many types of sociopathic behaviors. During the first epidemic flagellants and Jew-murdering mobs exploited society's fears and its intensified religiosity. They achieved the upper hand at certain times and places, but the flagellant movement faded quickly under active repression, and the pogroms against Jews came to an end—for a time at least. The poison libel was never widely broadcast again. Criminals of all sorts took advantage of the temporary societal breakdown, but courts and law enforcement officials restored the old order in most locales.

> After this, when the plague, the flagellant pilgrimages, the pilgrim-
> ages to Rome, and the slaughtering of Jews were over, the world
> once again began to live and joy returned to it, and men began to
> make new clothes.
>
> (*Chronicle of Limburg*, 1350)[28]

Over the longer run Christianity thrived, but the epidemic of 1347–
50 initiated broader changes in European people's attitudes and behaviors, especially among the working and lower classes. England, which
had suffered neither pogroms nor flagellant excesses, saw a rise in another type of antiauthoritarian attitudes and behaviors. The fictionalized
Robin Hood saw his stature as a champion of the downtrodden rise from
1350 to 1400; the town of Chester suffered riots of common folk in
1382, 1384, 1390, and 1393, which followed the larger-scale Peasants'
Revolt and march on London of 1381.[29] French peasants ("Jacques") in
the Paris basin rose violently against noble landlords in 1358 (the *Jacquerie*), and Florentine woolworkers (*ciompi*) violently demanded and
temporarily won a part in the guild-run government two decades later.
The massive death tolls had raised simultaneously the workload and the
economic expectations of many in the lower classes, and they challenged
the power structures to reduce the former and quicken the latter. The
medieval world was changing into the early modern age.

NOTES

1. William quoted in Christopher Harper-Bill, "The English Church and
English Religion after the Black Death," in *The Black Death in England*, ed.
W. M. Ormrod and P. G. Lindley (Stamford, Lincolnshire, England: Paul Watkins, 1996), p. 110; Sanudo quoted in Stephen D'Irsay, "Defense Reactions
During the Black Death, 1348–49," *Annals of Medical History* 9 (1927): p. 170–
71; Palfryman quoted in Christopher Daniell, *Death and Burial in Medieval England* (New York: Routledge, 1997), p. 194; Egilsson quoted in Gunnar Karlsson,
"Plague without Rats: The Case of Fifteenth-century Iceland," *Journal of Medieval History* 22 (1996): p. 269.

2. Rosemary Horrox, *The Black Death* (New York: Manchester University
Press, 1994), p. 3.

3. Quoted in Gene Brucker, *The Society of Florence* (Toronto: University
of Toronto Press, 1998), p. 48.

4. Kathleen Cohen, *Metamorphosis of a Death Symbol* (Berkeley: University of California Press, 1973), pp. 54–56.

5. Caroline Bynum, "Disease and Death in the Middle Ages," *Culture, Medicine and Psychiatry* 9 (1985): p. 100.

6. Papal Mass printed in translation in Horrox, *Black Death*, pp. 122–24.

7. Mary Henderson, "La confraternità e la catastrofe: La Confraternità francescana di Orvieto e la pesta nera," *Bollettino dell'Istituto storico artistico orvietano* 48/49 (1998/1999): pp. 91, 115.

8. Jean-Noël Biraben, *Les hommes et la peste en France et dans les pays européens et méditeranéens*, Vol. 2 (Paris: Mouton, 1976), p. 66.

9. Quote from the *Kalendarium* in Stuart Jenks, "The Black Death and Würzburg," (Ph.D. dissertation, Yale University, 1977), p. 89.

10. For translation of Henry see Horrox, *Black Death*, pp. 150–53.

11. Richard Kieckhefer, "Radical Tendencies in the Flagellant Movement of the Mid-Fourteenth Century," *Journal of Medieval and Renaissance Studies* 4 (1974): p. 159.

12. Anne Autissier, "Le sang des flagellants," *Médiévales: langue, textes, histoire* (Paris) 27 (1994): pp. 53–54.

13. Kieckhefer, "Radical Tendencies," 157; John Aberth, *From the Brink of the Apocalypse: Crisis and Recovery in Late Medieval England* (New York: Routledge, 2000), pp. 155–56; William McDonald, "Death in the Stars: Heinrich von Mügeln on the Black Plague," *Mediaevalia* 5 (1979): p. 91.

14. Quoted in Aberth, *Brink*, pp. 155–56.

15. Biraben, *Les hommes*, Vol. 2, p. 70.

16. Norman Cohn, *The Pursuit of the Millennium: Revolutionary Millenarians and Mystical Anarchists of the Middle Ages* (New York: Oxford University Press, 1990), p. 146.

17. Anna Foa, *The Jews of Europe after the Black Death*, trans. Andrea Grover (Berkeley: University of California, 2000), p. 19; Aberth, *Brink*, pp. 158–59; Steven Rowan, "The *Grand peur* of 1348–49: The Shock Wave of the Black Death in the German Southwest," *Journal of the Rocky Mountain Medieval and Renaissance Association* 5 (1984): p. 24.

18. David Nirenberg, *Communities of Violence: Persecution of Minorities in the Middle Ages* (Princeton: Princeton University Press, 1996), p. 233; Emmanuel Ladurie, "A Concept: The Unification of the Globe by Disease (14th to 17th centuries)," in *The Mind and Method of the Historian*, trans. Siân and Ben Reynolds (Chicago: University of Chicago, 1981), p. 54; Melanie V. Shirk, "The Black Death in Aragon, 1348–1351," *Journal of Medieval History* 7 (1981): p. 35.

19. Nirenberg, "Communities," p. 235.

20. Quoted in Ron Barkai, "Jewish Treatises on the Black Death (1350–1500)," in *Practical Medicine from Salerno to the Black Death*, ed. Luis Garcia-Ballester et al. (New York: Cambridge University Press, 1994), p. 1; for a fuller quotation in translation see Horrox, *Black Death*, p. 207.

21. Shirk, "Black Death," p. 36; Angus Mackay, *Spain in the Middle Ages* (New York: St. Martin's Press, 1989), p. 41.

22. Joseph Schatzmiller, "Les juifs de Provence pendant la peste noire," *Revue des études juives* 133 (1974): pp. 458–61 (quote at 460); Nirenberg, *Communities*, p. 237; J. Gautier-Dalché, "La peste noire dans les états de la couronne d'Aragon," *Bulletin hispanique* 64 (1962): p. 71.

23. Account of cleric Heinrich Truchess of Constance in Horrox, *Black Death*, p. 208.

24. See papal mandate in Horrox, *Black Death*, pp. 221–22.

25. Quoted in Rowan, "Grand peur," p. 23.

26. Rowan, "Grand peur," pp. 23–26; Norman Cantor, *In the Wake of the Plague: The Black Death and the World It Made* (New York: Harper, 2000), p. 155.

27. Quoted in Barkai, "Treatises," p. 1; Foa, *Jews*, p. 8.

28. Quoted in Johannes Nohl, *The Black Death: A Chronicle of the Plague*, trans. C. H. Clarke (New York: Ballantine Books, 1960), p. 260.

29. Colin Platt, *King Death: The Black Death and Its Aftermath in Late-medieval England* (Toronto: University of Toronto Press, 1996), p. 125; D. W. Robertson, "Chaucer and the Economic and Social Consequences of the Plague," in *Social Unrest in the Late Middle Ages*, ed. Francis Newman (Binghamton, NY: Medieval and Renaissance Texts and Studies, 1986), p. 58.

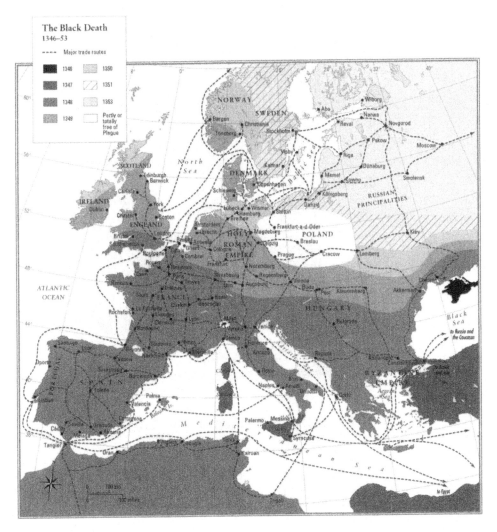

1. Map of major medieval trade routes and the spread of the Black Death.

Medice,cura te
ipíum.

LVCE IIII

Tu congnoys bien la maladie
Pour le patient secourir,
Et si ne scais teste estourdie,
Le mal dont tu deburas mourir.

F

2. "Physician, heal thyself: Luke 4." One of Hans Holbein's woodcuts of the Dance of Death, French edition of 1538. "Ailments thou understandest well, and healer of the sick canst be; But rash, vain man, thou canst not tell, in what form death shall come to thee." *Used by permission of Dover Publications.*

3. "St. Sebastian Intercedes during the Plague," by Josse Lieferinxe, 1497–99. While the burial procession is struck by the pestilence at the very church door, St. Sebastian kneels before God in Heaven seeking an end to the epidemic. *The Walters Art Museum, Baltimore*.

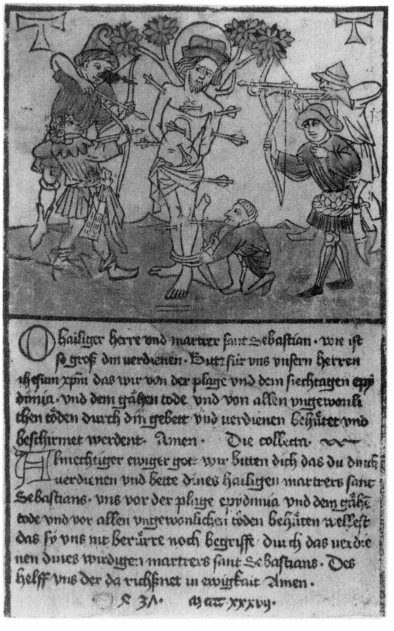

4. German single-sheet woodcut (1437) of the martyrdom of the "plague saint" Sebastian with a prayer to him asking for his intercession with God. Note the archers' medieval dress and crossbow. *Albertina, Wien.*

5. Flagellants, from the manuscript *Les Belles Heures*, by the Limbourg Brothers, 1412. Several standing "brothers" scourge themselves, while another scourges two who lie prostrate as they act out their penitential service. The dragon carried aloft symbolized the devil, and its position behind the cross represented Christ's triumph over him. These fifteenth-century flagellants are part of an authorized liturgical procession with its roots in 1348. *The Metropolitan Museum of Art, The Cloisters Collection, 1969 (69.86 f.74v). Photograph, all rights reserved, The Metropolitan Museum of Art.*

6. "The Three Living Meet the Three Dead," from the *Psalter and Hours of Bonne of Luxembourg, Duchess of Normandy*, probably by Jean LeNoir and his daughter Bourgot, before 1349. Bonne herself died of the plague, hence the date of the work. This macabre theme of the living conversing with the deceased was a reminder of human mortality and became ever more popular in the later Middle Ages. *The Metropolitan Museum of Art, The Cloisters Collection, 1969 (69.86 f.321v). Photograph, all rights reserved, The Metropolitan Museum of Art.*

7. Illustration of a transi tomb that accompanied the "Disputacion betwixt the Body and Worms"; from a fifteenth-century English manuscript. The sketch illustrates both the tomb described in the poem's text and the new tomb type introduced in the wake of the Black Death. The image of the decaying corpse was deliberately placed beneath that of the idealized body as a warning to passers-by of the vanity of earthly existence. *The British Library*.

Morte nihil melius. vita nil petus iniqua
O pma mors boim. reges eterna laboris
Zu semle iugum domino volente relaxas
Uinctoruiqz graues adimis ceruice carbenas
Eripis iudignis. iusti bona ptibus equans
Eripis indignis. iusti bona ptibus equans
Atqz immota manes. nulla exorabilis arte
A primo prefixa die. tu cuncta quieto
Ferre iubes animo. promisso fine laborum
Te sine supplicium. vita est carcer perennis

8. "The Seventh Age of the World: The Image of Death." Corpses in various
stages of decomposition abandon their graves and dance: "Nothing is better
than death. . . ." Like the mortality of the plague itself, this image served as a
reminder of death's ultimate triumph over the body. A woodcut by Michael
Wolgemut for Hartmann Schedel's *Liber Chronicarum*, printed by Anton
Koberger in Nuremberg, 1493. *Used by permission of Dover Publications.*

CHAPTER 6

EUROPEAN ART AND THE BLACK DEATH

The creation of art in the fourteenth and fifteenth centuries was a process that intimately involved patron and artist working within a cultural framework. This framework dictated the acceptable subject matter, style, and uses of artworks; it was shaped by the Church, political and economic elites, and traditions of artistic practice. For the student of the Black Death, art serves as a window into the past. Some works record the scenes of daily life as affected by the pestilence: the burial of victims, doctors with patients, religious processions. Others display people's fears and anxieties: images of rotting corpses, divine judgment, Death itself striking down the living. Still others embody the hope of the living and the thanks of survivors directed to saints such as St. Sebastian, St. Roch, and the Virgin Mary, who were believed to be able to intercede on behalf of humankind before God. Of interest, too, are changes in artistic style and production caused by the Black Death and its recurrences.

THE BLACK DEATH IN ART

Neither the Christian West nor the Islamic world had any way to express in visual images a catastrophe such as the Black Death. Artists struggled to create images that in some way captured this phenomenon, its various facets and meaning. Their works appeared in books, on church and cemetery walls, over altars, and on broadsheets with prayers or poems. Countless paintings and woodcuts depicted God, angels, or demons hurling spears or shooting arrows of the Plague at towns or among people. Some agents of death appear using lances, swords, hatchets, and the flagellum, a multistrand steel-tipped whip. But more than any other weapon, the arrow came to embody the direct cause of the disease itself: falling down from the heavens, killing some, wounding others, missing many. In Lavaudieu, France, a fresco personified the Plague as a woman with covered eyes holding arrows.[1]

The image of Death as an entity had a more standardized iconography in the West by the fourteenth century, and this evolved as the pestilence recurred. Before the Plague it may have been a snake or monstrous beast that devours the living. Death was sometimes portrayed as a small person, especially female, who is defeated by Christ (who brings eternal life). The female figure evolved into a more terrifying and potent savage woman stalking her prey. The use of corpse and skeletal figures for Death is ancient, but directly evolved from their use by Franciscans as a reminder of human mortality, or *memento mori.* The corpse image could be quite grisly, whether lying as it should be or walking about reminding people of Death's infinite mobility. The corpse is cloaked in its shroud, worms or snakes protrude from its eye sockets, and intestines tumble from its gaping abdomen. Skeletons were rather difficult to depict, but their angular limbs and eerily grinning skulls were soon common sights. These came to be armed with bow, sword, sickle, or scythe to mow down the living. In one terrifying image painted by Giovanni di Paolo in 1437 Death is a hairy, bat-winged, horse-riding archer bearing straight down on a mournful, praying man who stands alone before him.

Putting the living and the dead together, as in the "Three Living Meet the Three Dead" scenario or that of the Danse Macabre (see Photo 6 in photo essay), was fairly simple. In the first, which predated the Black Death, three young people, finely clothed, are out and about when they encounter three corpses, often in various states of decomposition. Verses generally accompanied the scene, but the point is that the Dead inform the Living: "We once were what you are now; what we are now, you will be." The sentiment was venerable, and may be found on Roman tombs and in early Arab poetry. During the Black Death the image appeared in churches and cemeteries from central Italy to northern England. The popularity of the scene stems from the usefulness of the message: people should repent and change their lives now, for all too soon, "they will be" among the corpses. A less positive note is sounded by the Danse Macabre genre. In a series of scenes, twenty-four or thirty-six people representing different classes and occupations are confronted or "danced away" to death by corpses or skeletons. The message that all are subject to and equal before Death comes across clearly, but the order often reflects the social stratification of the society, with the pope in full robes and tiara leading, and a child or mother and child at the end. Whether painted on church walls or printed on early pamphlets, the images often appeared with verses in Latin or the vernacular commenting on the character or scene. Scholars differ as to the theme's origins, but it seems to have come from Germany either before or during the initial outbreak of the Black Death. The earliest known mural of the scene was painted in 1424 on the wall of the Franciscan Cemetery of the Innocents in Paris.

Death comes for every individual at some point, which is why the themes outlined above are more generic than directly Plague-related. The massive presence of Death during outbreaks of pestilence made these messages immediate, however, and popularized the images. The "Triumph of Death" theme more closely reflects the social devastation of the Black Death expanding the horror of death from individuals or small groups to whole populations. In the wake of the Black Death the poet Petrarch borrowed the theme and title from the Camposanto mural in Pisa (c. 1340) and treated it poetically.[2] Illustrations accompanying the text show Death as a corpse or skeleton with a great scythe over his shoulder. He stands atop a huge heavy-wheeled cart that is drawn by oxen and rolling over a Danse Macabre–like population ranging from emperor to peasant. One variation sets a battalion of threatening skeletons against a terrified human army in Jean Colombe's vision from 1485 in the Burgundian *Tres Riches Heures*. In Flemish Pieter Brueghel the Elder's 1562 nightmare, hordes of the dead are unleashed against guilty and innocent alike in a smoldering, war-torn landscape. The battle is not man against man, but humans against death—and death always wins.

During outbreaks of pestilence many people were buried anonymously in unmarked or mass graves. Horrified by this sense of total disappearance, people with the means made certain that their graves would be properly marked. For about two centuries many among the wealthy and powerful had had full-sized sculptures of themselves, or effigies, made to be placed atop their tombs. In the 1390s a new form and message were attached to these monuments. Beneath the fully clothed bishop, cardinal, or noble appearing as he would at his funeral was carved a full-sized decomposing cadaver—what the finely dressed corpse would look like after several years. This new transi tomb type (see Photo 7 in photo essay)—vividly displaying the transition of the corpse—was first used by the French physician Guillaume de Harcigny of Laon, who died in 1393; Cardinal de La Grange was buried beneath one in Avignon in 1402. The trend spread: in England the decomposed figure was usually nude and emaciated. In German lands snakes and frogs crawled about and through it, and in France and Burgundy a shroud usually covered part of the cadaver. The table-like structure that separated the two images might have no decoration, small scenes of the Crucifixion or Resurrection, coats of arms, or inscriptions. That of Archbishop Henry Chichele of Canterbury (1425), the earliest in England, reads in part: "I was a pauper born, then to primate raised. Now I am cut down and ready to be food for worms. . . . You will be like me after you die: all horrible dust, worms, vile flesh." This quite pessimistic sentiment is hard to square with historian John Aberth's assertion that this tomb symbolized the triumph of resurrection over corruption; that after the final judgment all will be restored. Aberth sees the top, fully clothed effigy as the future, resurrected archbishop. Many transi tombs request the prayers of visitors on behalf of the dead, prayers that would lessen the time the deceased would spend in Purgatory preparing for Paradise.[3]

Art that depicts daily life and death during the pestilence is rare, but it is of great value as a record of the time. Physicians often appear in danses macabre or illustrating medical literature, especially in later woodcuts decorating printed editions. They are usually shown dressed in hat and doctor's gown and handling the large glass flask in which urine was placed for examination. They are often in the patient's room, which is one of the few times the sick are depicted. Artists also attached images of the stricken to some devotional images: as townspeople writhe in agony on the ground below, the saint prays for mercy before God enthroned in the clouds above. In the Lieferinxe painting *St. Sebastian Intercedes* a man is ironically struck down while helping to carry an enshrouded corpse into church (see Photo 3 in photo essay). Mourners on one side and the priest and his attendants on the other view the scene with resignation, as more corpses are carried or carted. The lack of coffins indicates the severity of the outbreak. Perhaps the most famous scene of mass burial is from the Gilles li Muisis manuscript (c. 1350), the only surviving image datable to the first outbreak. A crowd of men carries coffins or enshrouded corpses to the edge of the pit, where they are aided in laying the bodies in. Gravediggers continue their grim work in the fore- and background. In Giovanni di Paolo's *St. Nicholas Saving Florence* (1456) coffin-bearers trudge behind candle-bearers with clergy in abbreviated funeral processions through the otherwise empty city-scape.

THE ART OF INTERCESSION

The medieval Christian believed that all people sin and that all sinful people are unworthy of any gift from God. Rather, because of sin and disobedience, they are justly deserving of any punishment God deems appropriate, including the Black Death. Only those who had pleased God and received his mercy could effectively intercede with God, invoking his boundless divine mercy to temper his justice on behalf of humanity. These men and women, who had left this world, lived with God in Heaven as his saints, or holy ones. From early times the Church in both East and West had taught that the saints continued to care for and respond to those on earth who recognized and were devoted to them. The prayers of unworthy people could be augmented by those of the saints in Heaven, who could act as advocates for the poor sinners below. The Bible teaches that Christ is the perfect advocate before the Father, but if the Judge is Christ, who is there to advocate? If Christ sends the arrows of the Plague, then whose prayers are worthy enough to be heard? The saints' are, of course.

People had been praying to saints, venerating their relics, and painting images of them for countless generations before 1348. By the fourteenth century the "cult of the saints" was in full swing. Artistic representations of saints decorated churches, houses, town halls, and even city gates. The merchant Francesco Datini had St. Christopher, who was supposed to keep the traveler safe from harm, painted beside his palazzo's front door as a talisman to safeguard his family and guests. Over time the role of saint as intercessor who prayed for God's help changed to saints who served as protectors, who had their own power to help whom they willed. Individuals, craft guilds, parishes, and even cities had their patron saints on whose spiritual support people depended. The most effective of saints, because of her relationship to Christ, was his mother, Mary, and by 1348 Christians in the East and West had been seeking her protection and support for a millennium.

Mary was "humanity's most powerful advocate" in the face of the pestilence. As in the omnipresent depictions of the Last Judgment, Christ embodied divine justice, but Mary embodied mercy and was thought to provide protection to those who sought divine mercy through her. The Catholic prayer "Ave Maria," directed to her, asks only "pray for us sinners." But Mary emerged as a protector in her own right, too. This is manifested in the Catholic image known as the *misericordia*, or merciful image of Mary. The earliest of these images seems to have been painted in 1372 by Barnaba of Modena for the Cathedral of Genoa. In this image, Mary stands as a huge figure wearing a broad cloak that she holds out around and above a specific group of people, who are often kneeling in prayer, or a specific city. From above, Christ, angels, or demons hurl down spears or arrows, and these break upon or bounce off her protective mantle. In some depictions other people are shown outside her mantle, unprotected, often being struck down with arrows. Theologically the image has its problems, since it appears that Mary can thwart God's will, and this image was suppressed by the Catholic Church's Council of Trent in the mid-sixteenth century.[4]

Some *misericordias* make no visual reference to the pestilence, reflecting Mary's role as a protector in general. For saints specifically associated with the Black Death many Catholics turned to St. Sebastian (see Photo 4 in photo essay) or St. Roch (Rocco, Roche, Roccus). Sebastian was a Christian soldier who was to be executed for his beliefs in the early fourth century. He survived a shower of arrows and, having been left for dead, was nursed back to health. He returned to confront the pagan emperor and was brutally beaten to death. His association with the pestilence stems from his having survived the shower of arrows. The association of arrows with divinely sent disease is ancient. The Old Testament repeatedly mentions arrows as metaphors for God's punishments, as at Deuteronomy 32:23, "I will spend mine arrows upon them," or at Psalm 64:7, "But God shall shoot at them with an arrow; suddenly shall they be wounded," or Psalm 7:12, "he hath bent his bow and made it ready." The celestially afflicted Job laments: "For the arrows of the almighty are within me," (6:4) and "his archers compass me round about" (16:13). Classical authors spoke of pestilence as arrows, as did Christian writers during the First Pandemic. While at Rome in 590 Honorius of Autun wrote of "arrows falling from Heaven." The earliest known appeals to Sebastian were made in Pavia and Rome in the mid-seventh century, as recorded by Paul the Deacon. One of the Catacombs in Rome, along the Appian Way, has long been associated with Sebastian, though his relics were moved to Soissons, France, in 826.

The fourteenth-century notary Gabriele de' Mussis summed up the popular belief in Plague-stricken Italy: "For among the aforesaid martyrs, some, as stories relate, are said to have died from repeated blows, and it was therefore the general opinion that they would be able to protect people against the arrows of death." At the same time Abbot Gilles li Muisis described the devotion of fearful northwestern Germans and French people specifically to Sebastian:

> When the mortality was at its height an enormous number of people
> . . . flocked to the monastery of St. Peter at Hennegau, when it was
> discovered that there were relics of St. Sebastian in a shrine there.
> . . . While the pestilence raged in France pilgrims of both sexes and
> every social class also poured from all parts of France into the mon-
> astery of St. Medard at Soissons, where the body of that martyr St.
> Sebastian was said to lie. But when the disaster came to an end,
> the pilgrimage and devotion ended too.[5]

A patron chose Sebastian—or Mary *misericordia*—as a pictorial sub-ject either as a prophylactic to ward off the disease or as a token of thanks for having done so. In the few surviving depictions of him painted before the 1370s, Sebastian is portrayed as an older, bearded man. After two bouts of pestilence he changed into a very young man, shown nearly nude, tied to a pillar or stake, and perforated by anywhere from three to over a hundred arrows (often lodged in the pelvic, armpit, and neck areas). Though Renaissance Italian artists often include the executioners, medieval versions have him alone, alive, and suffering sto-ically very much like contemporary images of the suffering Christ. The image was formally reminiscent of the flagellation scene from the Pas-sion, and the effect was to turn Sebastian into a self-sacrificing "lightning-rod" for God's arrows. This was a much more complicated role for a saint to play than intercessor or even protector. Sometimes, however, he is shown interceding with God, arrows firmly in place. In one unique and striking image, by Benozzo Gozzoli at San Gimignano, Italy, he is shown in the *misericordia* pose shielding the townspeople. Chapels or altars dedicated to him could be found from Oslo, Norway

(1349), to Knockmoy, Galway (paired with the "Three Living meet the Three Dead" image, c. 1400), to Ragusa in Dalmatia (1465), to French Normandy, where some 564 memorials to him remain.

St. Roch's first appearance as a Plague saint is a matter of debate. Early tales have him born in Montpellier, France, anywhere from the 1290s to 1350. He was a nobleman who made a pilgrimage to Rome. Pestilence struck while he was on the road and he stopped to aid the sick at Aquapendente in Tuscany. After three years in Rome helping others he made for home via Piacenza, where he contracted the disease. He stayed alone in a forest, fed by a dog, his affliction healed by divine aid. Returning to Montpellier he was cast in prison as a spy and died there after five years. An "angelic inscription" found by his body informed the world that from Heaven he would serve as a patron of the Plague-inflicted. Evidence of reverence for him appeared as early as the 1410s. His story became popular around Venice, and the legend crystallized in 1478 in a formal, humanistic biography by the governor of Brescia, who promised, "Those suffering the plague, fleeing to the protection of Roch, will escape that most violent contagion." Portraits usually show Roch standing, a robust man with pilgrim's hat, staff, scallop shell, and the dog who fed him. His left leg is bared to reveal a bubo very high up, and in some pictures an angel delicately lances it. His image is virtually always a passive icon, and his role that of intercessor before God.[6]

Medieval people used art to embody, and not merely reflect, their spiritual hopes, joys, sorrows, and fears. By depicting their spiritual intercessors and protectors during times of the Plague they admitted their vulnerability, but also gave form to and energized their hope in a way that was very real to them, if rather alien to the modern mind. Though this art is often viewed as a pathetic and superstitious response to the Black Death, recent scholarship by Louise Marshall and Samuel Cohn interprets it as part of a positive, proactive spiritual defensive strategy that psychically empowered patrons.

THE MEISS THESIS AND ITS RECEPTION

In 1951 art historian Millard Meiss published a groundbreaking study of the Black Death and its impact on artistic style and content in the Italian cities of Florence and Siena. As Meiss saw it, the horrors of the pestilence shocked patrons of religious paintings into abandoning a half-century of artistic development in favor of an older and perhaps more reverent and spiritually effective style. Pre-1348 painters such as the Florentine Giotto and Siena's Lorenzetti brothers had created both religious and secular art that depicted humanity in natural rather than supernatural or spiritual terms. They portrayed human emotions such as fear, anger, and sorrow and set their stories in pictorial spaces that were meant to mimic the physical world. They treated humanity with optimism, finding it to be morally good and worthy of careful observation; they found the environment to be "orderly, substantial, extended, traversable."[7] Their patrons loved their work because they shared the artists' optimism and positive outlook on humanity.

As Meiss saw it, patrons and artists believed that God rebuked this orderly world and its good people through the punishment of pestilence. Human arrogance and pride may have been the very sins targeted by the divine arrows. Post-Plague art was now meant "to magnify the realm of the divine while reducing that of the human." The miraculous and mysterious replaced the natural, familiar, and human. Guilt-ridden merchants and bankers expressed their newfound penitence in paintings that glorified the divine and properly humbled humanity. For Meiss this art was "more religious in a traditional sense, more ecclesiastical, and more akin to the art of an earlier time."[8] New elites who emerged from or immigrated into urban society joined the old elites in preferring art of an older fashion: their tastes had not been formed in the stylish big city, but in cultural backwaters. In Meiss' view, the Black Death retarded the artistic evolution toward Renaissance-style realism and humanism for several decades. His is a bold thesis that seems to make clear linkages between societal change and anxiety and artistic style and content.

While praising Meiss's scholarly contribution overall, critics have undermined his big picture by attacking it in detail. Several specific paintings on which he relied, including the famous "Triumph of Death" mural in the Camposanto in Pisa, have been proven to predate the Black Death. Such revision is important for showing that certain morbid artistic themes that Meiss thought were prompted by the Black Death actually predated the pestilence.

A post-1348 Florentine panel painting called the "Strozzi Altarpiece" provided Meiss with the perfect example of a powerful divine image that supported his claim of a reversion to older style and content supposedly typical of the "sober post-plague culture." Against a gold background a rigidly seated Christ stares statically out at the viewer while handing the keys of Heaven to St. Peter on one side and a book representing correct doctrine to St. Thomas Aquinas—the Dominican theologian—on the other. The Virgin Mary presents Thomas to her Son and a frontally staring John the Baptist stands behind Peter, while four other standing saints fill out the wings. Art historian Bruce Cole emphasizes the connection of the altarpiece to the chapel in which it still hangs. He relates the somber tone to the Strozzi family burial chamber beneath the chapel rather than the Black Death more broadly, and the style to that of a Last Judgment depicted on the chapel's wall. The theme and specific saints were actually chosen not by the "guilt-ridden" banker Tommaso Strozzi who paid for it, but by the Dominican friar and scholar Piero Strozzi, who ran Santa Maria Novella, in whose church the chapel and painting are located. Another art historian, Diana Norman, demonstrates that the work combines qualities that are both naturalistic (treatment of clothing) and spiritualized (the staring, unapproachable Christ figure). For her, if one considers Cole's points, the painting fits in perfectly with works immediately preceding it and does not reflect any major changes claimed by Meiss. A third critic, Louise Marshall, finds nothing neurotic or fearful in depicting the formal, unapproachable Christ. She notes in the work "hierarchical relationships of mutual obligation between worshipper and image." She sees here embodied the idea that Christ is distant but can be approached, and interprets this, as she does other works, as proactive: people are taking steps toward lessening God's anger and regaining the proper, humble but positive relationship with him.[9]

Despite criticisms of specific cases, Meiss' observation that art changed stylistically because of the Black Death has been supported in part by art historian Henk Van Os. Van Os, however, discredits the idea that any change was due to cultural gloominess or a shift in spirit. Rather, Van Os believes it stemmed from the demographic fact that many key artists and patrons died. In hard-hit Siena large workshops in which artistic training took place collapsed as masters such as the Lorenzettis died suddenly. New partnerships formed among artists, changing creative relationships. Also, the Sienese government—a major patron— changed radically in the mid-1350s, ending an era of great public commissions that helped shape artistic taste. Suddenly wealthy "new men" (*novi homines*) entered public life, bringing with them simpler and more traditional artistic tastes. According to Van Os, it was for these reasons, rather than any new religious spirit, that Sienese painting became less sophisticated and more rustic. Picking up Van Os' theme, art historian Judith Steinhoff argues that surviving Sienese painters actually reshuffled themselves quite consciously into new partnerships. The sudden deaths of artistic leaders and the decline in new commissions and income— prices for works fell 50 percent—resulted in artists combining their styles, talents, and even tools on what few new projects there were. The "previous norms of stylistic unity" fell away as individuals' styles inter-mingled and affected one another. Steinhoff agrees with Van Os that art patronage by less sophisticated "new men" fostered the creation of less sophisticated art, but she thinks that these patrons ignored style rather than reshaped it.[10]

As Steinhoff points out, this Sienese trend of collaboration ended after the second outbreak of pestilence in 1363, largely because the art market revived. Historian Samuel Cohn has done much to demonstrate that a real shift in cultural values and artistic expression occurred after this second outbreak, when people realized that the great menace could return. Meiss had claimed that the "denial of the values of individuality" was reflected in post-Plague art, but Cohn finds no such denial in the culture. Italians developed a great concern with being remembered that expressed itself in chapel-building, art patronage, and gift-giving. They had witnessed the mass graves swallow hundreds who left not a trace behind; they had watched as entire families died off. During their life-times, and especially in their last wills, people of means associated their wealth and names with religious and charitable donations and the foun-dation of hospitals and orphanages. Their names, coats of arms, and images suddenly appeared on religious artworks of all kinds: paintings, vessels and vestments for Mass, candlesticks, banners, windows, and altar cloths. Identification of oneself with the church or saints ensured not only spiritual benefits, but also the earthly benefits of being remembered and hopefully prayed for. Cohn found that after 1363, Italian wills be-came much more specific in detailing how money was to be spent on forms of commemoration: instead of lots of small bequests to churches or monasteries or the poor, the wills now often contained directions for large building projects or works of art. Not every person could afford to commission a painting, but Cohn found that butchers, cobblers, bakers, blacksmiths, and even a gardener could.[11]

Florentine merchant Francesco Datini fit this pattern perfectly. His father's will of 1348 scattered bequests across every religious establishment in Prato (see Document 7). Francesco's will, however, specified in great detail how his enormous wealth was to be used to create a well-appointed foundation named for him to support the same town's orphans. Shortly after Francesco's death in 1410 his wife had huge frescoes of him performing charitable activities painted on the outside of their grand palazzo in Prato, near Florence.[12] The outlines can still be seen. This concern for commemoration of the individual person in the face of the Plague led directly to the humanistic concern for artistic realism that will be the hallmark of Renaissance art of the fifteenth and sixteenth centuries.

Meiss' thesis may have its flaws, but its bold assertions have drawn scholars to confront them creatively and thus reshape our view of the Plague's effects along more accurate—and perhaps even more interesting—lines.

NOTES

1. Christine Boeckl, *Images of Plague and Pestilence: Iconography and Iconology* (Kirksville, MO: Truman State University Press, 2000), pp. 46–48; Marie-Madeleine MacAry, "La peste et saint Roch en Bas-Limousin," *Bulletin de la Société scientifique, historique, et archéologique de la Corrèze* 94 (1972): p. 83.

2. He had earlier written Triumphs of Chastity and Peace, celebrating these two virtuous abstractions.

3. Kathleen Cohen, *Metamorphosis of a Death Symbol* (Berkeley: University of California Press, 1973), pp. 1–2, quote at p. 16; John Aberth, *From the Brink of the Apocalypse: Crisis and Recovery in Late Medieval England* (New York: Routledge, 2000), pp. 232–34.

4. Jérôme Baschet, "Image et événement: l'art sans la peste (c. 1348–c. 1400)?" in *La pesta nera* (Spoleto: Centro italiano di studi sull'altro medioevo, 1994), p. 35; Louise Marshall, "Manipulating the Sacred: Image and Plague in Renaissance Italy," *Renaissance Quarterly* 47 (1994): pp. 506–14, quote at p. 511.

5. Rosemary Horrox, *The Black Death* (Manchester, England: Manchester University Press, 1994), pp. 26, 54.

6. Jean-Noël Biraben, *Les hommes et la peste en France et dans les pays eu-*

ropéens et méditeranéens Vol. 2 (Paris: Mouton, 1975), pp. 78–79; Marshall, "Manipulating the Sacred," quote at p. 504.

7. Millard Meiss, *Painting in Florence and Siena after the Black Death: The Arts, Religion, and Society in the Mid-fourteenth Century* (Princeton: Princeton University Press, 1979), p. 60.

8. Meiss, *Painting*, pp. 38, 70.

9. Bruce Cole, "Some Thoughts on Orcagna and the Black Death Style," *Antichità viva* 22 (1983): p. 29; Diana Norman, "Change and Continuity: Art and Religion after the Black Death," in her *Siena, Florence and Padua, I: Art, Society and Religion 1280–1400, Interpretative Essays* (New Haven: Yale University Press, 1995), pp. 186–87; Marshall, "Manipulating the Sacred," p. 488.

10. Henk Van Os, "The Black Death and Sienese Painting: A Problem of Interpretation," *Art History* 4 (1981): pp. 242, 245; Judith Steinhoff, "Artistic Working Relationships after the Black Death: Sienese Compagnia, c. 1350–1363," *Renaissance Studies* 14 (2000): pp. 6–9.

11. Meiss, *Painting*, p. 31; Samuel Cohn, *The Cult of Remembrance and the Black Death* (Baltimore: Johns Hopkins University Press, 1992), pp. 235–56.

12. See reconstruction in Editors of Time-Life Books, *What Life Was Like in the Age of Chivalry* (Alexandria, VA: Time-Life Books, 1997), p. 145.

CHAPTER 7

INDIVIDUAL AND CIVIC RESPONSES IN CAIRO AND FLORENCE

The Black Death struck the great cities of Cairo and Florence with terrible fury. Their populations, clergy, and administrators reacted in ways shaped by their common humanity and very different cultures. Cairo was the center of the Muslim Mamlūk empire of Egypt and Syria, and said to be the largest city west of China. A major center of trade, Cairo was controlled tightly by the Turkic Mamlūk (slave) rulers and their foreign soldiers. Christian Florence was one of several city-states that competed for political and economic power on the Italian peninsula. Beyond the Alps lived the Holy Roman Emperor, who ruled Florence in name only. Florentines had developed civic self-rule by councils drawn from powerful commercial and crafts guilds. Both cities were located upriver from important seaports hit early by the pestilence, and their people watched in horror as the pestilence moved up the Nile and Arno Rivers.

CAIRO, EGYPT

The well-traveled fourteenth-century philosopher and historian Ibn Khaldûn described Cairo as "the metropolis of the universe, the garden of the world, the anthill of the human species, the portico [sheltered porch] of Islam, the throne of royalty." To another world traveler, his contemporary, Ibn Battuta (see biography), it seemed that "The number of inhabitants is so great that they seem to move in waves, making the city look like a choppy sea."[1] Cairo was actually a conglomeration of four urban areas along the Nile: Old Cairo, or Fustat; the city of Cairo built further north under the Fatimid rulers in the tenth century; Bulaq, a Nile island that served as the main commercial port; and Qarafa, dominated by cemeteries. It was a center of education and scholarship, replacing Baghdad, which the Mongols had destroyed in 1258. The Mamlūk Sultan Baybars made it the center of his caliphate, or Islamic empire, in 1261, and the city reached its apex at the end of the long reign of Sultan Nāsir Muhammad ibn Qalāwūn (r. 1293–1340). It boasted fifty-one bath houses, eighty-seven markets, thousands of shops, and fifty-eight caravanserais, or large enclosed courtyards with lodging and storage areas for caravans, for their camels, cargo, and personnel. As in most of the Muslim world, Cairenes did not use wheeled carts, but the streets bustled with human feet and animal hooves. A French-man visiting in 1322 remarked that although the city was four times the size of Paris, the streets were "narrow, tortuous, dark, rich in recesses, full of dust and other refuse and unpaved." The poor lived as they could, the rich in fine houses centered on open courtyards, and the middle class in *urbu*, or multistoried apartment complexes. The Mamlūk aris-tocracy controlled villages like feudal lords thanks to the *iqta* system, supporting themselves on the backs of peasants though living in the imposing Citadel in Cairo. Pre-Plague Egypt had perhaps 4.5 million inhabitants, and something over 10 percent lived in Cairo, which ab-sorbed a huge fraction of Egypt and Syria's wealth.

The Black Death hit Egypt in the fall of 1347, about the same time Sicily was struck. The fifteenth-century chronicler Muhammad al-Maqrizi claimed that a pestilence-stricken merchant ship originally stocked with 300 slaves landed at Alexandria, beginning the horror. At its peak 200 burials were taking place each day; the ports, markets, and customs houses were shut down. Cairo and much of lower Egypt fell prey in April 1348, the epidemic reaching its peak from October to January 1349 and subsiding in February.[2] Al-Maqrizi reported 300 deaths a day in late summer, and 3,000 daily by late October. Some think that pneumonic plague hit in December, as reports of 10,000 to 20,000 deaths per day began to surface. The Muslim world traveler Ibn Battuta visited Cairo and noted that the daily death toll was 21,000, and that all the scholars he had known were dead. He didn't stay long. In the end, al-Maqrizi made claims of 900,000 deaths in Fustat alone, or about twice the original population of all of Cairo. Modern estimates of the death tolls for Alexandria and Cairo run around 100,000 and 200,000, respectively.

Cairo was a Muslim city, and Islamic doctrines on the Plague and proper responses prevailed. Muhammad had taught that the Plague was entirely the will of Allah: it is a mercy to the faithful victims, since they will go immediately to Paradise, and punishment for the infidels. Muslims were to neither flee nor enter a place where the Plague raged; but there was no contagion, since God struck down only whom he willed. An early Muslim commentary stated that "God has created every soul: He has ordered its span of life on earth and the time of its death, the afflictions it will suffer and the benefits it will enjoy."[3] Some considered even prayer for relief to be a faithless act. The simple and strict Muslims had no use for science, but educated physicians tried to reconcile the theories of Hippocrates, Galen, and Avicenna on poisoned air with the operation of God's will. Ibn Hajar in the 1440s, for example, declared that the angel-like spirits or *jinn* pricked the skin of the chosen victims, opening it to the miasma. Bleeding could be an effective remedy, but only if God willed it: "God has as a result of this enlightenment (bleeding) caused great effects to follow in those whose sparing was ordained." The Andalusian Ibn al-Khatib dismissed the *jinn* and embraced contagion, finding that other rational people did as well: "Already, in fact, have pious people arisen in Africa, who retracted their earlier opinion, and formally proved by document that they withdrew from the earlier legal/religious decision (*fetwa*), since they considered their consciences burdened by the view that it is permitted them to surrender themselves to destruction."[4] In other words, if they can flee, they will and should.

And people did flee, including the sultan and his entourage, who left the Citadel in September 1348 for Siryāqūs. Some abandoned the city for the countryside, and rural folk fled their fields, seeking out urban centers with their physicians, religious centers, and food and medicines. Some sought to avoid the pestilence by following the diets prescribed by doctors, or coating their bodies with clay—presumably to dry it out. In the 1362/3 outbreak Sultan Ibn Abī Hajalah built fires of aromatic woods to dry out the Citadel's putrid airs. Besides these bonfires communal religious services were about the only public measures the rulers ever took to deal with the Black Death. On November 28, 1348, hundreds lined up behind the empire's banners and carriers of the Qur'an. As the procession wended its way out of town, its members prayed for the lifting of the increasingly deadly scourge. On their own, people prayed and fasted and scrupulously followed requirements for ritual purity. In the mosques they heard readings from the Sahīh of al-Bukhari, which outlined how the good Muslim should act in a crisis. When neither religious practice nor medicine worked, some Muslims turned to magic. Written incantations were worn around the neck, or the ink used was washed off into a glass of water and drunk. Recitation of the sentence "The Eternal, there is no destruction and cessation of his Kingdom" 136 times a day was said to keep the Plague away. Though Muslims recognized certain holy men as "saints," these played no role as spiritual advocates like Christian saints did. Yet the Christian appeals to St. Sebastian or the Virgin Mary played roles similar to those of Muslim magic, which was directed at the spiritual *jinn*. If one views the Christian practices as positive and proactive, perhaps one should view the Muslim ones the same way.

During Plague-times funerals in Cairo proceeded without ceasing. One Friday at the huge Mosque of al-Hākim there was a long double line of scores of coffins over which prayers were said. After the service, confusion reigned as to who was in which coffin: bodies were typically wrapped in shrouds and thus anonymous. Funeral processions for prominent victims often crossed one another in the narrow streets with mourners mixing and scuffling. As time passed, coffins disappeared; bodies were piled with rubbish in the streets; corpses were thrown into the Nile. The enshrouded dead were transported to the great cemeteries at Qarafa on planks, boards, ladders, and shutters and in baskets; camels carried several at a time as they swayed through the narrow streets.[5] Mass graves for thirty and more were dug and filled, time and again. Historian Michael Dols has suggested that the Muslims' failure to lash out violently against scapegoats, as some Christians did by targeting Jews, was due to a "psychic numbing" born not only of the disaster and its details, but also of the submission to God's will demanded of Muslims[6] (see Document 8).

The deaths and flight that depopulated Cairo had lasting social and economic impacts. Food prices fell as demand fell, but rose again as urban supplies were depleted. The harvest in 1348 was poor, laborers were few, and transportation of produce to the city very difficult. Fleeing peasants abandoned crops, animals, and the precious Nile irrigation apparatus, leaving it to crumble. In the rural Asyūt region where around

6,000 people usually paid taxes, in 1349 only 116 remained to do so. This radical depopulation kept food supplies low and prices high, and plagued the sultans until the sixteenth century.[7] In Cairo wages soared: those of a stable boy rose from thirty to eighty *dirhams* per month; millers' and bakers' wages increased by 113 to 160 percent. The prices of manufactured goods and processed foods rose, but demand for new items such as furniture, cookware, and clothing fell as the property of the deceased entered the market. Cairo's long-distance trade also suffered, both within the Islamic world and with the European Christians, as these foreign markets dried up. Over time the Black Death also hastened the end of the quasi-feudal *iqta* system of land control through which the sultan had rewarded his Mamlūk soldiers: with the massive death tolls and redistribution of wealth a cash market for the villages developed, and the sultans lost their control over them.[8]

Over the succeeding decades, however, demand in the construction trades rose, as wealthy and newly wealthy survivors built hospitals, schools, and mosques as acts of piety that were meant to please Allah. From 1341 to 1412, forty-nine new mosques were built in Cairo, as well as forty palaces for high Mamlūk nobles (*amirs*). Hundreds of houses, shops, and caravanserais had been abandoned, looted, or vandalized and needed rebuilding. In the 1350s the sultan spent lavishly on the new central mosque, which could accommodate 400 students—who would presumably replace the scholars, clerics, and judges who had died. From 1384 to 1386 Barquq, the first sultan of the Circassian dynasty, also built a new mosque, though on a smaller scale. Even though much of the sultans' normal revenue had dried up, they profited greatly from the Islamic legal requirement that the wealth of intestate victims, those who died without a will, was forfeited to the state.

Despite new outbreaks of pestilence in 1362–63, 1374–75, and 1379–81, a flood in 1354, and famine in 1375, by the early 1380s Cairo had largely recovered, earning praise from Italians and Arabs alike.[9] The respite was short-lived, however. European economic recovery, the military threats of the aggressive Mongol leader Tamerlane, high taxes, internal revolts, and recurrences of the Plague struck the Near East down (see Document 9). By the early 1400s Cairo's suburbs were desolate, industries crippled, mosques and markets empty or in ruins. There was little to buy and there were few to buy what little there was. Cairo lost its entire textile industry and half of its sugar processors.[10] In the rather light outbreak of 1419 an average of 193 people died daily from mid-March to late April, excluding those in hospitals. In 1428 ibn Zuhaira lamented that Cairo was "but 1/24th of what it had been."[11]

During the heavy epidemic of 1429–30, Mamlūk historian Abu l-Mahasin ibn Taghrî Birdî reported, the city government counted the number of coffins that left the city for Qarafa's graveyards, and that 12,300 did so on a single day. His estimate for that outbreak was a total of 100,000 victims in Cairo alone. People called it "the Great Extinction," and he noted that it was "greater and worse" than any outbreaks since 1348. "It differed from past plagues in many respects; one is that it occurred in the winter and disappeared in the spring season, whereas plagues used to occur in the spring and be lifted in the beginning of summer." The religious leaders declared a three-day fast, and a procession of townsmen was led out into the desert where there was preaching and praying. Drawing from al-Maqrizi's chronicle, ibn Taghrî Birdî tells "of eighteen fishermen who were in one place fourteen died on one day; the remaining four went to carry them to the graves, and as they were walking three died; so one went to attend to them all and bring them to the graves, and he died too." Despite the carnage, the duties of the living to the dead were performed. Ibn Taghrî Birdî wrote of how people "were unable to bury their dead, and passed the night with them at the cemeteries, while the gravediggers spent the whole night digging; they made large trenches, the dead in each one reaching a large number. Dogs ate the extremities of them, while the people searched eagerly all the night for washers [to prepare the corpses properly], porters, and shrouds."[12]

When pestilence struck Cairo in 1438 the sultan's religious lawyers told the ruler that Allah was specifically punishing the sin of fornication and that women should be forbidden to appear in public at all, lest they tempt the men. He agreed and imposed the law until the wealthy complained that their female servants could not shop for food. When he allowed this exception, other women dressed like servants and broke the law. Ibn Taghrî Birdî mocked this rare but futile attempt at intervention as "the result of the ineptitude of the rulers."[13]

Egypt continued to suffer epidemics. Of the 170 years between 1347 and 1517, when the Mamlūk regime fell to the Ottoman Turks, fifty-five were Plague years in Egypt, and twenty were serious outbreaks. Though there was another physical revival, like that of the 1380s, in the mid-fifteenth century, the city did not surpass its old glory until the late eighteenth or nineteenth century.

FLORENCE, ITALY

The Florentines were a proud—some would say arrogant—people who held their civic destiny in their own hands. From the late eleventh century they had negotiated and wrested the power to manage their own civic affairs away from the Holy Roman Emperor and his feudal lords in Italy. By the fourteenth century, for all intents and purposes, Florence was the center of a self-governing city-state that minted its own coins, levied its own taxes, conducted its own foreign policy, and controlled the countryside and towns for miles around—its *contado*. Family for family, it was one of Europe's wealthiest cities, its prosperity being based on the wool cloth trade and banking. Citizenship depended upon one's participation in one of the city's guilds, the organizations of Florence's craftspeople, merchants, and professionals; and representatives of the major guilds ran the city government. Civic pride and economic success went hand in hand in Florence, and the wealthy were as likely to build a church as they were to erect a townhouse.

Christianity was a public as well as a private matter. Religious processions filled the streets every year, and the huge churches of the Franciscan and Dominican friars overflowed when popular preachers came into town to fire up the slackers and make the pious feel good about themselves. Sin, and punishment for it, was a serious part of every Florentine's consciousness: Dante, who so vividly described the pains of Hell in his *Divine Comedy*, was her favorite son, and on the ceiling of the Baptistery building, where every new citizen-to-be was baptized, sat Christ in Judgmental majesty, and Satan, chomping hungrily on the damned. Florentines knew they were sinners—the clergy reminded them often enough—but, like Christians everywhere, they felt they could make their peace with God through the good works and charity that proved their faith and the repentance prescribed by their priests. Many belonged to religious brotherhoods (confraternities) that prayed and helped the poor; others supported the city's hospitals and charitable organizations, while all supported the Church through their parishes, the cathedral, and the city's monasteries and convents. They took sin and virtue, Heaven and Hell, divine reward and divine punishment very seriously, and when the pestilence hit, they knew what it meant.

Florence had been growing briskly for two centuries, despite famines and some types of epidemic earlier in the fourteenth century. On the eve of the Black Death, in 1346–47, she suffered a famine that killed about 4,000 people.[14] In the late 1330s Florence had between 90,000 and 120,000 people living in the city itself. At the same time its *contado* held about 300,000 people,[15] making Florentine territory one of the most densely settled regions in Europe. When the pestilence struck, in late March or early April 1348, probably arriving from Pisa or Genoa, the Florentine government had already begun to respond. They had long believed that vile odors caused sickness, and from the thirteenth century they had regulated the location and operation of smelly businesses; sewers were even cleaned out twice a year. In 1319 they had prohibited the slaughter of livestock in specific locations, because butchered animals "provoked illness among [neighborhood] inhabitants through their pestiferous exhalations." In March 1348 they passed a law concerning the "corruption and infection of the air." To limit the amount of "putrefaction and corruption of things and bodies" in the city, Florentines were "to remove and carry away from the city of Florence and from its suburbs any putrid thing or things and infected persons and similar things, from which might [proceed] corruption of the air and infection."[16] On April 3 they passed further laws that suggested a lack of belief in poisonous miasma. The clothes of sick people were to be destroyed, not sold or worn by others; prostitutes were expelled—probably for both moral reasons and to reduce the amount of sexual activity that physicians considered conducive to infection; and visitors from Pisa or Genoa were barred, with violators owing 500 lire (a small fortune) as a fine. None of these measures stopped the sixty to eighty deaths that were occurring each day, so on April 11 a temporary eight-person commission was formed to enforce these laws and oversee burial.[17] This last, very reasonable step was not repeated in Florence, however, until the fifteenth century.

Venice had set up a three-man health board in March, for "the conservation of the health [of the city] and the elimination of the corruption of the land." In Perugia, Italy, the noted physician Gentile da Foligno strongly urged that "some good men" meet with the College—or guild—of Physicians to "make arrangements for preserving the health of the city."[18] Most European cities were slow to make such arrangements: Barcelona in 1408; Ragusa (Dalmatia), 1426; Avignon, 1479; Milan, 1485. Marseille, hit so hard in 1347, did not establish such a board until 1472. By the mid-fifteenth century such health boards in European cities were sequestering, or quarantining, strangers, issuing and checking "health passports" that certified one free of disease, isolating the ill, managing or regulating charities, medical services, and burial practices, keeping records on the victims, and keeping up to date on where the plague was being reported.[19]

According to a chronicler of Ferrara, Florentine daily death counts began to rise in mid-June to around 100, and much more drastically in July and August when they "started to climb to 300, 380 and 400."[20] It was probably during the cruel days of high summer that Giovanni Boccaccio set the Introduction to his renowned collection of short stories, *The Decameron.* As the pestilence raged around them, a mixed group of ten young well-off Florentines met and decided to take the physicians' advice and flee to a country estate where the air would be healthier and their spirits lighter. Here they relate, over ten consecutive days, the 100 tales that make up the work. In setting the initial scene Boccaccio painted the classic portrait of human reaction to the Black Death. He brilliantly described the symptoms and the physicians' helplessness, the disease's contagiousness, and most famously the "fear and such fantastic notions among those who remained alive that almost all of them took a very cruel attitude in the matter: that is, they completely avoided the sick and their possessions; and in doing so each one believed he was protecting his good health." The breakdown in family ties that Boccaccio relates echoes descriptions of the First Pandemic: "brother abandoned brother, uncle abandoned nephew, sister abandoned brother." In his pages we find the sick dying unattended, the greedy corpse-carriers (*becchini*), and the unmarked graves. "The city was full of corpses."[21] Boccaccio's readers—for two centuries, in fact—knew the horrors firsthand, but his hellish picture was both a commentary on the weaknesses of human nature and artistically a grim background against which the beautiful, charming, and seemingly unscathed storytellers told their amusing tales.

Flight from the pestilential carnage and all of the suffering victims was, as Boccaccio admits, advised by physicians for self-preservation, but nonetheless presented a moral problem for this Christian group, and many others, no doubt. Unlike Islam, Christianity did not prohibit flight in such a circumstance, but it did expect people to love and aid their neighbors, even to be self-sacrificing. Boccaccio's group concluded that they could protect their own lives by fleeing for a time, but could really do no good by staying. Later in the century the Florentine moralist and city's chancellor, Coluccio Salutati, denounced flight as immoral and vile treason against the fatherland; those who flee often die in any case, he observed (he did not believe in miasma theory). In 1374 there were not enough city councilors for a quorum to conduct business, so the government imposed a fine of 500 lire on those who had fled and refused to return. Sometimes physicians followed their own advice, but Venice put an end to this in 1382, threatening such fugitives with loss of citizenship.[22] Concerning the 1383 epidemic, Florence's fourth, her son Marchionne di Stefano related that "many laws were passed that no citizens could leave because of the said plague. For [the rulers] feared that the [common people] would not leave, and would rise, and the malcontents would unite them." Florentine woolworkers had indeed risen up and held the government hostage during the Ciompi Revolt of 1378. Did the rich and powerful remain in the city to intimidate any Plague-time revolutionaries? Marchionne tells us no: for "it is always so that large and powerful beasts jump and break fences."[23] In the same year, for the first time, Florence posted civic guards, perhaps as much to keep people in as to keep Plague-carriers out.[24]

The issue of flight puts popular attitudes about the causes of the pestilence in an interesting light. If the Plague is punishment for sin, and punishment is inevitable, then how can one successfully flee it? If God uses the cloud of miasmic air only to punish the unrepentant, then he should preserve the properly pious, whether they flee or not. But flee people did, at least those with the resources. Salutati's student, the Florentine historian Lionardo Bruni, relates that in 1383 so many of the upper class left the city or died that nothing worthy of recording happened that year. In the Plague years 1390 and 1400 the Florentine citizen and merchant of Prato, Francesco Datini, bundled up most of his household and relocated to Pistoia and Bologna, respectively. His correspondence relates the care with which he chose his destinations, and though he weighed the options, he did not follow the advice of the physician da Tossignano, who wrote in his *consilium*: "It is safer to move to a region where there has never been an epidemic than where pestilence has reigned even six months back, since the *reliquae* (residue) will remain and, acting like a ferment, will infect those who come into the locality."[25] From our modern perspective, the biggest problem with flight was that it very probably spread the disease from place to place.

Boccaccio emphasized the social disruption caused by the deaths and the continuing presence of death and chaos. Many after him painted similar pictures, but more recent research on Florence and other cities has altered this image. Wills, for example, were still being attested to in the presence of many witnesses, a sign that the dying were not simply abandoned wholesale. While there are gaps in the records of city government activities, nowhere in Europe is there evidence of the collapse of the government or civilized life. Though in cities corpses were often dumped in mass, unmarked graves, the same was done after battles. The sheer number of bodies overtaxed the society's ability to dispose of them in both a traditional and timely manner. When the crisis was over, people quickly returned to their customary practices.

Disruption did occur, of course, in the lives of individuals and families. Women often died in childbirth, and children commonly passed away early in life, but the heads of households were expected to survive these occurrences, and life would carry on. When fathers, grandfathers, and uncles disappeared, they left wives, children, servants, and even slaves at the mercy of circumstances. Scoundrels, often called "false friends," took unfair advantage of widows or orphans, fleecing them of what little they might have inherited while claiming to protect it. Even while the Plague raged, legal disputes over inheritances and wardship brought misery to many. In post-Plague Florence, the great Confraternity of Orsanmichele, whose treasury brimmed with gifts and legacies from wills, made a point of targeting their charity to needy women and minors, rather than to down-and-out men. Their average individual gifts grew from one half lira (1348) to fifteen lire (1350) and twenty-three lire (1351). The Florentine Confraternity of the Roast Chestnuts concerned themselves with burying the dead during the Plague year, but in 1350 shifted their efforts to providing the poor, especially women, with financial support.[26] Similar activities picked up all over the Christian world.

In general, the rates of poverty dropped as fewer people shared the same amount of resources, and the demand and wages for even the lowliest workers rose dramatically. What also rose was the rate of vulnerability: legally unprotected orphans, and widows with minor children. The poor were much more likely to be women now, and fortunately the society realized this and provided appropriate relief. Women were also literally the future of the society. As much as anyone, Florentines recognized the need for an increase in births to compensate for the enormous death toll. When actively supporting marriage and childbirth becomes a policy, it is called natalism. Through both official and private initiatives natalism became Florentine policy. A woman's share of her birth family's wealth traveled with her into marriage and was called her dowry. Prospective husbands insisted and relied upon these financial resources; rarely were marriages arranged without them. Poor young women whose families had little or nothing relied upon the aid of others to provide part or all of a respectable dowry. To help a prospective bride was "good charity": the act itself was pious and the woman would, presumably, pray for the salvation of her patron's soul. During one Plague year Francesco Datini, who usually gave when asked, refused to help a specific young woman because he had just aided another but she had died very soon after. A widow legally still had access to her dowry, so she was unlikely to get aid. Orsanmichele's gifts may have supported as many as 20 percent of post-Plague marriages. As might be expected, the age at first marriage dropped significantly after 1350, but crept back up as the century drew to a close. In the early fifteenth century the Florentines initiated the *Monte delle doti*, or Dowry Fund, into which new fathers of girls paid small amounts toward a handsome payoff when the child wed. The fund operated successfully until the government raided it for needed revenue.

The civic government also responded by invoking divine aid and seeking medical knowledge, with no apparent sense of irony. It allowed the annual public gathering on June 24 for the feast St. John the Baptist, the city's patron saint. Religious processions were held and wound their way through the city's neighborhoods despite doctors' warnings against the dangers of crowds and infections. These same physicians, however, did receive the license to conduct autopsies of victims in the hope of better understanding the nature of the disease.[27] If the crisis had both natural and supernatural causes, then the authorities had to respond accordingly. Individuals did so as well: they assaulted Heaven with their prayers, but took their medicines, watched their diets, burned their aromatic woods to fumigate their rooms, and did all they could to avoid melancholy. Some, as Boccaccio vividly reminded his readers, took the last too far, losing their inhibitions, reveling in drunkenness and immoral activity. Abandoned shops and houses found few guardians even among the civic-minded, so that criminals and the unscrupulous helped themselves to what they desired, "doing everything that amused or pleased them the most."[28]

By the end of the pestilence, in early September, the death toll in Florence was terrible. Historian Gene Brucker says that the 1352 tax survey "suggests" that the city had only about 50,000 residents; historical demographer Massimo Livi Bacci claims that the death rate in 1348 was twenty times normal, with an abnormally high grouping of deaths in the high summer that distorts these figures even more. "We have only scattered notices here and there, certainly indicative of the general effects of the plague, but, in themselves, of little value for determining the number of the dead."[29] Most scholars accept a death rate in Florence of about 55–60 percent, or about 60,000 people.

Epidemic disease recurred in Tuscany in 1363, 1371, 1383, 1390–91, 1400, 1410, 1417, 1422–23, 1429–30, 1439, 1448–50, 1456, 1478–79, and 1495–98. Each of these outbreaks took a far smaller toll than the great one, in both number and percentage of the population, but the cumulative effect was to keep her population below pre-Plague levels until the eighteenth century. By 1427 the city's population had dropped to 37 percent of its pre-Plague size, and only increased significantly in the last part of the century. Despite their natalist policies, Florentines were not reproducing themselves fast enough, nor did they allow large numbers to immigrate into the city. The Florentine peasantry worked under much better terms and conditions than did the Egyptian; these, and high prices for food, gave them little incentive to leave the countryside for the city. Even so, perhaps 12,000 moved within the walls between 1354 and 1364 to take advantage of high wages and abundant charity.

The chronicler Matteo Villani, who survived his elder brother, Giovanni, described the economic expectations generated and the problems Florence faced:

> It was thought that depopulation would bring with it an abundance of all the fruits of the earth, but it was not so; human ingratitude was such that there was a great lack of everything, and this lasted

for a long time. In some parts . . . there was terrible and extraordinary famine. And it was thought also that there would be clothing in plenty, and an abundance of all other things, which, besides food, the body has most need of; but again this was not so and these things were lacking for a long time. But payment for labor and the cost of such things as are wrought by craftsmen and artisans of all kinds more than doubled compared with their customary price.[30]

Wages of skilled labor rose nearly 200 percent, and even unskilled laborers commanded three times their previous salaries. Yet Florentine economic recovery was rapid and impressive. Wealthy Florentines bought up rural farmland after 1348 and quickly profited from high prices, eventually bringing them down in good years with high production. They made *mezzadria*—or sharecropping—contracts with their laborers, so that both parties benefited from increased yields. In this way, and in general, the independent Florentine entrepreneurs were far more capable than their Cairene brothers of shifting their capital to put it to best use.[31] Young Francesco Datini learned early to do this after he took his and his brother's inheritance to Avignon in the 1350s and, by trading in a wide variety of goods, built up a fortune. Florentines had built their city and their fortunes by taking rational risks and by taking opportunity of formal and informal associations from family to partnerships to confraternities, guilds, patron-client relationships, and the communal government itself. Yet despite this web of relationships, Florentines exhibited self-assurance based on self-reliance that would set the tone for the Renaissance of the next century.[32] They also reinstated legal slavery after the Plague of 1363.

If the Florentine government all but disappeared between April and August 1348, it recovered rapidly. It raised taxes to make up for lost revenues and encouraged artisans from elsewhere to settle in Florence but limited immigration from its own farms, and its courts sorted out sticky matters of inheritance and wardship. As early as August 1348 they felt optimistic enough to announce the founding—or refounding—of a university, the *Studio fiorentino*. The government saw it as a way not only of replacing lost intellectuals and better educating its shrunken populace, but also of drawing students from elsewhere.[33] Guilds relaxed their membership requirements—as did monasteries and convents—to entice merchants, craftsmen, and professionals. The physicians' guild, however, tightened theirs, since so many quacks and frauds practiced medicine during the Plague; with the communal government they also far more tightly regulated the prescription and sale of medicines.

Over the 150 years following the first outbreak of the Black Death, Florentines, often working through their government, took many important and far-reaching steps to control the pestilence, or at least its impacts, and some whose effects were more dubious. Some of these measures were moralistic and sought to control or eliminate certain sexual behaviors: public prostitution (1403), immorality in women's religious convents (1421), and sodomy (1432).[34] From 1385 until the eighteenth century the Grain Office maintained the *Book of the Dead*, in which civic deaths were recorded. From 1424 causes of death appear, allowing for some modern analysis. For example, from 1424 to 1430, 68 percent of recorded deaths were from pestilence (seven from intestinal disorders, seven from old age, and four from fevers).[35] The Grain Office also oversaw prostitutes, gravediggers, parish burial records, and compliance with sumptuary laws.[36] These last targeted two types of behavior: lower-class people dressing out of their class in cheap, secondhand upper-class clothes, and overly lavish funerals. Fancy funerals were acceptable for civic heroes or important people, and the post-Plague trend really began in 1353 with the return of the corpse of wealthy Nicola Acciaiuoli's son from Naples. The lower classes began to imitate the upper, with flamboyant displays of candles, fancy cloths over the casket, and crowds of paid mourners. In 1374 laws restricting the numbers of candles (four) and mourners went into effect.[37]

More importantly, in 1448 the civic committee called the Eight Guardians, "for the conservation of health and preservation from the said pestilence and avoidance of contagion [one of the earliest uses of the word in a public document]," provided publicly distributed bread for the poor, four public physicians and four barber-surgeons to treat the poor, and sixty men and women to visit—and monitor—the sick. Florence already had one large hospital, the 200-bed Santa Maria Nuova, but in 1464 they began to build a new one in the city. They quickly built two in the port cities of Livorno and Pisa, in an attempt to isolate future sea-borne cases.[38] The new foundation in Florence itself was to be an isolation hospital (*lazaretto*) specifically for pestilence victims and based upon older leper-houses. It would have a staff that included a priest, physician, barber-surgeon, pharmacist, and servants. Venice had opened one in 1424, expanded it in 1429, and built a second in 1471; Milan began their first in 1468. The Florentine government reauthorized their project in 1472 and 1476, and construction finally began in 1479. It was not until 1497 that the hospital's twenty-six beds held their first Plague victims. In 1494 the Florentine government reconstituted the health board with which they had experimented in 1348. Five men with six-month terms kept watch on where the Plague was being reported, provided clean bills of health for Florentine travelers, and condemned violators of sanitation laws. As Luca Landucci pointed out in his diary (see Document 12), during the epidemic of the late 1490s they also expelled poor victims of disease from the city, an action taken by many cities in Europe. The board was made official in 1496 as the Ufficiali del Morbo (Officials for Disease), but was staffed by permanent officers only after 1527.[39]

COMPARING CAIRO AND FLORENCE

The reader may have noticed that the section on Florence in this chapter is rather longer than that on Cairo. In part this is because the documentary record on Florence is richer, but it is also because the range of responses made by Florentines over the years was wider. Muslims and Christians alike relied upon flight and medicines, both groups prayed privately and en masse for divine mercy, and both suffered deeply the pangs of loss and the terrible fear of sudden illness and death. In neither culture did social norms disintegrate or governments crumble. Despising God never rose to the level of fearing (or loving) him, so traditional religion and its leaders retained their spiritual and cultural holds on both peoples. When the dead had been mourned and buried, Muslim and Christian alike sought life as it had been.

Yet Florence, and Christian Europe more generally, recovered far more quickly and completely than did Cairo and the Muslim world more generally. Although in both cultural regions rebuilding the population remained dampened by relatively low birth rates and recurrent epidemics with high death rates, the Florentine economy quickly became aggressive and increasingly capitalistic—carefully reinvesting its wealth in making more wealth. The Cairene and Florentine were both highly competitive and wonderful bargainers, but competition among the Italians led not only to lower prices but also to better products. By 1400 Florence was selling its high-quality wool cloth in Cairo, putting the city's own weavers out of business. The relatively greater mobility of capital—the ability to make or change investments of wealth rather easily—encouraged placement of resources, in northern Italy at least, where profits would be highest and most certain. This made for a wealthier and more optimistic society.

Christians and Muslims both believed that they thrived when God smiled and failed when he was displeased, but the Christians had a broader sense of their ability to bargain with the almighty. God's will was malleable, able to be shaped by the intercession of saints and the survivors' prayers and acts of charity. Allah was considered most merciful, but Muslims tended to have a more predestinarian view of his will: what would happen was already determined. Their reactions betray a certain fatalism that Catholic Christianity felt it could overcome. This difference was further reinforced by the differences between Christian and Muslim governing systems. In Cairo the full integration of governance and religion (including secular and religious law) that created the Islamic state left no room for individual participation or influence or initiative. In the Catholic world the Church and State intersected, but neither had absolute power over the other, nor over the individual. Competition between them allowed for plenty of individual participation, influence, and initiative in society. In cities such as Florence, these three were at the very root of civic governance. When it came to the Black Death and its many recurrences, the Florentine, and by extension European, responses were thus more fluid, innovative, creative, and evolutionary than those of the Islamic states. This may help explain why the Black Death disappeared from European countries one to two centuries earlier than it did from the Near East.

NOTES

1. Quoted in Gaston Wiet, *Cairo* (Norman: University of Oklahoma Press, 1964), pp. 63, 73.

2. Abraham Udovitch et al., "England to Egypt, 1350–1500," in *Studies in the Economic History of the Middle East*, ed. M. Cook (New York: Oxford University Press, 1970), p. 119.

3. Lawrence Conrad, "Epidemic Disease in Formal and Popular Thought in Early Islamic Society," in *Epidemics and Ideas*, ed. Ranger and Slack (Cambridge, England: Cambridge University Press, 1992), p. 93.

4. Quotes in Anna Campbell, *The Black Death and Men of Learning* (New York: Columbia University Press, 1931), pp. 59, 73.

5. Michael Dols, *The Black Death in the Middle East* (Princeton: Princeton University Press, 1977), pp. 237–43.

6. Michael Dols, "The Comparative Communal Responses to the Black Death in Muslim and Christian Societies," *Viator* 5 (1974): p. 286.

7. Dols, *Black Death*, pp. 160–63; Dols, "Comparative," p. 277.

8. Dols, *Black Death*, pp. 271–72.

9. Janet Abu-Lughod, *Cairo* (Princeton: Princeton University Press, 1971), p. 37.

10. Abu-Lughod, *Cairo*, p. 39; Eliyahu Ashtor, *A Social and Economic History of the Near East in the Middle Ages* (Berkeley: University of California Press, 1976), p. 306.

11. Quoted in Ashtor, *Social and Economic History*, p. 304.

12. Abu l-Ma·hasin ibn Taghrî Birdî, *History of Egypt 1382–1469 AD*, Vol. 18 part 4, ed. and trans. William Popper (Berkeley: University of California Press, 1915–64), pp. 69, 70, 73, 182.

13. Ibn Taghrî Birdî, *History*, pp. 146–47.

14. Antonio Ferlini, *Pestilenze nei secoli a Faenza e nella valli del Lamone e del Senio* (Faenza: Tipografia Faentina, 1990), p. 51.

15. David Herlihy and Christine Klapisch-Zuber, *Tuscans and Their Families* (New Haven: Yale University Press, 1985), pp. 65, 69.

16. John Henderson, "The Black Death in Florence: Medical and Communal Responses," in *Death in Towns*, ed. Steven Bassett (New York: Leicester University Press, 1992), p. 143.

17. Henderson, "Black Death," p. 144; Ann Carmichael, *Plague and the Poor in Renaissance Florence* (New York: Cambridge University Press, 1986), p. 99.

18. Henderson, "Black Death," pp. 142–43; Jon Arrizabalaga, "Facing the Black Death: Perceptions and Reactions of University Medical Practitioners," in *Practical Medicine from Salerno to the Black Death*, ed. Luis Garcia-Ballester et al. (New York: Cambridge University Press, 1994), p. 271.

19. Jean-Noël Biraben, *Les hommes et la peste en France et dans les pays européens et méditeranéens*, Vol. 2 (Paris: Mouton, 1976), pp. 138–39; Ann Carmichael, "Bubonic Plague: The Black Death," in *Plague, Pox and Pestilence: Disease in History*, ed. Kenneth Kiple et al. (New York: Marboro Books, 1997), p. 63.

20. Quoted in Ann Carmichael, "Plague Legislation in the Italian Renaissance," *Bulletin of the History of Medicine* 57 (1983): p. 514.

21. Giovanni Boccaccio, *The Decameron*, trans. Mark Musa and Peter Bondanella (New York: Norton, 1977), pp. 5, 6, 8.

22. Francesco Gianni, "Per una storia letteraria della pesta," in *The Regulation of Evil*, ed. Agostino Paravicini Bagliani and Francesco Santi (Sismel: Galluzzo, 1998), p. 100; Samuel Cohn, *The Black Death Transformed: Disease and Culture in Early Renaissance Europe* (Oxford: Oxford University Press, 2002), p. 125; D. W. Amundson, "Medical Deontology and Pestilential Disease in the Late Middle Ages," *Journal of the History of Medicine* 23 (1977): p. 410.

23. William Naphy and Andrew Spicer, *The Black Death and the History of Plagues, 1345–1730* (Stroud, Gloucestershire, England: Tempus, 2001), pp. 59–60.

24. Carmichael, *Plague*, p. 99.

25. Quoted in Ann Carmichael, "Contagion Theory and Contagion Practice in Fifteenth-century Milan," *Renaissance Quarterly* 44 (1991): p. 226.

26. John Henderson, "Women, Children and Poverty in Florence at the Time of the Black Death," in *Poor Women and Children in the European Past*, ed. Henderson and Richard Wall (New York: Routledge, 1994), p. 170; Henderson, "The Parish and the Poor in Florence at the Time of the Black Death," *Continuity and Change* 3 (1988): pp. 259–60.

27. Gian Maria Varanini, "La Peste del 1347–50 e i governi dell'Italia centro-settentrionale: un bilancio," in *La pesta nera* (Spoleto: Centro italiano di studi sull'altro medioevo, 1994), p. 295.

28. Boccaccio, *Decameron*, p. 5.

29. Gene Brucker, "Florence and the Black Death," *Boccaccio: secoli di vita*, ed. Marga C. Jones and Edward Tuttle (Ravenna: Longo Editore, 1977), p. 22; Massimo Livi Bacci, *The Population of Europe: A History*, trans. Cynthia and Carl Ipsen (New York: Blackwell, 1999), p. 42; quote from Alberto Falsini, "Firenze dopo il 1348," *Archivio storico italiano* 129 (1971): p. 434.

30. Quoted in Bronislaw Geremek, *Poverty: A History* (New York: Blackwell, 1994), pp. 80–81.

31. Henderson, "Women," pp. 163–64; Samuel Cohn, "Florentine Insurrections, 1342–1385, in Comparative Perspective," in *The English Uprising of 1381*, ed. R. H. Hilton and T. H. Aston (New York: Cambridge University Press, 1987), pp. 143–45; James Powell, "Crisis and Culture in Renaissance Europe," *Medievalia et humanistica* 12 (1984): pp. 208–9.

32. Brucker, "Florence," p. 28.

33. Brucker, "Florence," p. 23; Katherine Park, *Doctors and Medicine in Early Renaissance Florence* (Princeton: Princeton University Press, 1985), p. 40.

34. Naphy and Spicer, *Black Death*, p. 73.

35. A. L. Morrison, et al., "Epidemics in Renaissance Florence," *American Journal of Public Health* 75 (1985): p. 534.

36. Carmichael, *Plague*, p. 27.

37. Sharon Strocchia, *Death and Ritual in Renaissance Florence* (Baltimore: Johns Hopkins University Press, 1992), pp. 55, 59, 62.

38. John Henderson, "Epidemics in Renaissance Florence," in *Maladies et société (XIIe–XVIIIe siècles)*, ed. Neithard Bulst and Robert Delort (Paris: Editions du C.N.R.S., 1989), pp. 171–72; Varanini, "La Peste," p. 316.

39. Carmichael, *Plague*, 101, 103, 105; Henderson, "Epidemics," pp. 172–74.

CHAPTER 8

EPILOGUE: THE END OF THE BLACK DEATH AND ITS CONTINUING FASCINATION

Between the 1650s and the 1720s, region by region, pestilence disappeared from Europe. The pattern is clear—Scotland, Italy, and England by 1670, Spain in the 1680s, Scandinavia, the Netherlands, and central Europe by 1720, and France in the following decade—but the reason or reasons for it are not. Ultimately the explanation must be biological, but did human intervention help nature? Most scholars are willing to consider several possibilities, often in combinations, while some have their favorites. The following discussion assumes the pestilence was the bubonic plague.

A few simply claim that the bacillus itself must have mutated into a more benign form. Stephen Ell suggests that $Y.$ *pestis* may have mutated slightly into the less deadly or pathogenic forms of $Y.$ *enterocolitica*, or $Y.$ *pseudotuberculosis*. But he immediately asks "Why?" and "Why only in Europe?" Mutation is a complex process that provides little advantage to the organism in this case. Perhaps the change was in the flea, as biologist L. F. Hirst posits without elaboration or explanation. On the other hand, humans may have developed a form of immunity by having contracted $Y.$ *pseudotuberculosis*, which confers temporary immunity to bubonic plague. French biologist and historian Jean-Noël Biraben thought this enough to break the cycle, but historian A. B. Appleby points out that this would lead to a gradual die-off of bubonic plague, not sudden cessations; and in any case, $Y.$ *pseudotuberculosis* seems to have appeared as an independent bacterial strain only in the nineteenth century.[1]

Most explanations focus on the rat. The replacement of weakened *Rattus rattus* with *Rattus norvegicus* was once a popular answer, since X. *cheopis* is far less fond of the brown rat. The problem is that *R. norvegicus* arrived in western Europe only in the mid-eighteenth century, after the pestilence ended, and the two currently live side by side. Some think that immune variations of *R. rattus* may have replaced more susceptible rats through invasion, while Appleby sees the lack of an epizootic as due to development of immunity within the rat population itself. But why did this not occur earlier? He answers, "I have no idea." In another scenario, the rat population may have simply dropped below levels necessary to sustain an epizootic. Some connect this to changes in European trade patterns that broke overland contact with central Asia and shifted maritime shipping from the Mediterranean Sea to the Atlantic. Contrarily, Ell claims that there never has been an enzootic plague focus in Europe, so there is no question of its disappearance, taking the Plague with it, so to speak. Finally, Hans Zinsser's venerable answer from 1935 is that rats became more sedentary with better urban food supplies and more secure homes, and thus migrated—and encountered strange fleas—less often.[2]

Human progress may have changed human susceptibility, incidentally or consciously. Many, like biologist J. F. Shrewsbury, point to new brick houses with slate or tile roofs as keys to the question: no more black rats living in thatch roofs or plastered walls. Others claim better personal hygiene in general kept fleas away, and biologist Henri Mollaret specifically credits flea-repelling soap. He also cites more frequent changes of clothing, especially in winter, which stranded fleas without human body heat. Some suspect that better nutrition helped strengthen human resistance, but others counter that the rich always ate well and still died.[3] Historian David Herlihy and others see people's conscious efforts to stem the tide as proving effective in the long run. Contagion theory progressed and public health efforts gained in potency, they claim. Historian Paul Slack gives credit specifically to quarantines strengthened by early notice of Plague outbreaks elsewhere and firm action by local authorities. Travel regulations and blockades of people and goods from infected areas may well have stopped feeding the susceptible rat supply, and isolation of the sick may have limited exposure to pneumonic versions of the

Plague. Advances in public sanitation—sewers, garbage control, and even the use of disinfectants—may have played their part, but Appleby reminds us that both Naples and London (even after the city fire of 1666) were still quite foul when the Plague ceased. Perhaps the truth lies in historian Kari Konkola's discovery that the large-scale use of arsenic as rat poison began in Europe at the same time that the Plague began to disappear.[4]

THE BLACK DEATH AND THE WESTERN IMAGINATION

Six hundred and fifty years after the first chroniclers and physicians recorded the opening stages of the Second Pandemic, Western society retains an uneasy fascination with the Black Death. Though living in the shadow of the man-made Holocaust and the development and use of nuclear and other types of weapons of mass destruction, we still reel at the thought of Nature's destructive capability. That people might unleash something as terrible as the Black Death on other people seems both unthinkable and closer to reality than ever before in history. As the Rand Corporation study cited in the Preface suggested, the Medieval Plague might just be a distant mirror for our society, making all the more disturbing the conclusion that human society can withstand such a blow and remain intact.

Popular culture has harnessed the Black Death's horrors in solemn and dark films such as Ingmar Bergman's *The Seventh Seal*, and callously mocked it in Monty Python's irreverent *Holy Grail*. Via the Internet one may purchase "Black Death on Tour" T-shirts and coffee mugs, while another vendor sells Black Death Vodka. Images of rats and dirty medieval peasants, maybe dancing skeletons, and the call of "Bring out your dead!" remain embedded in our social consciousness. Yet as we become ever more accustomed to human suffering and violent and mass death in the mass media, the realities described by Boccaccio and chroniclers become both more familiar and less horrific, taking on the unreal reality of a Halloween haunted house.

And so the student of the medieval Black Death has to navigate between the equally popular tendencies on the one hand to emphasize the gross and disturbing elements for the purpose of titillation and on the other hand to arouse the fear of an uncontrollable outbreak of deadly disease behind every newly discovered contagious ailment. Especially in its initial outbreak, the Black Death was the worst natural disaster known to human history. Biological and social scientists and historians have recently been revisiting the event and revising our shared understanding of it: what used to be stated with confidence must now be changed, or at least carefully qualified. Demographers have been raising their estimates of death tolls, while social historians have been downplaying the event's impact of social and political order from Syria to Ireland. In the short run, recovery seems to have been quite rapid and complete, though with repeated recurrences both human behavior and social structures appear to have been reshaped. Finally, historians more generally have begun to conclude that the Black Death's great impact was to intensify certain political, economic, cultural, and social trends rather than to initiate them.

Since the 1930s lone voices have questioned the fit between the actual epidemiology of bubonic plague as uncovered early in the century and the disease(-s?) experienced and written about in the fourteenth and fifteenth centuries. More recently, lone voices have become an increasingly loud chorus: no one mentioned rats; it spread too swiftly and in the wrong seasons; death tolls were too high; the symptoms do not all add up: it probably was not bubonic plague. Then what was it? At this the chorus breaks up again and their answers range from anthrax to an unspecified viral hemorrhagic fever. When bubonic plague DNA was found in dental pulp many felt vindicated, others questioned the procedures and conclusions, and still others said, "Fine for southern France, but in England it was not plague, it was . . ." Advances in biological and medical science will continue to shape this debate, as Chapter 2 suggests.

In the 1350s medieval chroniclers estimated the loss of life locally or across the land as anywhere from one-third to 90 percent of the population. Modern historians, rightly wary of such figures, generally set the toll at "from 25 to 33 percent." English researchers, and to a lesser degree continental ones, have been concentrating on locales, and their studies, taken together, demonstrate that the overall death toll estimate and the local figures need to be raised. Death in the countryside seems to have been quite as common as death in the more densely populated cities. There is a growing consensus that, however one views initial population levels, on a broad scale—regional, national, even continental—the toll was closer to 40 percent of the population, with local variations. Such reassessments make the whole event appear even more ghastly in its effects and support those who believe it was not bubonic plague but some other disease, since no modern outbreak of bubonic plague comes close to such a toll.

The emphasis on local studies, especially of legal and governmental sources, has also reshaped the older picture of a Christian and Islamic world reduced to social and political chaos by the enormous and terrifying death tolls. The flight and deaths of authorities of all types were thought to have left cities and countries without guidance or social controls. Recent research demonstrates that, on the contrary, councils did meet, notaries did file wills, the dead were buried, and criminals were noted and—eventually—punished. Deaths and flight did affect the ability of local governments to collect needed revenues, and leadership, especially in the Church as an institution, did decline in quality, but nowhere did the prepestilence authority structure disintegrate. This is certainly directly related to the observation that in many places economic and social recovery from the first outbreak of the Black Death was quite rapid and in many ways rather complete. In many other places, of course, the immediate effects were devastating: French and English villages disappeared forever; in Italy today visitors to San Gimignano discover a town that looks today as it did before 1348, a victim of economic dislocation that neither grew nor died. Overall, however, the Christian West took advantage of the positive aspects of lower population and movements in wealth; this in contrast to the Mamlūk world's relative lethargy, which resulted in its economic and political decline. The depressive state of the Christian West set in after the recurrence of the pestilence, as people realized that the scourge would be with them indefinitely.

In the end, contemporary scholars are reaching the conclusion that the Black Death, for all its hype and horror, was much more a catalyst for change in the West than an instigator of it. Students of demography are finding that Europe's population had been declining for thirty years before 1348. Students of European art are agreeing that the Plague's effects on style and content were relatively small, given the psychic shock of the event. Students of English feudalism are finding the roots of its demise further and further back in time, making the Black Death responsible for speeding up but not initiating its disappearance. Scholasticism was already declining, use of the vernaculars was already in-creasing, and dissatisfaction with Catholicism was rife, but the Church survived—without any kind of reform, let alone reformation—until the 1520s. Fewer today than in the past are willing to see the Black Death even as a major turning point, an event after which everything was different. This trend in scholarship, however, is likely to evoke cries of disapproval from those who will dig even deeper and continue to shape and reshape our view of the nature and meaning of the Black Death.

The Black Death was both more and less than an event in late me-dieval history. It was an amoral epidemic disease without intention or motivation. It was neither anyone's fault nor the result of anyone's evil. The disease, whatever it was, was natural and inescapable, and the cur-rent fascination for many is in understanding the natural event as a natural event: as a geologist studies earthquakes, a meteorologist hurri-canes, or a climatologist droughts. For most, though, the fascination lies in understanding people's reactions to it, both individually and as a society. The event, then, was the interaction of the natural disease with the people and their societies and the effects that flowed from this in-teraction. Historians seek to order, understand, and give meaning to some of the enormous range of these experiences, reactions, and effects. The questions they ask, the assumptions they make, the type of evidence they choose to study all shape the conclusions to which they come; and their studies will shape the questions, assumptions, and research projects of others, and so goes the historical project. There will never be a "last word" on the Black Death unless and until it has been forgotten. Part of the historian's task is to see that this never happens.

NOTES

1. Stephen Ell, "Immunity as a Factor in the Epidemiology of Medieval Plague," *Review of Infectious Diseases* 6 (1984): pp. 869, 876; A. B. Appleby, "The Disappearance of the Plague: A Continuing Puzzle," *Economic History Review* 33 (1980): p. 165; on Biraben and Hirst see Leslie Bradley, "Some Med-ical Aspects of Plague," in *Plague Reconsidered* (Matlock, Derbyshire, England: Local Population Studies, 1977), pp. 20–21.

2. Appleby, "Disappearance," p. 171; Ell, "Immunity," p. 869; Hans Zinsser, *Rats, Lice and History* (Boston: Little Brown, 1934), pp. 206–7.

3. J. F. Shrewsbury, *History of Bubonic Plague in the British Isles* (New York:

Cambridge University Press, 1970), p. 35; Henri Mollaret, "Introduzione," in *Venezia e la peste, 1348/1797* (Venice: Marsilio Editori, 1979), p. 14.

4. David Herlihy, *The Black Death and the Transformation of the West* (Cambridge, MA: Harvard University Press, 1997), p. 17; Paul Slack, "The Disappearance of Plague: An Alternative View," *Economic History Review* 34 (1981): pp. 469–76; Appleby, "Disappearance," p. 167; Kari Konkola, "More Than a Coincidence? The Arrival of Arsenic and the Disappearance of Plague in Early Modern Europe," *History of Medicine* 47 (1992): pp. 187–90.

BIOGRAPHIES

Abu Abdullah ibn Battuta (1304–68), *Moroccan Legal Scholar and Traveler*

At the end of his twenty-four years of travel from Tangier, Morocco, to the farthest reaches of the Islamic world, Ibn Battuta returned home through the Near East and North Africa, which had been ravaged by the Black Death, and recorded his observations in his *Rihla* (*Book of Travels*). Born into a family of Islamic legal scholars in Tangier in 1304, Ibn Battuta received what education in the Muslim religious law (*Shari'a*) that he could. When he was twenty he set out eastward to perform the required pilgrimage to Mecca (Hajj), study the law further, and see the world. Supporting himself on pious donations, he traveled through Tunis to Cairo, then on to Jerusalem and Damascus, where he caught a caravan bound for Mecca. After performing the required rituals he headed north to Baghdad, from which he visited other Muslim cities in Iraq and Iran. In the company of the Ilkhan (ruler) of Baghdad and his entourage Ibn Battuta returned to Mecca, where he remained as a student from 1327 to 1330. With India as a goal he traveled by boat down the Red Sea and African Coasts as far as Zanzibar, returning to Arabia and the Persian Gulf. From here he turned north, moving through Syria to Turkey, the Crimea, and the Kipchak Khanate; in the Volga region he used carts for the first time to carry his great wealth and growing entourage of wives, slaves, and hangers-on. He lived among "infidels" for the first time in Constantinople, then retraced his steps eastward through the Golden Horde and Afghanistan and finally crossing into India, reaching the Indus in September 1333. He entered the service of the sultan of Delhi as an Islamic *qadi* (judge); there nearly eight years, he reports having judged but a single case (drunkenness: eighty lashes). In August 1341 Ibn Battuta accompanied a Chinese delegation returning to Peking. Along the way, however, a storm destroyed the hired ships and killed many in Calicut Harbor. He worked his way to the Maldive Islands, where he served as *qadi* and married and divorced six wives; then on to Bengal, Ceylon, and the Chinese coast, from which he visited Peking and Hang-chou in 1346. He returned to southern Arabia in April 1347 and, traveling north, reached Baghdad in January 1348.

Come spring, Ibn Battuta visited Damascus and Aleppo, where he first heard of the Plague then raging at Gaza: "the number of dead there exceeded a thousand a day." Returning south he encountered the Plague at Homs, where, he claimed, 300 people died the day he arrived. He reached Damascus in July, and reported a daily death toll of 2,400. People had been fasting for three days, and after prayer on Friday, "God alleviated their plague." Staying no longer than necessary nonetheless, he decided to perform the Hajj one more time. He arrived in Jerusalem after the Plague had passed, and attended a banquet whose host had sworn "he would give a banquet if the plague were to cease and a day were to pass during which he did not pray over a corpse . . . 'Yesterday I did not pray over a corpse.' " Gaza they found mostly "deserted because of the numbers that had died during the plague. The *qadi* told me that only a quarter of the eighty notaries there were left and that the number of deaths had risen to eleven hundred a day." In Egyptian Abu Sir he stayed in a hospice where he was visited by a holy man who stayed the night huddled in a corner. In the morning he "went over to him and found him dead. We prayed over him and buried him. May God have mercy upon him!" At Alexandria he was told the deaths had reached 1,080 a day, and at Cairo they "had risen to twenty-one thousand a day. I found that all the *shaikhs* (scholars) I had known were dead." He completed his Hajj and returned across North Africa to Morocco, where he learned that his mother, whom he had not seen in twenty-four years, had died of the Plague.

Further excursions took him to Granada and Sardinia and south to the kingdom of Mali and Timbuktu, the only part of the Islamic world he had not seen. All told, he visited parts of forty-four modern countries and traveled some 73,000 miles. He died in Fez, Morocco, in 1368.

Charles IV (Charles of Luxembourg) (1316–78), *Holy Roman Emperor*

Holy Roman Emperor Charles IV ruled the empire during the initial outbreak of the Black Death and two successive epidemics. He was born in Prague on May 14, 1316, the son of John of Luxembourg and Elizabeth of Bohemia. Baptized Wenceslas, at age seven he was sent to Paris to be raised at the court of King Charles IV, and took this monarch's name when he was confirmed in the Church. While in Paris he was deeply affected by the preaching of Pierre Roger, who would go on to become Pope Clement VI, ruler of the Church during the Black Death of 1347–52. Young Charles also studied briefly at the University of Paris, where he gained an appreciation of formal education, and perhaps astrology specifically. In his late teens he administered the kingdom of Bohemia from Prague, and when his father went blind, in 1340, he managed the family's Luxembourg holdings. The emperor, Louis the Bavarian, had long fought with the papacy and angered many of the German princes. In 1344 Louis was excommunicated by the pope and told he would be dethroned if not cleared within two years. Two years later Louis was deposed and Charles elected as king of the Romans in Bonn, the last step toward the imperial throne. His early friendship with the pope certainly helped matters. A year after that he was crowned king of Bohemia after his father's death at the Battle of Crécy, and in 1355 as emperor, in Rome.

The Black Death first arrived in imperial territories when it struck northern Italy, but Charles did nothing to intervene in this self-sufficient land. For the most part, he could do little outside his own ancestral lands, and with regard to these, he did little. He followed the pope in decrying the persecution of Jews as "Plague-spreaders," but tarnished this moral act by offering to the archbishop of Trier the goods and property of all Jews in Alsace that were killed or to be killed in future. This may have been a baldly political ploy to curry favor with one of the empire's electors, and it certainly gave the churchman no incentive to stem the violence. On the other hand, this may have been meant to deter the murders and looting by the mobs of lay people, who could not legally benefit from robbing that which now belonged to the Church. Charles is also said to have promised the margrave of Brandenburg the three best Jewish houses emptied in the next pogrom in Nuremberg. This gentleman was also one of the electors, and there is no way to preserve Charles' integrity in this instance. Charles also echoed the pope in speaking out against the flagellants, but he played little role in their eventual disappearance.

Before the Black Death Charles established the university in Prague (papal bull of January 1347; imperial charter of April 1348), central Europe's first university. Its dual models were those of Paris and Bologna, Europe's centers for the study of theology and law, respectively. The breadth of his intellectual interests was rare for the time, and those interests were no doubt fostered by his time in Paris. Over the three decades that followed the initial epidemic Charles spent lavishly on imperial building projects in Prague, the empire's new capital. He was also firm in his support for intellectuals and writers, such as the poet Heinrich von Mügeln, at his court. Heinrich's poem, "Whoever wants to know," is an explanation of the origins of the Plague in astrological terms, and was firmly in line with Charles' interests. The fact that it was written in German also reflects Charles' concern for his empire's vernacular languages, especially Czech and German. Among many other projects, he had the University of Paris' *Compendium* on the Plague translated for circulation.

Much of his activity later in his reign concerned the consolidation of his dynasty. He married four times, absorbing new territories with each union. After returning from his coronation he issued the edict known as the Golden Bull in 1356, a key constitutional document that made only seven of the empire's chief nobles—including the margrave of Brandenburg and archbishop of Trier—responsible for electing the king of the Romans and removed any role for the pope in the process. He died in Prague on November 29, 1378.

Clement VI (Pierre Roger) (1291/2–1352), *Pope*

Clement VI was the Roman Catholic bishop of Rome (and Avignon) and pope (1342–52) during the Black Death. Pierre was the second son born to members of the lower nobility at Maumont in Corrèze, France.

In 1301 he entered Chaise-Dieu Abbey in the Auvergne region, formally becoming a Benedictine monk five years later. Shortly afterward he was sent to study at the University of Paris, where he completed work in the arts, philosophy, theology, and canon law. He taught and preached in Paris, drawing the attention of prominent clergy and the French king, Charles IV. In his later twenties he provided intellectual support for Pope John XXII in his struggle over who had authority over bishops. With the popes now located nearby in Avignon, Pierre came to Pope John's immediate attention as well. Pope and king saw to it that Pierre received his Master's degree in theology, his license to teach, and a teaching position in canon law and theology at the University of Paris several years before he was eligible. As a scholar he continued to support the papal positions against members of the Franciscan order who attacked the Church's ownership of property, and against the French king over the respective jurisdictions of Church and secular courts. In recognition of his support and service, the pope appointed him abbot of the Norman monastery of Fécamp in 1326, bishop of Arras in 1328, archbishop of Sens in 1329, and archbishop of Rouen in 1330. A loyal Frenchman, Pierre also served the king as a councilor and diplomat in the early stages of the Hundred Years War with England. In addition, he did his best to promote a new crusade to the Holy Land, with French King Philip VI at its head. In early 1338 he entered the College of Cardinals and was elected by its members as pope on May 7, 1342; he was crowned on May 19, taking the name Clement.

As pope, Clement did his best to defend papal power and authority and to glorify the Church by making its papacy more magnificent. In Avignon he accomplished this by adding new and grand sections to the Papal Palace. He spent lavishly on decorating it and in supporting the new *Ars nova* style of music of Philippe de Vitry at his court. In fact, he created the most brilliant court in the Latin West. He was an avid book collector who had Petrarch searching on his behalf, and he studded his sermons with classical quotations. Clement also cared for the poor, indeed tripling the number of free bread loaves distributed by his predecessor, John, to 30,000 per day. He tried to broker peace between France and England, hoping to direct both toward a crusade against the aggressive Turks, but to no avail. His relations with the Holy Roman Empire were strained as he refused to recognize the claims of Louis of Bavaria, whom he and his predecessors considered a heretic, and he even denied coronation to his own candidate, Charles of Bohemia, whom he did manage to get elected king of the Romans (1346), the last step before the imperial dignity. In addition to all of this, there were loud cries from Rome demanding his return, which were amplified during the revolutionary government of the "Tribune of the People," Cola di Rienzo (May 1347).

When the Plague hit Europe, Clement had to act as the spiritual father of all of Christendom; when it reached Avignon in early February, he had the special task of caring for his own diocese. His personal fascination with astronomy and astrology, which at the time were far more closely linked than in modern times, led him to seek the connections between the heavenly bodies and the disease. His need to understand the disease itself led him to order postmortem medical autopsies on victims. As spiritual leader of the diocese, he granted full indulgences to the dying, which removed the spiritual penalty for sins that they were unable to confess to a priest. He felt that God's punishment for sin was the root of the pestilence, and he preached fervid sermons that made this point and warned against the penalties for living a sinful life. One contemporary source claims that he encouraged a procession through Avignon of barefoot local flagellants. He felt that their personal suffering and example of penitence would help placate an angry God and draw others to repentance. Clement aided the sick by providing care with his own funds and arranged for burials of many victims at his expense. He purchased land for a new cemetery when the old ones filled to capacity, and even blessed the Rhône River to receive the bodies of the dead.

On a broader front Clement encouraged prayer and repentance throughout Christendom, and even wrote a special Mass for time of Plague, which circulated throughout western Europe. When he heard of the popular reactions against Jews and Jewish communities he responded quickly and fervently. On July 4, 1348, he published a bull, or official statement, that noted the fact that Jews died no less frequently than Christians and were to remain unmolested in Christian lands. A second blast was required and was proclaimed on September 26. While he hated the fact that, as he saw it, Jews refused to recognize Christ and the Gospel, he did respect them as the Chosen People of God, and he sought to protect them as such. When flagellant groups began to circulate in central Europe, however, he condemned the flagellants formally. His confirmation of the Holy Year for 1350, during which spiritual gains were to be had by those who made a pilgrimage to Rome, was in part a thanksgiving for the lifting of the Plague, in part a way of rechanneling the flagellants' energy, and in part a way of placating the people of Rome who had lost so much business and revenue in the papacy's forty-year absence.

Clement died on December 6, 1352, and is buried in his old monastery of Chaise-Dieu. He lies beneath a white marble effigy of himself in full papal regalia, which is surrounded by statues of forty-five of his closest family and friends.

Francesco di Marco Datini da Prato (c. 1335–1410), *Tuscan Merchant*

Orphaned in the Black Death of 1348, Francesco Datini went on to live through six additional outbreaks of the Plague, amass a major fortune, and, through his will, establish two foundations for orphaned or abandoned children. Born to an innkeeper and his wife in Prato, about ten miles from Florence, Italy, Francesco received a small but not insignificant inheritance when both his parents died in 1348. At age fifteen he left Prato for Avignon, the center of papal government, in the company of other Tuscan merchants. Hit hard by the pestilence, the city no doubt welcomed the businessmen. Over the next thirty years Datini amassed a small fortune, trading in a wide variety of goods from cloth to armor to small devotional paintings. In 1376 he married an expatriate Florentine noblewoman, Margherita Bandini, but the couple never produced any children. Following the pope's return to Rome, the couple returned to Tuscany in 1382. Francesco continued trading through agents in Avginon and soon established branch offices in Barcelona, Milan, Majorca, Genoa, Pisa, and Florence. His ventures flourished, and they prospered. In Prato Margherita set up housekeeping in the palazzo they were building, and which still stands today, housing the huge archive of Datini's letters and account books. These priceless materials allow a rare glimpse of daily life in the time of the Plague.

After their return the Datinis, their household, and their associates experienced the Plague years of 1390 and 1399/1400. Three letters from Margherita's Florentine brother-in-law confirm that the Plague was raging in Florence in May and June 1390: "the air has been corrupted"; "the air is not healthy." Prato was threatened, and he questioned why

Datini had not moved his family to a safer region: "are you waiting for someone in your household to die?!" Ironically, at the same moment Datini's agents in Florence were writing concerning housepainters and pigments that had not yet arrived. By early July he had decided to re-locate to Pistoia, and a letter from Bartolomeo di messer Nicolao wel-coming him reflected a mood common to the Datini correspondence of the time: "May God have mercy not according to our merits, but ac-cording to His infinite goodness. Though death is a natural thing, and cannot be cured or loathed, yet we must strive to become and live well now. This cannot be through human power, but must come from God. From grace promised us comes hope. Yet we loathe when dangers occur, or those things that shorten the life of man." After his move in July, friends wrote from Prato concerning the deaths of mutual friends. On October 1 Francesco Angiolini sent a list of the ill and recently de-ceased. Two days later Datini wrote the suffering notary Bartolomeo that "I do and will pray to God that He return you to health, and all of your friends, too." He was certain, he said, that the suffering was due to man's sinfulness, and "there seems to me to be no other remedy except to pray to God that he not regard our sins." Soon after, Datini's good friend the pious notary Lapo Mazzei drew this lesson for the merchant: "You see your and our friends and neighbors and how they are cast down by death; and you can judge how much good their possessions did them, aside from their good works. We who remain ought to see well, if the veil is not drawn over our eyes, that 'life is a race with death'" (Dante, *Pur-gatorio*, 33.54). The family returned after only a few weeks.

In the heat of August 1399 Datini, along with hundreds of other Italians, made the Bianchi pilgrimage to nearby Arezzo, with hopes of pleasing God and fending off the Plague, the rumors of which were trickling down the peninsula. They failed. On November 17 Datini's oldest friend, Niccolo Giunta, wrote him from Florence: "Here every day people go in procession and fast, and all this week no meat is eaten. And every morning Mass is said for fear of the pestilence, and everyone stays in church with a candle for as long as it takes to say Mass and for each one to pray to God that he might lift this pestilence from us. God will do it if it is best for our souls." The attack was light, and unpaid bills due to sick children Datini's greatest burden. By spring 1400 the toll was rising; on April 23 Niccolo wrote: "The plague is doing great damage here and is giving us many sick people." Subsequent letters chronicle the deaths of friends, relatives, and associates. His notary Ser Schiatta's belated letter of condolence for Datini's loss of his Genoese partner asks pardon for the delay, but Schiatta's own wife had died at about the same time: "She took all the sacraments of Holy Church with great devotion, and with good and perfect judgment, as ought every faithful Christian; and I spoke [with her] up to the end, and she kept her reason as long as she had life in her body . . . may it please God to have received her soul into the glory of eternal life through [His] holy mercy." Datini had been inquiring into places to which to flee from Prato. Arezzo and Bologna were prime candidates, and he had strong support in both, especially from local Franciscans, who looked forward to his patronage. At Bologna "the air [was] very healthy and no one [was] dying," many Florentines had already migrated by mid-June, and most had brought ample supplies with them. At Arezzo, reported one of his friends, "We find everything here to be advantageous with respect to Bologna: the air, and food, wine, water, natural conditions and every other thing. There is only this: that the plague has been there [Bologna] and passed, and it has not been here." He made his choice after receiving advice from several others, including Stefano Guazzalotti of Pistoia: "It would appear to be better for you to go to Bologna than to Arezzo because the plague has been there and has spent all its force, and it has not yet been at Arezzo. And the places it has passed, it would seem, reasonably, would be safer than where it has not yet made its course." Two days later they were on the road to Bologna, from which they returned about a year later.

This Plague was especially hard on Datini. He lost Ser Schiatta, Niccolo Giunta, and his banking partner, who died shortly after arriving in Bologna. Stefano Guazzalotti lost his eldest son, and Lapo buried at least three of his children: "three days ago I watched two of my children die, the eldest and the middle one, in my arms, within a few hours [of each other]. God knows how much hope I had in the first, who was like a partner to me and a father with me to the others."

Over the next decade Lapo helped Datini formulate his will, in which the merchant set aside 1,000 florins to help found the Ospedale degli Innocenti in Florence and most of his great wealth to create and fund the Datini *Ceppo*, a foundation for rejected or orphaned children. He died and was buried in Prato in August 1410, on the threshold of yet another outbreak of pestilence.

Galen of Pergamum (129?–199/229), Greco-Roman *Physician*

A physician and student of the medical thought and practices of the Greek physician Hippocrates of Cos (469–399 B.C.E.), Galen wrote medical works that had an enormous impact on the theories and practice of medicine in both the Christian and Islamic worlds of the Middle Ages. His father was a mathematician and architect who arranged to have young Galen formally exposed to Greek rhetoric and philosophy, as well as to what he himself could teach the boy. When he was about sixteen years old Galen began the study of medicine in Smyrna, and a few years later finished it in Alexandria, Egypt. He returned home to Pergamum, in modern-day Turkey, to practice medicine in 157 C.E. Galen began his career working at the Asklepion medical facility and tending the medical needs of gladiators. From the latter he no doubt learned a great deal about human physiology and the art of healing. Gladiators were slaves, and slaves property, and their owners wanted the best care for their money. Around 161 he relocated to Rome and practiced as a physician, giving public anatomy lessons with cadavers and healing a prominent philosopher. This last caught the attention of the emperor, Marcus Aurelius, but either an epidemic outbreak or nasty rivals forced Galen to leave Rome in 166. He returned to Pergamum, but was called back to Rome for imperial service three years later. Marcus Aurelius wanted his company on a campaign in Germany, but Galen ended up staying in Rome and attending to young Commodus, who was then eight years old. Galen was noted for his intellectual as well as his healing powers, and no doubt served as a tutor to Commodus and intellectual companion to his father, who was known for his philosophical interests. While in the imperial household Galen wrote his large body of works, not all of them medical. He wrote on theories of teaching, on grammar, and on moral philosophy. His works on medicine, however, have earned him his fame.

Although a student of many thinkers, including Hippocrates, Aristotle, Plato, and a raft of lesser lights, Galen emphasized to his readers the need to draw independent judgments from knowledge and observation. The practicing physician needs to have generally applicable information and theories, but each case is unique in its combination of circumstances and symptoms. His writings contain detailed case studies of people suffering from a range of diseases and ailments; these provide information on feces and urine conditions, on body temperature and temperament (agitated, listless, calm), and on changes in these over time. He was no specialist, but felt rather that the body as a whole should be known intimately by the physician. He dissected not only human corpses but also those of animals to deepen his understanding of the workings of life. He believed that there was no useful distinction between surgeons and physicians, an attitude developed, perhaps, in his days treating gladiators. In his work *On My Own Opinions* Galen stressed the relationship between medicine and philosophy, thus universalizing the former and basing it on an intellectual and not merely pragmatic basis. On the other hand, the observation and experimentation of the physician influenced his philosophical works, which seem far more practical and based on life as it is lived than most works of the period.

Galen's acceptance of the four humors discussed in the Hippocratic writings—blood, phlegm, and black and yellow bile—and his reduction of the human systems of organs to three—heart, brain, and liver—ensured that these incorrect doctrines would be passed along to medieval physicians. Since most disease was considered a matter of an imbalance of humors, cures involved addressing this imbalance by diet or directly adjusting the levels by such means as exsanguination (controlled bleeding). Connection of these humors with conditions (hot, cold, moist, dry), "elements" (earth, air, fire, water), and even planets provided a kind of seductive universal model that prevented clearer thinking until the seventeenth century.

Because Galen wrote in Greek his works remained alive in the Byzantine and Islamic worlds, and only hints of his thought remained in the Latin-speaking West. From the ninth century Islamic physicians and scientists moved furthest ahead in both incorporating and adjusting Galenic ideas and practices in their own medical works. Western European scholars now absorbed much of Galen's thought through these Arabic sources, as is clearly noted in many of the Latin medical texts that survive from the thirteenth and fourteenth centuries. By the time of the Black Death the Western world had yet to reconcile the positive influences of Galen's diagnostic material and his humoral theories and the ineffective practices that sprang from them.

Gentile da Foligno (c. 1275–1348), *Italian Physician and Medical School Professor*

Gentile was one of the fourteenth century's most famous physicians and medical writers. His early tract on the Plague had a major influence on subsequent works. He was born in either Perugia or Foligno, Italy, around 1275, to Gentile, who was probably also a physician. Young Gentile junior married Iacoba Bonimani, and they had four sons, two of whom became physicians. He was probably educated at the University of Bologna, and probably studied under Taddeo Alderotti, the era's greatest medical educator. At some point he also learned to appreciate the classical Roman literary figures, such as Seneca, whose works were just then being revived and studied in northern Italy. He remained in Bologna as a teacher and practitioner until 1322. Over the previous year or two many teachers and students had left the city, and Gentile moved to Siena to help the government establish a university. After the Sienese effort failed, the leaders of Perugia invited him to teach—and perhaps serve as a public physician—at the respectable salary of sixty gold florins. He relocated and seems to have remained there for the rest of his life, with the possible exception of a short stay in Padua.

Like most Western physicians of his day, Gentile had been taught, and he himself taught, the major Greek and Arabic medical authorities. Medical schools taught what was known as scholastic medicine, in which mastery of a traditional text was the main goal. A student learned to be critical, but to seek resolution of problems or apparent contradictions, not to question the authority seriously. As in the arts, law, and theology, educators in medicine produced commentaries on these authorities to aid other experts and their own students. Gentile wrote over ninety practical and theoretical medical works, medical tracts or *consilia*, speeches, and commentaries that survive. His great work, on which his reputation still rests, was his *Commentary* on Avicenna's eleventh-century *Canon of Medicine*. He had begun this by 1315, and only finished it before the Black Death. The enormous *Canon* was itself the era's most respected medical textbook, having been translated from Arabic to Latin by Gerard of Cremona in the later 1100s. It remained an authority in Europe until the seventeenth century and in the Arab world until the nineteenth. Gentile's commentary interpreted the work in light of intervening scholarship on Galen in Western universities and Gentile's own experience. He could and did argue with his source, as over the role of experience in gaining medical knowledge. Avicenna, despite his clear reliance on his own experiences, taught that his conclusions could be taught and would suffice, whereas Gentile felt strongly that the student could learn certain things only from trial and observation.

When the Plague hit, Gentile was an elderly man, yet he wrote at least five *consilia* (medical tracts) on the disease. The first was for the Guild of Physicians at Genoa, which had been struck by the Plague in the fall of 1347. He wrote the most detailed for the commune of Perugia, and it may have been the last thing he wrote, as he succumbed to exhaustion (and not the Plague) on June 18, 1348. Because his work arrived on the scene early and because of his reputation, Gentile had many disciples. His *consilium* quickly passed over divine and celestial causes, and began in earnest with treating the Plague as a poison. Gentile admitted not knowing exactly how this poison worked, but he did note that it turned everything it touched to itself and destroyed the heart. Plague was "spread from man to and from place to place." The best advice for avoiding the disease, he admitted, was flight (quickly, far, and for a long time), but he also counseled purification of the air, moderation in physical activity, diets that help keep the body "dry," and maintenance of an upbeat mood. He presented very specific diets and regimens of herbs and medicines to keep one's body "dry." For the victim, he recommended heavy bloodlettings from very specific points, or cauterizing of the buboes by red-hot metal or "plasters" made of such things as a paste of crushed crabapple and bird-droppings to release the poison. Ever the good teacher, he ended with an academic discussion of broader matters such as personal susceptibility to the disease.

Lisad-ad Din ibn al-Khatib (1313–75), *Andalusian Physician and Bureaucrat*

Along with Abi Gafar Ahmed ibn Khatimah, al-Khatib was one of the two major authors of Plague tracts to come from Andalusia (Muslim Spain). His ancestors had migrated from Syria to Andalusia shortly after the Arab invasion in 711. Al-Khatib studied medicine in Muslim Granada and there entered the service of the ruler Yusuf I around 1341. He served as a secretary under the vizier, or chief minister, Ali bin al-Djayyab, and when the vizier died of the Plague in 1349, al-Khatib replaced him as head of the royal chancery. He survived the change of rulers in 1354 when Yusuf died and Muhammad V took power. In 1359 Muhammad's enemies had him deposed and he fled to Morocco; al-Khatib was imprisoned, released, and then allowed to join Muhammad. When Muhammad regained power in 1362, the loyal al-Khatib returned to the chancery as vizier and was honored as the chief dignitary at court. By 1372 his own enemies, however, had gotten the upper hand and, while on a tour of inspection of the kingdom's defenses, he slipped across the Strait to Ceuta in Morocco. In his absence he was charged with heresy and treason. In 1375 al-Khatib was seized and returned to Granada. His trial in a private court resulted in an unclear verdict, and, since he could not be executed legally, he was strangled in prison.

Like some other prominent Muslim physicians, al-Khatib was more scholar than practitioner. He wrote on many subjects, including philosophy, religion, history, and medicine. He probably wrote his plague treatise, *Muqni'at as-sa'il an marad al-ha'il*, while exiled in Morocco from 1359 to 1362. More than any contemporary Muslim and most Christian physicians, he trusted his own experience and reason more than he did the models blessed by tradition. He wrote, "One may not ignore the principle that a proof taken from tradition, if observation and inspection show the contrary, must be interpreted allegorically." This meant that while the Qur'an or other religious sources were not incorrect when their words seemed to contradict simple observation, they were also not literally true. Their deeper truth and meaning lay hidden beneath the words, to be released by correct interpretation. Al-Khatib rejected the theory of a miasma poisoning people and, at least implicitly, the doctrine of Allah's direction of the Plague. Since he clearly had observed contagion (*al-adwa*), this random factor, rather than bad air or divine direction, he reasoned, must be responsible for the Plague's spread, even though this contradicted specific Islamic teaching against contagion. "That infection [contagion] exists is confirmed by experience, investigation, insight, personal observation and reliable reports. These are the elements of proof." This bold challenge to the medical and religious orthodoxy of the day probably accounts for the charges of heresy from which he suffered.

Al-Khatib distinguished between the bubonic and pneumonic forms of the disease and discussed it in purely humoral terms. His suggestions for avoiding the Plague reflect his concern for contagion, and his recommended treatments follow the accepted understanding of the effects of the disease on the body.

Francesco Petrarch (1304–74), *Italian Poet*

Petrarch, often considered the "first modern Man," lived through three episodes of the Plague in Italy, lost many loved ones, and through his intensely personal poetry embodied the anxieties and grief of the time. Born in Arezzo, near Florence, in 1304 to Ser Petracco, a notary and friend of Dante, young Francesco was exposed to classical Latin literature, which shaped his future life as a humanist scholar. In 1313 his family moved to Avignon, then the seat of the papacy, and eventually to nearby Carpentras, where Francesco was formally educated. He went on to law school in Montpellier, France, and in 1323 to Bologna, Italy, for legal studies that left him hating scholastic education and lawyers in general. After his father's death and subsequent events deprived him of both support and inheritance, he joined the clergy and went to Avignon—"Babylon of the West"—to seek a position. Here he gained the patronage of Cardinal Giovanni Colonna, on whose behalf he traveled to Rome and around northern Europe in the 1330s. In Avignon, in 1327, he first saw Laura, the woman who inspired reams of his groundbreaking Italian poetry. His sonnets circulated and grew in popularity, and he received offers of the poet laureate's coronation from both Rome and Paris; he chose Rome, seat of the Apostles and, more importantly, of ancient glory. Hating Avignon but relying on the papal court for support of his scholarship and poetry, Petrarch settled in the nearby rural Vaucluse, where he pursued his poetry, studies, and gardening.

"This year, 1348, I now perceive to have been the beginning of sorrow." He was shuttling between Verona and Parma in north-central Italy when the Plague struck. On May 19 his great friend Louis Heiligen ("Socrates") informed him of Laura's death in Avignon. In July Cardinal Colonna died, and soon thereafter Paganino de Bizzozzero, a very close friend, with all his family. These and similar reports of others' passing led Petrarch to pen his Latin poem *Ad te ipsum*, which includes the lines

> Time rushes onward for the perishing world
> And round about I see the hosts of the dying,
> The young and the old; nor is there anywhere

In all the world a refuge, or a harbor
Where there is hope of safety. Funerals
Where'er I turn my frightened eyes, appall;
The temples[1] groan with coffins, and the proud
And the humble lie alike in lack of honor.
The end of life presses upon my mind,
And I recall the dear ones I have lost . . .
The consecrated ground is all too small
To hold the instant multitude of graves.

(Trans. by Ernst Hatch Wilkins)

"Life is one long agony," he commented elsewhere. He had written the poetic *Triumph of Cupid* and *Triumph of Chastity*, and now he turned his pen to the *Triumph of Death*, intertwining Laura's death with those of so many others and creating a lasting poetic and pictorial theme. This he would follow with the *Triumph of Fame*, setting the stage for the Renaissance cult of the individual. Meanwhile, his brother Gherardo, who lived in a Carthusian monastery, tended his dying brothers' needs, burying them with his own hands. He alone survived to request a new abbot and reestablish the community. In a famous letter to Gherardo, Francesco expressed his horror:

How will posterity believe that there has been a time when without the lightnings of heaven or the fires of earth, without wars or other visible slaughter, not this or that part of the earth, but well-nigh the whole globe, has remained without inhabitants. When has any such thing been even heard or seen; in what annals has it ever been read that houses were left vacant, cities deserted, the country neglected, the fields too small for the dead and a fearful and universal solitude over the whole earth? . . . Oh happy people of the future, who have not known these miseries and perchance will class our testimony with the fables. We have, indeed, deserved these [punishments] and even greater; but our forefathers also have deserved them, and may our posterity not also merit the same.

(Trans. by George Deaux)

Petrarch remained in northern Italy, and he decided to stay in Milan when the Plague hit again in 1361. When invited to flee to a country estate to wait out the carnage, Petrarch declined, claiming stoically that "to face [death] in fear is a base weakness." His twenty-five-year-old illegitimate son, Giovanni, succumbed in July: "He died in Milan in the unexampled devastation wrought by the plague, which hitherto had left that city immune from such evils, but now has found it and invaded it." In August he heard of the deaths of dear "Socrates" and his friend Philippe de Vitry in Avignon; joy drained from what life he had left.

Always one torn between solemn monastic idealism and unfettered freedom to pursue his classical studies, Petrarch grew in somberness as age and the Plague took their tolls. He lived out his last years in and around Venice and Padua, dying peacefully on July 18, 1374.

Alexandre Emile John Yersin (1863–1943), *Swiss/French Microbiologist*

The microbiologist Alexandre Yersin is credited with being the first to isolate successfully the bacillus responsible for the bubonic plague and produce a vaccine against it. Yersin was born on the shores of Lake Geneva in Lavaux, Switzerland. Yersin's father predeceased him, and his mother raised him while running a finishing school for girls. Though brought up a Calvinist Christian, Yersin eventually rejected all religion, but he did take up as a hobby the study of insects. As a young man he quitted the Academy of Lausanne, where he had finished a year of premedical training, going to Marburg, Germany, in 1884 to study botany. While there he switched his studies to human anatomy and pathology. In 1885 Yersin relocated to Paris, where he worked first in the Hotel Dieu hospital and then in the private bacteriological laboratory of André Cornil. While there he met the famed bacteriologist Louis Pasteur, at whose institute Yersin served first as a volunteer in studies of rabies and later as the assistant of Emile Roux in the study of diphtheria and tuberculosis. Yersin's work with tuberculosis led directly to his prizewinning University of Paris doctoral thesis of 1889. He spent part of the summer of this same year studying bacteriology even further in Berlin under Robert Koch, Pasteur's rival for preeminence in the field. Returning to Paris Yersin taught the institute's first course on microbiology, did further research on diphtheria, and was naturalized a French citizen. At the end of the year he decided to take a vacation.

During his one-year leave of absence he was to serve as a ship's doctor on a regular run between Manila and Saigon, in French Indochina. Once in the region he took a profound interest in exploring the interior of Indochina: he mapped the landscape, collected plant and animal species, and studied the local people. Though asked to work as partner in a research laboratory with Pasteur-trained Albert Calmette, who later discovered the vaccine for tuberculosis, Yersin declined, deciding—for the moment—against a career in medicine. In 1893 he returned from Paris for further exploration and to conduct a census of diseases that were endemic in southeast Asia. Meanwhile, plague had broken out in China, and Yersin was determined to study it at first hand. Denied access to the mainland, he arrived at the British colony of Hong Kong on June 15, 1894. Immediately he enlisted the aid of the Italian missionary Father Vigano, who had spent thirty years on the island. On June 12, however, Shibasaburo Kitasato, the famous Japanese student of Robert Koch, had arrived with a great entourage and was presented by the British authorities with full access to all medical facilities and all plague corpses. Yersin lived in a bamboo hut and worked with corpses stored in quicklime that he obtained through Vigano's bribery of British sailors who were supposed to dispose of them.

Yersin reasoned that the buboes themselves should contain the organism responsible for the disease. He studied material drawn directly from buboes and found a very high density of previously unidentified bacilli. When he injected these into animals, they died. He had isolated the deadly agent after less than a week's work. On June 22 Yersin approached the authorities with these findings and obtained their cooperation and access to facilities and plague victims. Kitasato, meanwhile, had isolated a virus that he believed to be the culprit, and later a bacillus, but one that his own associates identified as probably a type of streptococcus. Kitasato's own teacher, Masanori Ogata, admitted that Yersin's find was genuine and unique. The bacillus was formally dubbed *Pasteurella pestis* (*P. pestis*), but, because Kitasato continued to press his claim to a share in the discovery, it was commonly referred to as the Kitasato-Yersin bacillus. In 1971 the formal name was changed to *Yersinia pestis* (*Y. pestis*). Yersin also discovered the relationship of the bacillus to the rat and the possible rat-human connection and that the bacillus can live in the soil on its own for some time, but he did not find the relationship of the flea to the bacillus' spread.

Although British authorities wanted Yersin to remain in Hong Kong, the French sent him to Madagascar to work on "blackwater fever," a case he could not crack. In 1895 he returned to Paris to produce a vaccine from the cultured live bacilli. His experiments with live bacilli failed, but when he killed the organisms with 58°C heat and waited an hour, the resultant matter, when injected, protected a variety of animals, even as large as horses. He quickly returned to Viet Nam to produce serum at a research station at Nha Trang, which later became an official outpost of the Pasteur Institute. In the spring of 1896 the plague broke out again in Hong Kong. On June 26 the first human victim of the plague was cured: an eighteen-year-old Chinese seminary student. Over the next ten days, twenty-three victims were treated with the serum, and twenty-one lived. Interestingly, these results were not repeated in India during a massive outbreak the following year: a success rate of only 50 percent was achieved with the Indochinese formula. There was more work to be done. Though he made Nha Trang his home, Yersin shifted away from microbiology to cattle-raising and -breeding, growing rubber trees he imported from Brazil, and growing cinchona trees from which quinine is derived. He established a medical school there, but his native students were accepted by the French colonial medical authorities only as nurses, a development that disgusted him and led him to close the school. He last visited Paris on the eve of the German occupation in 1940 and died peacefully near Nha Trang, under Japanese occupation, in the winter of 1943.

NOTE

1. Catholic churches.

PRIMARY DOCUMENTS

The Black Death in Constantinople (1347)

The Plague hit the Byzantine Empire with no less ferocity than it did the West. The emperor John VI Cantacuzenos retired in 1355 to a monastery in which he wrote a history of the empire over the years 1320– 56. His description of the Plague episode of 1347 discusses a range of issues: its origins and spread, its symptoms and course, and people's reactions to it. Though no physician, his eye for medical detail is quite sharp, as is his observation of popular response. Since he was educated in classical Greek literature, he knew firsthand the description of the ancient Athenian plague in Thucydides' History *(Book II: pp. 49–53; c. 300 B.C.E.), and its influence on his own work is detectable. Embedded in it are intriguing details that both link it to other works in the genre and distinguish it: its origins in southern Russia rather than China, its contagiousness, the deaths of domestic animals, apparent immunity of those who survive, the different forms the same disease can take, and the social-psychological effects on the populace: fear, anxiety, and intensified piety.*

DOCUMENT 1
The Description of the Pestilence: From the *Historiarum* (after 1355)
Emperor John VI Cantacuzenos

Upon arrival in Byzantium the Empress found Andronikos, the youngest born, dead from the invading plague, which, starting first from the Hyperborean Scythians [of southern Russia], attacked almost all the sea coasts of the world and killed most of their people. For it swept not only through Pontus, Thrace and Macedonia, but even Greece, Italy and all the islands, Egypt, Libya, Judea, and Syria, and spread throughout almost the entire world.

So incurable was the evil, that neither any regularity of life, nor any bodily strength could resist it. Strong and weak bodies were similarly carried away, and those best cared for died in the same manner as the poor. No other [major] disease of any kind presented itself that year. If someone had a previous illness he always succumbed to this disease and no physician's art was sufficient; neither did the disease take the same course in all persons, but the others, unable to resist, died the same day, a few even within the hour. Those who could resist for two or three days had a very violent fever at first, the disease in such cases attacking the head; they suffered from speechlessness and insensibility to all happenings and then appeared as if sunken into a deep sleep. Then, if from time to time they came to themselves, they wanted to speak but the tongue was hard to move and they uttered inarticulate sounds because the nerves around the back part of the head were dead; and they died suddenly. In others, the evil attacked not the head, but the lungs, and forthwith there was inflammation which produced very sharp pains in the chest.

Sputum suffused with blood was brought up, and disgusting and stinking breath from within. The throat and tongue, parched from the heat, were black and congested with blood. It made no difference if they drank much or little. Sleeplessness and weakness were established forever.

Abscesses formed on the upper and lower arms, in a few also in the maxillae, and in others on other parts of the body. In some they were large and in others small. Black blisters appeared. Some people broke out with black spots all over their bodies; in some they were few and very manifest; in others they were obscure and dense. Everyone died the same death from these symptoms. In some people all the symptoms appeared, in others more or fewer of them, and in no small number [of cases] even one of them was sufficient to provoke death. Those few who were able to escape from among the many who died, were no longer possessed by the same evil, but were safe. The disease did not attack twice in order to kill them.

Great abscesses were formed on the legs or the arms, from which, when cut, a large quantity of foul-smelling pus flowed and the disease was differentiated as that which discharged such annoying matter. Even many who were seized by all the symptoms unexpectedly recovered. There was no help from anywhere; if someone brought to another a remedy useful to himself, this became poison to the other patient. Some, by treating others, became infected with the disease. It created great destruction, and many homes were deserted by their inhabitants. Domestic animals died together with their masters. Most terrible was the discouragement. Whenever people felt sick there was no hope left for recovery, but by turning to despair, adding to their prostration and aggravating their sickness, they died at once. No words could express the nature of the disease. All that can be pointed out is that it had nothing in common with the everyday evils to which the nature of man is subject, but was something else sent by God to restore chastity. Many of the sick turned to better things in their minds, by being chastened, not only those who died, but also those who overcame the disease. They abstained from all vice during that time and they lived virtuously; many divided their property among the poor, even before they were attacked by the disease. If he ever felt himself seized, no one was so ruthless as not to show repentance of his faults and to appear before the judgment seat of God with the best chance of salvation, not believing that the soul was incurable or unhealed. Many died in Byzantium [Constantinople] then, and the king's [emperor's] son, Andronikos, was attacked and died the third day.

Source: Christos Bartsocas, "Two Fourteenth Century Greek Descriptions of the 'Black Death.'" *Journal of the History of Medicine and Allied Sciences* 21 (1966): pp. 394–400.

A Poetic Vision from Prague of the Origins of the Black Death (1348–52)

> *Heinrich von Mügeln was a poet at the imperial court in Prague. Paris-educated Emperor Charles IV had a strong interest in astrology and science, and Heinrich's poem, perhaps written with him in mind, certainly reflects this. The responsibility of the Great Conjunction of Jupiter and Saturn in the House of Aquarius for pestilence outlined here has roots in Greco-Roman and Arabic medicine and scholastic science; the specific reference is to the celestial event reported in 1345. Neither the pestilence nor the "science" of astrology was considered proper poetic fare, but*

Heinrich uniquely combines them in the German vernacular. Around 1350 Simon de Covino of Liège wrote De iudicio Solis, *a much longer, fuller, and more complex treatment in Latin of the same astrological allegory.*[1] *It remains unclear whether Heinrich's poem preceded this or was influenced by it. Where Simon clearly places his celestial characters under the ultimate authority of the Judeo-Christian Godhead, Heinrich does not, leaving the door open to interpretations of his work as being purely naturalistic.*

DOCUMENT 2
"Wer wil nu wissen das" (c. 1349–55)
Heinrich von Mügeln

*Whoever wants to know
whence the Great Death came,
let him follow the manner of my poem:
this will lead him on the right path.
The sky has twelve signs,
according to my knowledge, called the houses of the planets.*

*Now Aquarius is
a sign and the largest in Saturn's house,
in which it finds distinction. This I pledge.
If I speak falsely, may I burn!—
for I have read this information.*

*When now Saturn was
in his domicile, it happened that
Lord Jupiter sat linked
with him in power and dignity.
Owing to the might
of his house, Saturn took victory there,
and pressed Lord Jupiter severely:
He injured creation, brought suffering to animals.
Saturn is cold and dry like the earth;
Jupiter the noble one is moist and warm.
In such a climate of enmity,
Saturn roused the ravages of death.*

*Now I speak in truth:
since Aquarius possessed the human form,*

so it had to transpire
that humankind would suffer death.
If, however, their joining together had occurred
in other signs—this I hear tell—
for instance, in Pisces, undoubtedly
many fish would be dead.
Albumazar and Ptolemy[2] ordained
these rules; thus I'll let them stand here.
He who wants to refute them,
that desire derives from a foolish heart.

Source: William McDonald, "Death in the Stars." *Mediaevalia* 5 (1979): pp. 89–112.

An Explanation of How the Plague Worked: Corrupted Air (1348)

Andalusian (Spanish-Arab) physician Abi Gafar Ahmed ibn Ali ibn Khatimah of Almeria wrote one of the most straightforward medical tracts on the Plague of the fourteenth century, the Tahsil al-gharad al-qasid fi tafil al-marad alwafid *(1348). In this excerpt he explains the way in which the air we breathe, which is a mixture of the element air plus other "accidental" substances, is corrupted by the Plague vapors and made fatal to people and animals. Water, too, can be "plague-stricken" and become poisonous. This notion of "corruption" was key to his understanding of the pestilence. He carries on a dialogue with a silent detractor, answering his objections as he builds his case. While not identical in detail to Christian medical works, Ibn Khatimah's is similar in many ways, reflecting both Christian and Muslim reliance on Greek sources, especially Hippocrates, Galen, and Aristotle. The modern reader finds much of this discussion to be not only incorrect, but also very strange; even so, it provided the theoretical basis on which many elements of medical practice and public policy were founded.*

DOCUMENT 3
Plague Tract (1348)
Ibn Khatimah

Understand that the immediate cause is usually the corruption of the air, which surrounds people and which people inhale. This corruption can be [either] partial or total. Partial corruption results from the degradation of all or some of the air's accidental characteristics, without changing or spoiling the element [air] itself. This can take place by adding to or reducing the number of the air's [accidental] characteristics—changing its natural condition—or by mixing and combining it with foreign things, which will be mentioned below.

Total corruption, however, is due to the corruption of the elemental components [of the air] by rotting, in such a way that the air takes on a completely different mixture. This is done by means of substances that we will mention below.

If you ask what the difference is between the two kinds of corruption, the answer reads as follows:

In the first case, the air does not change in kind: none of its elemental components is missing; rather, all are kept intact. However, the changing agent is corrupted through mixture or contact, but without the [corrupting] agent's nature being changed, lest we have to redefine "air." An example of this: whenever good air is mixed with heated, dry, and foul vapor, so that the [foul vapor] changes the insignificant characteristics of the [good air, it does so] without making the air putrid or corrupting its element, since the vapor has not yet completely taken possession of the air. In the second case, however, the air is corrupted through the corruption of all or some of the substantial components, so that the nature of the air is completely changed, and the definition [of "air"], which previously had been suitable, no longer applies. Anyone who still uses the same name for both types of air, does so because he links together the components in the first case, and uses the word allegorically in the second case [i.e., it really is not "air" anymore]. An example of the second case is good air mixed with heated, dry fumes, so that the proportion of the latter outweighs that of the former, making the good air putrid, and changing its components, so that such [good] air becomes more like putrefied fumes, just as pure elemental air becomes merely good air [by adding substances to it]. One sees this [process] in old dining rooms with old [tarnished] silverware, in the black slime that appears on ships and in wells, anywhere animals are found dead, and wherever their stench remains trapped. The air found in these places is putrefied, completely changed; specifically, changed into fumes that are deadly for animals. If a man is exposed to them and breathes them in, he dies immediately. No flame burns in the presence of such fumes, rather it would expire immediately; whenever a flame is applied to the fumes, they reach the highest degree of rot and corruption of the air. From this kind of change, or something similar, the air is changed as described in accounts of the epidemic disease, in which historical writers claim that thousands of people died for this reason. The same thing can happen to cattle, for whenever a process of change takes place in the air, it is particularly harmful for the temperament of this type of animal. A trustworthy man informed me from the report of Christian merchants who had recently arrived at Almeria from the east, that in the lake opposite the Turkish coast, where this plague also raged, mutilated and putrefied fish were found floating upon the water, and that large quantities of them accumulated there, and the strong stench and vile odors spread. They thought that these fish were struck by lightning and thereby destroyed; however, that is absolutely wrong. Lightning is extinguished by the water. Even if we were to assume that lightning goes into the water, it would only destroy the fish it struck, and that would not play a major role [in causing the Plague], even if many lightning bolts had struck. It seems to me, however, that if air was so changed and putrefied that land animals would die from it, then water could also be changed and putrefied so that sea animals are destroyed, as the water is transformed into another mixture and condition. This takes place frequently in calm waters, in enclosed, shallow lakes. Whenever such a lake becomes plague-stricken putrefied air rushes downward, simultaneously mixing with air currents that stir up the surface [mixing putrefied air with the water]. This process of change is the one that took place in those lakes [near Turkey].

You say, however, "The change, which you determine to be air and water putrefying and changing into perishable substances, contradicts what has been determined by science. This means that the four elements[3] can only be spoiled in part, and this takes place through [a large amount of] one [element] mixing with another one: for example, air in water, water in earth, and so on; however, if they transform into other things, they are now compounds and no longer pure elements. From this, Hippocrates came to the conclusion that humans are made up of [a compound of] four tempers. If people were of the same nature and consisted of the same element, that wouldn't make any sense." The answer to this is:

The air, which is healthful for us and necessary for life, is not an entirely pure element; rather, it is a compound of aqueous fumes, dry smoke developed from the earth, fine particles of fire, and mostly [elemental] air. All of this has been blended into what we call "air." For this reason, a process of rotting can shrink the [amount of elemental] air [in "air"] into a smaller and smaller portion in relation to these [other] substances. In regard to pure elemental air, this cannot occur. But if elemental air were in its pure condition, perhaps it would be above the atmospheric level where the air currents are circulating—possibly.

The same can be said of water, particularly in those lakes where calm water is found, generally in shallow waters. These are penetrated by atmospheric air currents, stirred up by storms and therefore become putrid as well.

Source: Translation by Patrick Gann of Ibn Khatimah in Taha Dinānah, "Die Schrift Ahmed ibn ʿAlī ibn Mohammed ibn ʿAlī Hātimah aus Almeriah über die Pest." *Archiv für Geschichte der Medizin* 19 (1927): pp. 34–38.

French Medical Advice for Avoiding the Plague (1348)

In the summer of 1348 France's King Philip VI commanded the medical faculty of the University of Paris to write a treatise, or consilium, on the pestilence that was rapidly approaching the capital. Utilizing the writings of earlier Greek, Roman, and Arab physicians, they cobbled together a scholastic exercise in Latin that bore no relation to the realities of the epidemic. Even so, it was translated into French, Italian, and German, and it influenced countless other plague-tract authors for decades to come. The advice on avoiding the disease is founded on the notion that it is caused by corrupted air (see Document 3) and that the corrupted air most easily sickens people whose "humoral balance" is moist and warm (replete). Though the advice, like the "science" on which it was based, was flawed, there is an admirable internal consistency between cause and cure. Unfortunately, the strength of this connection kept the Western world ignorant of the real causes and cures until only a century ago.

DOCUMENT 4
Compendium de epidemia, Book 2 (1348)
Medical Faculty of the University of Paris

CHAPTER ONE: ON THE CHOICE OF AIR AND ITS PURIFICATION

He who wants to protect himself from this epidemic should choose air as clean and pure as possible; dry, with no mixtures of corrupting vapors. This suggests two considerations: one on the choice of air in the place of habitation, the other on the general nature and substance of the air. When talking about the first point, let's follow the advice of Halys, who expresses himself in these terms: "The inhabitants should leave any place where and in which [the air is mixed with corrupting vapors], if possible. If not, they should choose a dwelling away from the wind channels that carry these corrupt vapors, as in humid houses, where air is stagnant." With those considerations, in these gloomy and suspect times, low-built houses are best.

Therefore, it is necessary to have such a dwelling, far from marshy, muddy, and stinking places with bad, stagnant waters and trenches; one whose windows can be opened to the northern winds. Always be on guard that these winds do not blow across corrupt and infected places, and make sure that the windows facing the south stay closed and locked. If they must be opened, be sure that they are opened neither before sunrise nor before starting a fire. Windows should be protected with a border of coated string (caulking), so that air can not enter the apartment, unless the northern wind blows pure or the air blows in the middle of the day, when it is purified by the heat of the sun. As to whether one should live in the woods, we do not recommend it. Those who leave the woods for more northern locations and board-up the [new] house on the south side have the preferable situation.

On the subject of the purification of air in its substance and nature: if the air is impure, fetid, and hazy, one must choose to stay inside in a single room, correcting the corruption of the air with a fire made with dry and odoriferous wood. The choice wood for this fire is juniper and ash, vine and young and prickly oak. In winter, above all, correct the air by burning a smoky fire made of wood of aloes, of amber and musk, for the wealthy who are able; or with costmary, storax calamite, frankincense, marjoram, mastic, pistachio, tamarisk and other similar plants.

In winter, it is therefore necessary to avail yourself of these plants, be they mixed together, or separated one by one, provided that the fumigating fires are aromatic and pleasant without being too hot. The cyperus (galingale) and tamarisk likewise should be used in the fumigations because their acid content is better for correcting the bad air. One can also use lozenges, the description of which we reserved to the last chapter; this type of fumigation should be made at sunrise, sunset, and in the middle of the night. At the same time, rather advantageously, one can use frankincense and juniper-berry. Also, it is said that asa (an aromatic, resinous gum) hampers putrefaction of the air, and removes the stench of the air and the corruption [caused by] the stench. Another way to correct the corruption of the air is to put pieces of fresh figs in the fire, making sure to throw them on the hot coals until entirely burned.

In the summer, on the contrary, the corruption of the air should be corrected by the cold. It is then necessary to moisten the room or habitat with rose water and vinegar or with very cold water [mixed] with vinegar. One must scatter about branches, leaves, and "cold" flowers, like green plants, willow branches, roses, seaweed, vine leaves, and other odiferous plants, some rose water and vinegar, or keep a sponge soaked with vinegar.

SECOND CHAPTER: ON EXERCISE AND BATHING

On exercise and bathing, there are two things to consider. First of all, with regard to exercise, those not used to it should not start in times of epidemic. As long as the air is calm, those who are in the habit [of exercising] should do a little less than normal so that they do not intensify the need to breathe. However, if the air is not calm, but troubled and infected, do not go out of the lodging, but do a little exercise in the room or in the court. Some authors prescribe exercise, but one risks doing it to excess in this present epidemic.

The second thing to consider is taking a bath, and according to us, it is best to avoid taking a hot one because it relaxes and moistens the body. A hot bath should be rare, and rarer still for those whose body is replete. Only those who are strongly habituated to it and those with a fat and compact build can do it to moisten themselves in trying to expel the sickness.

Third Chapter: Food and Drink

On the subject of eating and drinking, [we have] observed that one should avoid all excesses of food and drink because humid things are predisposed to the epidemic. One should eat lightly, choosing food that is easily digested, capable of enriching the blood, such as bread made with a high-quality tender wheat and of a good harvest, well cooked, sufficiently fermented, of one or two days at most and mixed with a little bran and barley.

Among meats, it is necessary to choose lambs of one year, tender pieces of veal, kid, rabbits, young chickens, hens, partridges, pheasant, starlings, capons, and small birds such as the lark, gamaleon[4] and others like them. However, all these meats should be roasted rather than boiled. Young mutton, if it has to be boiled, must be salted for one day first. And, boiled meats should be seasoned with aromatic spices like ginger, cloves, cubeb pepper, cardamom, nutmeg, mace, or powder and shell of nutmeg, and especially crocus and cinnamon, with some vinegar or verjuice.

Source: Translation by Jeffrey Williams of text from H. Émile Rébouis, *Étude historique et critique sur la peste* (Paris: Picard, 1888), pp. 95–105.

A Fifteenth-Century English Poet's Advice on Avoiding the Black Death

> *John Lydgate (c. 1370–1450) joined the monastery of Bury St. Edmunds early in life, and never left the monastic life. He is noted today as a prolific poet, the major figure in English literature between Chaucer and Shakespeare. Some 150,000 lines of his survive, touching many subjects in every poetic format. His most notable patron was Humphrey, Duke of Gloucester, owner of a huge library and pillar for many of the era's writers and scholars. At stanza 15 of this undated poem Lydgate advises against allowing "divisions to develop at your court," suggesting that the work may have been written for Humphrey, or at least for a noble and his household. The prices of many of the specific foods and herbs he recommends, including "potable gold," would not have been within the range of the commoner. Aside from the so-called "Canutus Plague Treatise,"[5] England produced no fourteenth- or fifteenth-century prescriptive Plague literature, either in Latin or in the vernacular. This makes Lydgate's Middle English contribution especially valuable as ver-*

nacular poetic medical advice. Like the Paris Compendium and similar
literature the poem opens in the third person—"Whoever wishes . . ."—
and presents an abstract or outline of the advice that follows, which is
presented in the second person through most of the rest. As a sort of
"bookend" he returns to the third person in summing up at the end.

DOCUMENT 5
"A Diet and Doctrine for the Pestilence" (Fifteenth Century)
John Lydgate

Whoever wishes to be healthy, protect himself against sickness,
And resist being struck down by the plague,
Should try to be happy and avoid sadness entirely;
Flee from bad air, indeed avoid the presence
Of infected places which can cause harm.
Drink good wine and eat healthy foods;
Smell sweet things and for his own protection
Walk in clean air and avoid black mists.

Do not dress to go out on an empty stomach;
When rising early, do so with the aid of a fire;
Delight in gardens for their wonderfully sweet smell,
But take care to dress yourself warmly.
Avoid excessive indulgence of any type,
Especially make not visits to brothels and baths:
The exchange of humors in such places causes great harm.
Walk in clean air and avoid black mists.

Do not eat meat out of greediness,
And abstain from eating fruit,
Eat poultry and chicken because they are tender—
Eat them with sauce and don't use sparingly
Verjuice, vinegar, and seasoning
With healthy spices. I even dare say
Morning sleep, called golden in proverbs,
Is a good protection against the black mists.

The Dietary

For the health of your body, protect your head from cold,
Take special care to eat no raw foods,
Drink wholesome wine and eat white bread.
Get up from eating while you are still hungry.
Have nothing to do with older, sensual women.
If you wish to go to bed and rise up in good spirits,
Never drink before sleeping
And never eat your supper late.

Eat good bread, cleanly mixed
And well made of good wheat flour—
More than a day and a half old will show in the taste.
Avoid excessive physical labor.
Walk in sweet-smelling gardens,
Calmly and taking care.
Repeated overeating causes sleepiness,
And always take care not to sleep at midday.

Put sage and rue in your beverages—
Both have good, healthful properties,
As does rose water, according to medicine.
And Hippocrates has recorded in his writing
That good wine is healthy for everyone,
Taken in moderation, with various additions—
Strong, fresh, and cold, tasting and smelling of herbs,
Highly recommended in all nations.

In brief, for good health, follow this policy:
Always avoid excess and overeating;
Practice abstinence from gluttony,
Late suppers, and belligerent drunkenness,
Yawning, twitching, and nodding sleepiness
Are sent as ambassadors for good reason—
Snoring, drowsing, and inability to move
Tell men it's time to go to bed.

A full stomach causes many problems—
Groaning, grumbling, and pacing in the middle of the night—
For young and old alike.
A light supper makes people lively in the morning.

Three remedies preserve a person's strength:
First, a glad heart, troubled by few cares;
A moderate diet, which is wholesome for all creatures;
And most importantly, not worrying about things.

Caraway is a good medicine,
Taken before meals, and prepared with gladness,
A healthful preparation, distilled from the vine
Of Bacchus' garden, which helps the heart.
Potable gold is good for chills or fever,
But it is too expensive for poor people;
For them, a watery gruel wards off nausea
And abates a burning fever from illness.

Eating greedily at supper and drinking late at night
Cause an excess of phlegm to develop;
Choler upsets the stomach;
Melancholy is an insistent guest, indeed!
All infirmity comes from too much or too little—
Lack of self-control in balancing these extremes
Drives one away from the mean, to excess or scarcity:
Set your sights on moderation.

By this I mean, if out of extreme pleasure
You give in to a desire to exceed natural appetites,
Overtaxing your digestion
With dangerous indulgence and excess,
Be warned that you may be attacked
By fever, chills, and unexpected aches.
As protection against all illness, a moderate diet
Is the best physician to balance your digestion.

All this leads to a timely conclusion:
A temperate diet, making pleasant digestion;
Golden sleep, taken at the appropriate hour;
Appetites which are natural to the season;
Food according to one's complexion
Governed by the four humors—phlegm, melancholy,
Blood, choler—guided by reason, these are the means of
Avoiding all the troubles caused by ungoverned illness.

And if leeches fail to help you
Follow these three courses of action:

Moderate diet, moderate labor,
Avoidance of melancholy regardless of adversity;
Accepting of one's troubles, content in poverty,
Feeling rich though having little, content with what is sufficient,
Never complaining and merry, as suits your status.
If medicine fails, let these govern you.

Do not immediately believe every tale;
Do not be hasty or suddenly vengeful;
Do not abuse the poor.
Be courteous in speech, measured in eating—
Not being greedy for varied foods at table;
Be gentle in your eating habits, prudent in affairs of the heart,
Not loose of tongue or deceitful
And always strive to speak well of others.

Disdain people who engage in double talk;
Don't permit negative speaking at your table;
Avoid people who sow trouble
Through false rumors and flattery.
Don't permit divisions to develop at your court,
As these can cause trouble in your household.
Regarding all pertaining to your welfare, property, and prosperity,
Live in peace, without unrest, with your neighbors.

Dress cleanly, and according to your status;
Don't exceed your limits; keep your promises faithfully,
Avoiding discord especially with three groups of people:
First, be wary of contests against your betters;
Don't seek quarrels with your fellows;
And it is shameful to fight with those subject to you.
Therefore, I counsel, seek all your life
To live in peace and acquire a good reputation.

While fire in the morning and in the evening before bed is useful
Against black mists and pestilential air,
Even better is being on time for Mass,
Doing God reverence upon first rising in the morning,
Diligently visiting the poor,
Having pity and compassion on all who are needy—
Then God will send you grace and influence,
To increase[6] you and your possessions.

Do not permit overindulgence in your house at night
Being wary of late suppers and overeating,
Nodding heads, candle light,
Laziness in the morning, and sleepy idleness—
This is the chief gateway of all vice.
Avoid drunken liars and lechers,
Drive away the mistress of profligacy,
That is, dice players and bettors.

Be careful after eating: do not sleep;
Always protect your head, feet, and stomach from cold.
Don't be too pensive, don't worry—
Maintain your household in accordance with your status.
Suffer when necessary, but be bold when you are in the right.
Don't swear oaths to deceive others.
Be lusty when young and sober when older—
Worldly joys only last a brief while.

Don't eat in the morning before you are hungry;
Clean air and walking help the digestion.
Don't drink between meals for pleasure
But rather let need or hard work be the reasons.
Salty foods can overtax weak stomachs
Especially when people can't refrain from
Eating things that don't agree with their constitution.
Frequently, greedy hands cause the stomach great distress.

Therefore, the well-being of soul and body depends
On two things, for those who heed them:
Moderation in eating gives men good health,
Which overindulgence can take away;
Charity is a balm to the soul.
This recipe, though purchased from no apothecary,
Not from Master Anthony or from Master Hugh,
Is the richest of diets, and free to all.

Source: Translation by Margaret Monteverde of John Lydgate, "A Diet and Doctrine for Pestilence," in *The Minor Poems of John Lydgate*, vol. 2, ed. Henry Noble McCracken (London: Early English Text Society, 1934), pp. 702–7.

The Medical Signs of Pestilence (c. 1447)

> *By the mid-fifteenth century distinguishing the signs, or symptoms, of pestilence from those of other diseases was vital not only for the health of the patient, but also for the community. If cases of pestilence were not identified, the community would be unprepared; false positives could result in panic, flight, and unnecessary civic measures. Michele Savonarola was born in Padua, Italy, in 1385. He studied and practiced medicine there, and he was active in civic affairs. He wrote on moral and political philosophy as well as medicine. Savonarola was called to the d'Este court at Ferrara as physician in 1441, and died in either 1462 or 1468. In this vernacular consilium Savonarola combines his own experience—one must assume—with the teachings of Avicenna, whom he calls il Principo (the Prince—variously spelled). He begins with the signs of the fever itself, then briefly describes signs indicative of recovery and those that are mortal, or indicate impending death.*

DOCUMENT 6
The Treatise on the Pestilence in Italian: Chapter 2 (c. 1447)
Michele Savonarola

The signs of pestilential fever, briefly speaking, are these:

First: that the fever has slackened a little to the touch; internally, the person is very disturbed, especially on the left side, and is thus in great distress: and to others it might seem inexplicable that such a mild fever should cause such great distress. As *lo Principo* says, there are times when such a fever occurs that neither the doctor nor the patient considers it high enough to be a problem, and likewise the pulse does not appear to have changed, nor the urine, but still the patient is going to die. Thus pestilential fever is a fever about whose essence physicians have many doubts. But when such a sign is seen, and the patient appears to be greatly weakened and to have lost all strength in his limbs, and does so on the first or second day, and he feels utterly debilitated without manifest reason, then there is clear reason to believe that it is pestilential fever. And especially, when these other signs accompany it: the appearance of the face has changed; the tongue has blackened and dried out; he vomits, has impure sweat, and stinking breath for which he has to gasp; when patches or blotches appear [on the skin] that are red or another color; small pustules [appear and] suddenly disappear [because] they discharge constantly. They have headaches, a terrible time catching their breath, sudden loss of appetite; they are stricken, cannot sleep; there is great swelling; the patient seems demented and dull-witted. Sometimes in the body there is breakdown as in dropsy (edema), and, as *il Principo* says, pestilential fever increases the tension in the hypo-chondrium. Sometimes, in the early stages choleric flux of the body appears, and the pulse is commonly rapid but weak, though at night it becomes stronger.

One cannot place much faith in the urine. *Il Principe* says that it rather often happens in pestilential illnesses that the urine is good, nat-ural in its substance, of good color and sediment, and nonetheless, the patient dies. Therefore, the "sign" of the urine is very misleading. But, as it is written, sometimes it appears watery, that is it does not have good substance; sometimes it is quite discolored, and in most cases cloudy, called *subiugale*. The emissions are watery, stinking, and foamy. Sometimes such signs are accompanied by swellings and carbuncles, and then there is no doubt. All of these signs are matters of speculation, most of which for the sake of brevity I leave aside at the present.

Thus we have laid out the signs that indicate the fever. Let us now discuss signs that signify its termination, and by which they ought to make judgments. These will be useful, that thus seeing the dangers to mortals, they comfort friends, the relatives get the patient to confess, to make a will and similar things. But it must be said that most of the time such a fever ends badly, often making fools of the doctors; and therefore, whoever is thus tried, would be wise to confess himself and put his affairs in order.

But when one sees such good signs as slight fever with the symptoms in remission, the appetite getting stronger, especially in the first days, and also with strengthening of the limbs, and with strengthening of the spirit and no loss of mental faculties, one can be comforted and have hope in a full recovery.

But when the patient is the face of death, that is worn out, skin color tending to brown and some blotches appear on the face, which begins to turn green, then death is probably not far away. Later, when in the early stages appear some bodily evacuations, sweat, vomit, urine similarly it is a mortal sign. When the urine is thick, cloudy, and does not leave a sediment, it is a very bad sign, especially if the [bodily] strength should be weakened. A mortal sign is watery urine that perseveres, and becomes stinking, black or livid. Also, when the emissions are very fetid, of several colors, especially in the early days, and likewise, when it is also choleric, because of this the patient does not recover. Also, if the emission is greasy, stinking, and over it there appears a greenish tinge, it is mortal. Stinking sweat in the early stages is a matter of concern, and it is bad. Stinking vomit, either the green, like a leek leaf and stinking, or the red darkened with blackness like a *fior di ramo*,[7] is mortal. Likewise some pustules appear and later become less evident. Soon after, when the headaches persevere with weakening of [bodily] strength: with these there will be other bad signs with a lightening of the symptoms, it will be a mortal sign. [And if the flux of blood should appear on the seventh (day), and it does not appear on the fourth (day) with a lightening of the symptoms, it will be a mortal sign.] Variations in the pulse with the weakening of bodily strength are a matter of great concern. I hope these present [observations] suffice.

Source: Translation by the author of selection from Michele Savonarola, *Il trattato in volgare della peste*, ed. L. Belloni (Rome: For the Società Italiana di medicina interna, 1953).

Will-Making in the Midst of Plague: Prato, Italy (1348)

Historian Samuel Cohn makes the case that before the 1360s, Italians tended to spread their wealth around widely through their wills, while after about 1363 they began to consolidate their gifts for the sake of being remembered. In many ways Marco's will is very typical. Most of his wealth goes to his children, to be shared among them as they survive the raging epidemic. Gifts of one lira (twenty soldi) or one-half lira went to each of ten churches, convents, or lay religious brotherhoods (confraternities) so that they would pray for the salvation of his soul at Mass. His wife was to raise their children and continue running the wine-tavern without remarrying. Were the children to die, Prato's main church became his main heir: the amount to go to the chapel in Santo Stefano went from one-half lira to twenty-five lire. In fact, his pregnant wife Vermillia, Vanna, and Nofrio died before he did, facts reflected in his amended testament. Stefano survived, and Francesco, with his modest fortune of fifty florins, became a wealthy merchant and the town's most famous citizen.

DOCUMENT 7
Last Testament of Marco Datini of Prato, Italy, June 1, 1348

In the name of God.

Marco, son of the late Datino, of [the neighborhood] Porta Fuia, by the grace of Christ healthy in mind and body, wishing to arrange orally [for the disposition of] his goods, established this testament in this manner without having written it down [himself].

Firstly, he chose and willed that his body be buried within the church of San Francesco in Prato.

Likewise he left for [the sake of] his soul for the saying of masses, to the chapter of the church of Santo Stefano Maggiore, in the territory of Prato, 10 soldi. Likewise he left for his soul to the altar of the new chapel of the Belt of the Blessed Virgin Mary, which is located in the said church of Santo Stefano, 20 soldi. Likewise he left for his soul to the priest of the church of San Piero of Porta Fuia in Prato, for the saying of masses for his soul, 10 soldi. Likewise he left for his soul to the Confraternity of the Virgin Mary of the church of San Piero of Porta Fuia in Prato, 20 soldi. Likewise, he left for his soul to the convent of the Order of St. Francis of Prato, for the saying of masses, 20 soldi. Likewise he left for his soul to the Confraternity of the Virgin Mary of the said church of San Francesco, 10 soldi.

Likewise he left for his soul for the saying of masses to the convent of the brothers of San Domenico (Dominicans) of Prato, 10 soldi. Likewise he left for his soul to the convent of the brothers of Sant'Agostino (Augustinians) for the saying of masses, 10 soldi. Likewise he left to the brothers of the convent of Santa Maria of Carmel (Carmelites) of Prato for the saying of masses for his soul, 10 soldi. Likewise he left to the brothers of Santa Maria (Servites) of Prato, for the saying of masses for his soul, 10 soldi.

Likewise he left, for his soul, to the new altar of Saint Mary that is located in the church of Santa Anna across the Bisenzio [River], for adornment of the said altar, 10 soldi. Likewise he left for his soul to the Confraternity of St. John of Prato, 10 soldi. Likewise he left for his soul to the poor of the House of Dolce of Prato and to the house of Dolce itself, 20 soldi.

Likewise he said, ordered and willed and commanded that all of the above-written bequests are to be carried out in his behalf by his heirs, listed below, and by their guardians within three years computed from the day of his death. Likewise he left, ordered and willed that all of his goods be set aside for the restitution of evil gains or illicit dealings or retention [of funds] by this testator.

To all of his other property, both moveable and real, for rights and actions, present and future, he instituted as his heirs Francesco, Nofrio, Stefano and Vanna his children, and any sons or daughters, of either gender, born to his pregnant wife Donna Vermillia; and to each of them in equal shares. And should it happen that any one of his children {gap in text} die before reaching the age of eighteen years without [having] legitimate children born from a licit marriage, then and in that case the surviving wards will take the place of him who has thus died, as regards the trust, as is done with minors.

Likewise, he left Donna Vermillia, his wife, control (and) use of all his property as long as she lives chastely, honorably [and] with her said children, and {gap in text} if she will maintain and lead the life of a widow and preserve her honor and does not reclaim her dowry.

And if it should happen that all of his children and heirs mentioned above should die while minors, he (Marco) substituted for them, or for the last one to die, Angelo Datini, his brother and the son of the said Datino. Likewise, then and in the said case[8] he left to the said Mona Vermillia his wife, his home and the use of the household of the testator himself with his place of business [legal description of its location]: including the bed, household goods and everything that is in the house itself, and place of business as long as she [Mona Vermillia] will live chastely and honorably and continue to live as a widow.

Likewise, then and in that case, he leaves for his soul and those of his kin 25 lire to the new chapel of the Belt of the Blessed Virgin Mary located in the church of Santo Stefano Maggiore, in the territory of Prato. Likewise, then and in that case, he leaves for his soul and [the souls] of his kin five lire to the operating fund of the church of San Pier Forelli in Porta Fuia, Prato. Likewise, then and in that case, he leaves for his soul and [the souls] of his kin five lire to the poor of the House of Dolce of Prato and to the House itself. Likewise he leaves, then and in the said case, for his soul and those of his kin to the poor of the Misericordia house in Porta Fuia in Prato and to the house itself five lire. Likewise, then and in that case, he leaves to Mona Caterina, wife of Bettino Bettini (and) his [Marco's] sister, each year twelve sacks of good and unadulterated grain. [This will continue] for as long as she should remain a widow and without her dowry, for the entire length of life of the same Caterina, as long as she should preserve her chaste widowhood and honorable life.

He constituted, bequeathed, and willed the guardians of his said children to be Barzalone di ser Guccio, Angelo di Datino, and Piero di Giunta, and Mona Vermillia of Porta Fuia in Prato, the wife of this present testator, releasing to them the necessity of putting together an inventory and of carrying out an account of the administration of their charges. . . .

All of these actions were taken in Prato at the house of the poor of the Misericordia in Porta Fuia in Prato.

[List of 8 witnesses follows]

I, Rinaldo di Banduccio of Prato, by imperial authority judge and notary was summoned and was present for all the aforesaid things and wrote them publicly.

Source: Translation by the author of Enrico Bensa's edition of "Il Testamento di Marco Datini." *Archivio Storico Pratese* (April 1925): pp. 74–78.

The Black Death Shakes the Islamic World: The View from Damascus, Syria (1348)

This poem (translated into prose here) by the noted Muslim Syrian geographer Abu Hafs Umar ibn al-Wardī is in the form of a prayer to Allah (a saj). In a short space Ibn al-Wardī supplies an abundance of observations on major themes of the Black Death: the spread of the pestilence, its destruction of urban populations, symptoms such as the spitting of blood, the pious prayers to Allah, the rejection of miasma theory and medicinal remedies, the suffering believer as martyr, the many metaphors for pestilence, and the activities of those resigned to death. Unexpectedly, Ibn al-Wardī provides a positive view of human responses: reconciliations, repentance, manumissions that were prompted by the Black Death. Ibn al-Wardī died on March 18, 1349, apparently of the pestilence, shortly after completing this work. His poem was the only extensive description of the Plague in Syria contemporary with the initial outbreak, and was used by many later Arab historians.

DOCUMENT 8
"Risālah al-Naba' 'an al-Waba'": An Essay on the Report of the Pestilence (1348)
Abu Hafs Umar ibn al-Wardī

God is my security in every adversity. My sufficiency is in God alone. Is not God sufficient protection for His servant? Oh God, pray for our master, Muhammad, and give him peace. Save us for his sake from the attacks of the plague and give us shelter.

The plague frightened and killed. It began in the land of darkness. Oh, what a visitor: it has been current for fifteen years. China was not preserved from it nor could the strongest fortress hinder it. The plague afflicted the Indians in India. It weighed upon the Sind. It seized with its hand and ensnared even the lands of the Uzbeks. How many backs did it break in what is Transoxiana! The plague increased and spread further. It attacked the Persians, extended its steps toward the land of the Khitai, and gnawed away at the Crimea. It pelted Rūm with live coals and led the outrage to Cyprus and the islands. The plague destroyed mankind in Cairo. Its eye was cast upon Egypt, and behold, the people were wide awake. It stilled all movement in Alexandria. The plague did its work like a silkworm. It took from the *tirāz* factory its beauty and did to its workers what fate decreed. Oh Alexandria, this plague is like a lion which extends its arm to you. Have patience with the fate of the plague, which leaves of seventy men only seven.

Then, the plague turned to Upper Egypt. It, also, sent forth its storm to Barqah. Then it attacked Gaza, and it shook 'Asqalān severely. The plague oppressed Acre. The scourge came to Jerusalem and paid the *zakāt* religious tax [with the souls of men]. It overtook those people who fled to the al-'Aqsā Mosque, which stands beside the Dome of the Rock. If the door of mercy had not been opened, the end of the world would have occurred in a moment. It then hastened its pace and attacked the entire maritime plain. The plague trapped Sidon and descended unexpectedly upon Beirut, cunningly. Next, it directed the shooting of its arrows to Damascus. There the plague sat like a king on a throne and swayed with power, killing daily one thousand or more and decimating the population. It destroyed mankind with its pustules. May God the Most High spare Damascus to pursue its own path and extinguish the plague's fires so that they do not come close to her fragrant orchards. Oh God, restore Damascus and protect her from insult. Its morale has been so lowered that people in the city sell themselves for a grain. The plague struck al-Mazzah and appeared in Barzah. The plague, then, came to Ba'labakk and compounded itself with the town as its name is compounded. It recited in Qārā, "Halt, friends both! Let us weep." The plague cleansed al-Ghasūlah. It eclipsed totally the sun of Shemsin and sprinkled its rain upon al Jubbah. In al Zabadāni the city foamed with coffins, and the plague brought misfortune on Hims and left it with three. The plague domesticated itself in Hamāh, and the banks of the river 'Asī became cold because of the plague's fever.

Oh Plague, Hamāh is one of the best lands, one of the mightiest fortresses. Would that you had not breathed her air and poisoned her, kissing her and holding her in your embrace. The plague entered Ma 'arrah al-Nu'mān and said to the city: "You are safe from me. Hamāh is sufficient for your torture. I am satisfied with that." It saw the town of Ma'arrah, like an eye adorned with blackness, but its eyebrow decorated with oppression. What could the plague do in a country where every day its tyranny is a plague?

The plague and its poison spread to Sarmīn. It reviled the Sunni and the Shi'i [Shi'ite]. It sharpened its spearheads for the Sunni and advanced like an army. The plague was spread in the land of the Shi'i with a ruinous effect. To Antioch the plague gave its share. Then, it left there quickly with a shyness like a man who has forgotten the memory of his beloved. Next, it said to Shayzar and to al-Hārim: "Do not fear me. Before I come and after I go, you can easily disregard me because of your wretchedness. And the ruined places will recover from the time of the plague." Afterward, the plague humbled 'Azāz, and took from the people of al-Bāb its men of learning. It ravished Tel Bashar. The plague subjected Dhulul and went straight through the lowlands and the mountain. It uprooted many people from their homes.

Then, the plague sought Aleppo, but it did not succeed. By God's mercy the plague was the lightest oppression. I would not say that plants must grow from their seeds. The pestilence had triumphed and appeared in Aleppo. They said: it has made on mankind an attack. I called it a pestilence.

How amazingly does it pursue the people of each house! One of them spits blood, and everyone in the household is certain of death. It brings the entire family to their graves after two or three nights. I asked the Creator of mankind to dispel the plague when it struck. Whoever tasted his own blood was sure to die.

Oh God, it is acting by Your command. Lift this from us. It happens where You wish; keep the plague from us. Who will defend us against this horror other than You the Almighty? God is greater than the plague which has captured and entered like an army among the peaceful, even as a madman. Its spearheads are sharpened for every city, and I was amazed at the hated thing [i.e., the Plague] which lies on the sharpened points.

How many places has the plague entered? It swore not to leave the houses without its inhabitants. It searched them out with a lamp. The pestilence caused the people of Aleppo the same disturbance. It sent out its snake and crept along. It was named the "Plague of the Ansāb." It was the sixth plague to strike in Islam. To me it is the death of which our Prophet warned, on him be the best prayers and peace. Aleppo— may God protect us from this disaster—is the land of toil. The plague became a serpent, an evil thing which kills her people with its spit.

Oh, if you could see the nobles of Aleppo studying their inscrutable books of medicine! They multiply its remedies by eating dried and sour foods. The buboes which disturb men's healthy lives are smeared with Armenian clay. Each man treated his humors and made life more comfortable. They perfumed their homes with ambergris and camphor, cypress, and sandal. They wore ruby rings and put onions, vinegar, and sardines together with the daily meal. They ate less broth and fruit but ate the citron and similar things. If you see many biers and their carriers and hear in every quarter of Aleppo the announcements of death and cries, you run from them and refuse to stay with them. In Aleppo the profits of the undertakers have greatly increased. Oh God, do not profit them. Those who sweat from carrying the coffins enjoy this plague-time. Oh God, do not let them sweat and enjoy this. They are happy and play. When they are called by a customer, they do not even go immediately. The Grey [Aleppo] became blackened in my eyes because of the anxiety and deceit. The sons of the coffins [the undertakers] are themselves about to follow death.

We ask God's forgiveness for our souls' bad inclination; the plague is surely part of His punishment. We take refuge from His wrath in His pleasure and from His chastisement in His restoring. They said: the air's corruption kills; I said: the love of corruption kills. How many sins and how many offenses does the crier call our attention to? . . . This plague is for the Muslims a martyrdom and a reward, and for the disbelievers a punishment and a rebuke. When the Muslim endures misfortune, then patience is his worship. It has been established by our Prophet, God bless him and give him peace, that the plague-stricken are martyrs. This noble tradition is true and assures martyrdom. And this secret should be pleasing to the true believer. If someone says it causes infection and destruction, say: God creates and recreates. If the liar disputes the matter of infection and tries to find an explanation, I say that the Prophet, on him be peace, said: who infected the first? If we acknowledge the plague's devastation of the people, it is the will of the Chosen Doer. So it happened again and again.

I take refuge in God from the yoke of the plague. Its high explosion has burst into all countries and was an examiner of astonishing things. Its sudden attacks perplex the people. The plague chases the screaming without pity and does not accept a treasure for ransom. Its engine is far-reaching. The plague enters into the house and swears it will not leave except with all of its inhabitants. "I have an order from the *qāḍī* [Islamic judge] to arrest all those in the house." Among the benefits of this order is the removal of one's hopes and the improvement of his earthly works. It awakens men from their indifference for the provisioning of their final journey. One man begs another to take care of his children, and one says goodbye to his neighbors. A third perfects his works, and another prepares his shroud. A fifth is reconciled with his enemies, and another treats his friends with kindness. One is very generous; another makes friends with those who have betrayed him. Another man puts aside his property; one frees his servants. One man changes his character while another mends his ways. For this plague has captured all people and is about to send its ultimate destruction. There is no protection today from it other than His mercy, praise be to God.

Nothing prevented us from running away from the plague except our devotion to the noble tradition. Come then, seek the aid of God Almighty for raising the plague, for He is the best helper. Oh God, we call You better than anyone did before. We call You to raise from us the pestilence and plague. We do not take refuge in its removal other than with You. We do not depend on our good health against the plague but on You. We seek Your protection, Oh Lord of creation, from the blows of this stick. We ask for Your mercy which is wider than our sins even as they are the number of the sands and pebbles. We plead with You, by the most honored of the advocates, Muhammad, the Prophet of mercy, that You take away from us this distress. Protect us from the evil and the torture and preserve us. For You are our sole support; what a perfect trustee!

Source: Michael W. Dols, "Ibn al-Wardī's Risālah al-naba' 'an al-waba'," in *Near Eastern Numismatics, Iconography, Epigraphy and History*, ed. Dickran Kouymjian (Beirut: American University of Beirut, 1974), pp. 443–55.

Plague and the Corruption of Mankind: A Muslim's View from Syria (1390s)

> *Christians were not the only ones to note the decline in morals that accompanied the Plague and its effects; Muslims, too, claimed that humanity had declined from an earlier state of goodness. Disaster had not made people better; rather, it had made them both less humane and less religious. In this qasida, which was recorded in the* Chronicle of Damascus *by Muhammad ibn Sasra, an unnamed Arab poet laments that it would have been better to die of the Plague than live under the current shameless corruption and immorality. The Mamlūk empire of Syria and Egypt had suffered from repeated blows of pestilence and political and economic disintegration that followed. Ibn Sasra introduced this piece by stating, "Men's occupations have ceased, the hearts of the rulers have become hardened, the rich have become haughty toward beggars, while the subjects perish and misfortunes increase."*

DOCUMENT 9
Anonymous Poem in the *Chronicle of Damascus*, 1389–97
Recorded by *Muhammad ibn Sasra*

*Say unto him who expects goodness from men, "Draw not
    near to them, lest you be miserable and distressed."*
*We are, by God, in an age of wonders, had we seen this in a
    dream, we would have been frightened.*
*In it, men have fallen into the worst state; it is fitting that
    one of them who has died be congratulated.*
*We have seen in this age wonders and things, at some of
    which we are amazed.*
*Among them there is no shame, no worship, and if you have
    survived to these [times] no quiet is yours.*
*By God, the effort of him who desires goodness of them was
    in vain, and he is disappointed in his opinion.*
*We have seen therein that the corrupt gain power and
    become high; it is fitting that we go mad.*
*We have reached the worst of times, so that we envy in them
    the one among us who has died.*
*We have seen what we had never seen, and heard what
    we had not heard.*
*He who died attained deliverance in death, while he who
    lives is tortured by anxieties.*
*Would that the times were reversed with their people, or
    that we were transformed in them!*
*People were formerly as pure as water, thus we observed
    them since we have lived.*
*They left us behind in a miserable state and went; would
    that we had not survived them!*
*For God was mindful of previous time, in which they were
    happy, and so were we.*

Source: Muhammad ibn Sasra, *Chronicle of Damascus, 1389–1397*, vol. 2, ed.
and trans. William M. Brinner (Berkeley: University of California Press, 1963),
p. 218.

An Early Fifteenth-Century English Poetic Meditation on Death

The macabre literary and artistic theme of the living meeting the dead became commonplace during the fourteenth and fifteenth centuries. This anonymous poem, however, breaks new ground in confronting the living interloper with a talking corpse and the vermin that were feeding on it. At the top of the manuscript page on which this Middle English poem was written is the drawing of a transi tomb that may have inspired the poet. Funerary depictions of the human corpse decomposing and literally providing a meal for worms originated in France in the 1390s and were seen in England in the early 1400s. Aside from the reference to the debate, the opening epitaph in iambic pentameter might easily have been posted on an actual transi tomb. As in similar dual poetic/artistic treatments of the Danse Macabre or Meeting of the Living and Dead, the message is clear: repent and live life well now, or harbor no hopes beyond the wretchedness of the grave.

DOCUMENT 10
"Disputation Betwixt the Body and Worms"
Anonymous

Epitaph

*Pay heed to my figure shown here above
And see how I, once finely dressed and gay,
Now am become the food of worms and corruption,
Both foul earth and stinking slime and clay.
Therefore, attend to the debate written below
And write it wisely in your noble heart
That from it you may acquire some wisdom
Regarding what you are and what you will be.*

When you least expect it, death comes to conquer you
While your grave is green, it is good to think on death.

A Disputation Between the Body and Worms

*In a time a wide-spread death
From various diseases, with the plague*

Reigning heavily throughout the country,
I was moved by my conscience to go on pilgrimage
And I went on my way in thoughtful haste.
One holy day in front of me I saw a church,
Where I went to set my rosary to work.

It was standing alone in a pleasant field—
My intentions were to hear Mass
But that was said and done before I got there.
I found the door open and I soon went in.
I knelt down and began my prayers.
With humble deference I bowed down
Before one image with great devotion.

Beside me I saw a tomb or sepulcher
Nobly made, painted and carved
All around and newly planned
With the imprint of various coats of arms.
I was not hesitant to look on the epitaph,
In gilded copper with gold showing through,
Regarding a fine and noble figure of a woman

Well clothed in the latest fashion.
Lulled by looking at this for a long time
I fell into a slumber in such a way
That rapt and taken out of myself
I heard debating between this body and worms—
Strangely, with each one replying to the other
Like a dialogue it seemed.
Therefore, pay attention to this sampling.

The body speaks to the worms:
"Worms, worms," this body said,
"Why do you act thus? What causes you to eat me thus?
By you my flesh is horribly decorated,
Which once was a figure noble and attractive,
Very pleasant and fragrant and sweet,
Best loved of all creatures
Called lady and sovereign, I assure you.

I was a lady of rare beauty
Descended of noble blood in a true line
From Eve and from proper beginnings well-endowed.

All hearts were glad to be in my presence—
Men of honor and great nobility did I decline—
And now in the earth, by mortal death do I come
Among you worms; naked I am brought low.

The most unkind neighbors ever made are you,
Food for dinner and supper all too little,
Now arguing, now eating, you have searched me through,
With a completely insatiable and greedy appetite.
No rest—since always you suck and bite,
No hour or time of day do you abstain,
Always ready to do violence to me again.

When you first began to make your way into me
It seemed to me you had been fed in a thin pasture;
Now you grow fat and ugly, round as well as large,
For courtesy and gentleness, remove me from your care
And dwell and remain with someone else
Who may reward you with better provisions,
For I am almost wasted away, consumed and gone."

Worms speak to the body:
"Nay, nay! We will not yet depart from you
Not while one of your bones hangs with another,
'Til we have scoured and polished them
And made everything between them as clean as we can.
For our labor we ask to extract nothing,
Not riches of gold or silver, nor any other reward
But only for we worms to feed on you.

We cannot smell or taste you in any way,
The horrible rotting and stinking of your flesh,
Something hated by all other creatures,
Excepting by we wretched worms alone.
If we, like beasts, had the ability to smell or taste
Do you believe that we would openly touch your carrion?
Nay, believe me, we would avoid it for certain."

The body speaks to the worms:
"Indeed, you are discourteous to me,
Thus strongly to threaten and menace me,
And to leave me thus, as nothing but bare bones.
Now, where are you, oh knights? Come to this place!

And you worthy squires, both noble and lower born,
Who once offered me your service,
The pledge of your heart for all the days of your lives

Asking me to permit you to place your life in my counsel,
Come do me service and defend me now
From these huge horrible worms, ugly to see
Gnawing here on my flesh with great cruelty,
Now devouring and eating me, as you can see,
Me whom you once loved so completely.
Succor and defend my body now!"

The worms answer the body:
"What could they do? Let them come—
We have no dread of them, nor of their complaints,
For we have had to contend with the words
Of all the mighty ones who have passed away and gone
Before this time, having divided them up,
Emperors, kings, and conquerors, all
Lords both worldly and spiritual

All the nine worthies: Judas Maccabeus,
Julius Caesar, Godfrey of Boulogne,
Alexander, David, Hector, and Arthur,
King Charles, Duke Joshua the captain,
With all the Trojan knights most noble
With fair Helen, beauteous of visage,
Polyxene, Lucretia, Dido of Carthage.

These and others were also as fair as you
Yet they dared not stir or move at all
Once we had taken possession of them,
For all venomous creatures are ordained
To take part in this service—
They are entirely set on siding with us
To devour and destroy you utterly.

The cockatrice, the basilisk, and the dragon,
The lizard, the tortoise, the ringed snake,
The toad, the mole, and the scorpion,
The viper, the snake, and the adder,
The crapaud toad, the ant, and the canker-worm,

The spider, the maggot, the dark things of nature,
The water leech and others not unlike them."

The body speaks to the worms:
"I can find no remedy to this in any way,
Neither succor nor release of any kind,
Except that in this situation I must follow their plan
To completely gnaw my flesh away and be bound to sorrow.
For they are deemed hateful to all living things.
What shall I do but let them have their way—
Chance has it I must remain, though they destroy me."

The worms answer the body:
"On the day you were born we sent our messengers;
To them we gave as our commandment,
A charge to follow that they not offend us,
Not to depart from you until you went to death.
It was our intent that they gnaw and annoy you
And later come with you into our realm,
Where they would have your flesh as their reward.

And since they obeyed our commandment
You cannot in any way say no to this outcome.
Some of them went to your womb and to your stomach,
Others, lice and nits, were always in your hair,
Worms in your hands, fleas in your bed—I told you
With other venomous things of various types
To be warned to make yourself ready for us."

The body answers the worms:
"Now I recognize your messengers well! They were
Those things which kept residence with me while I lived.
No longer will I dispute or debate this matter.
Rather I will endure your violence against me.
Do your will with me, in your benevolence.
Yet, in the Psalms, David says that all
Shall be obedient to man's call."

The worms answer the body:
"That power lasts while man has life—
In this wretched world only are they yours.
Now that your life is gone, you cannot strive against us.

You are but as the earth and as a thing gone to nothing.
What I have told you was also said in preparation
Of Lent coming, on Ash Wednesday,
When the priest crosses everyone with ashes.

And with the blessing of ashes to have remembrance
Of what you are and whence you shall return to again,
For ashes you were before this moment
And ashes shall you certainly be again afterwards,
Be you lord, lady, or mighty sovereign,
To powder and dust in time shall you come.
Your interval is but til you leave this world."

The body speaks to the worms:
"Alas, alas! Now I know full well
That in my life I was ignorant and unwise,
Ruled by a pride too great to associate with others,
Led to be so by my abundant beauty.
I have been too proud, too wanton, and too foolish,
Taking great delight in worldly pleasures,
Thinking no one worthy to be my peer.

And now am I become subject to worms,
Bearing their proven messenger daily
Spiders and lice, and other worms hospitably,
Not knowing truly from whence they came.
To this I absolutely can say nothing more.
Instead I must arm myself with patient endurance,
Abiding our Lord's will in all circumstances."

The worms answer the body:
"For this tolerance you will get no thanks from us,
For by your will have you lived ever as you wished.
With the desire of your noble heart, you should remember
Holy Scripture and behold there
That the beauty of women is said to be
But a vain thing and transitory.
Women who fear God shall be praised as holy."

The body speaks to the worms:
"Yes, it is now too late a time to complain,
As now, about my situation; instead I can only place myself
At the mercy of our Lord God, most sovereign;

This is truly what is best for me to do,
And those still living have time to ready themselves,
To remember in this same way as well,
Thinking continually of the time to come.

What he shall be and also what he is:
Be it he or she, be they never so fair, beware
Of pride over their fellows, that they don't become
That which often brings men to suffering.
As statements in Scripture truly declare
It is good to avoid fleshly temptation
Made and performed by the fiend, our foe.

Of this complaint that I have spoken
Take no displeasure for yourself:
Let us be friends, despite this sudden outburst,
Neighbors and lovers as we were before.
Let us kiss and dwell together forever,
Til God wills that I shall rise again
On Doomsday before his high justice.

To be glorified with the body
And that I may be one of that number
Which will come into the bliss of heaven as a reward
By meditation on and by the means
Of our blessed Lord, our true patron,
Able to be there by his desire.
Amen, Amen, your mercy grant this instance."

Now speaks he who saw this vision:
When I woke from a deep sleep,
Or from a sleeping meditation,
To a holy man of great renown
I related this dream and strange vision,
Who bade me put it into writing
As near and truly as I could remember it,
In as fine, well-shaped language as I could.

To give the readers something delectable
And an admonition able to both stir and move,
Man and woman to make themselves acceptable
Unto our Lord, and to leave behind all desires
For worldly things which will do them harm

And instead to call into mind
Our savior and bind ourselves to him. Amen.

Source: Translation by Margaret Monteverde of Karl Brunner's edition of "Dis-putacioun Betwyx the Body and Worms." *Archiv für deutsche Studien der neueren Sprachen* 167 (1935): pp. 30–35.

Finding Scapegoats: The Persecution and Slaughter of Jews (c. 1349)

> *Jews had long been involved in the economic life of European towns,*
> *often serving as money-lenders to whom local Christians went into debt.*
> *Fears of a Jewish role in the spread of the Plague were in the air from*
> *Spain to Germany. Supported by "confessions" and more or less official*
> *reports, they fueled existing resentments, and provided frightened folk,*
> *whether debtors or not, an excuse for eliminating local Jewish commu-*
> *nities. The religious and civic officials, who are at first unwilling to see*
> *the area's Jews maltreated, for they "knew no evil of them," relented and*
> *gave the mob what they wanted. For the reader familiar with the story*
> *of Jesus' Passion, these men certainly played the part of Pontius Pilate.*
> *This short description characterizes this mixture of motives and describes*
> *the fate of Jews in this city on the Rhine and suggests the fate of many*
> *others.*

DOCUMENT 11
The Jews of Strassburg, February 1349
From the Strassburg Chronicle

In the year 1349 there occurred the greatest epidemic that ever hap-pened. Death went from one end of the earth to the other, on that side and this side of the sea, and it was greater among the Saracens than among the Christians. In some lands everyone died so that no one was left. Ships were also found on the sea laden with wares; the crew had all died and no one guided the ship. The Bishop of Marseille and priests and monks and more than half of all the people there died with them. In other kingdoms and cities so many people perished that it would be horrible to describe. The pope at Avignon stopped all sessions of court, locked himself in a room, allowed no one to approach him and had a fire burning before him all the time. And from what this epidemic came, all wise teachers and physicians could only say that it was God's will. And as the plague was now here, so was it in other places, and lasted more than a whole year. This epidemic also came to Strassburg in the summer of the above mentioned year, and it is estimated that about sixteen thousand people died.

In the matter of this plague the Jews throughout the world were reviled and accused in all lands of having caused it through the poison which they are said to have put into the water and the wells—that is what they were accused of—and for this reason the Jews were burnt all the way from the Mediterranean into Germany, but not in Avignon, for the pope protected them there.

Nevertheless they tortured a number of Jews in Berne and Zofingen [Switzerland] who then admitted that they had put poison into many wells, and they also found the poison in the wells. Thereupon they burnt the Jews in many towns and wrote of this affair to Strassburg, Freiburg, and Basel in order that they too should burn their Jews. But the leaders in these three cities in whose hands the government lay did not believe that anything ought to be done to the Jews. However in Basel the citizens marched to the city hall and compelled the council to take an oath that they would burn the Jews, and that they would allow no Jew to enter the city for the next two hundred years. Thereupon the Jews were arrested in all these places and a conference was arranged to meet at Benfeld [Alsace, February 8, 1349]. The Bishop of Strassburg [Berthold II], all the feudal lords of Alsace, and representatives of the three above-mentioned cities came there. The deputies of the city of Strassburg were asked what they were going to do with their Jews. They answered and said that they knew no evil of them. Then they asked the Strassburgers why they had closed the wells and put away the buckets, and there was a great indignation and clamor against the deputies from Strassburg. So finally the Bishop and the lords and the Imperial Cities agreed to do away with the Jews. The result was that they were burnt in many cities, and wherever they were expelled they were caught by the peasants and stabbed to death or drowned. [The town council of Strassburg which wanted to save the Jews was deposed on the 9th–10th of February, and the new council gave in to the mob, who then arrested the Jews on Friday, the 13th.]

On Saturday—that was St. Valentine's Day—they burnt the Jews on a wooden platform in their cemetery. There were about two thousand people of them. Those who wanted to baptize themselves were spared. [Some say that about a thousand accepted baptism.] Many small children were taken out of the fire and baptized against the will of their fathers and mothers. And everything that was owed to the Jews was cancelled, and the Jews had to surrender all pledges and notes that they had taken for debts. The council, however, took the cash that the Jews possessed and divided it among the working-men proportionately. The money was indeed the thing that killed the Jews. If they had been poor and if the feudal lords had not been in debt to them, they would not have been burnt. After this wealth was divided among the artisans some gave their share to the Cathedral or to the Church on the advice of their confessors.

Thus were the Jews burnt at Strassburg, and in the same year in all the cities of the Rhine, whether Free Cities or Imperial Cities or cities belonging to the lords. In some towns they burnt the Jews after a trial, in others, without a trial. In some cities the Jews themselves set fire to their houses and cremated themselves.

It was decided in Strassburg that no Jew should enter the city for a hundred years, but before twenty years had passed, the council and magistrates agreed that they ought to admit the Jews again into the city for twenty years. And so the Jews came back again to Strassburg in the year 1368 after the birth of our Lord.

Source: Jacob R. Marcus, *The Jew in the Medieval World: A Sourcebook: 315–1791* (New York: Atheneum, 1979), pp. 45–47.

Pestilence in Late Fifteenth-Century Florence

Luca Landucci (c. 1435–1516) was an apothecary, or pharmacist, in Florence, Italy. He lived the life of an average guildsman and knew the recurring scourge of the Plague throughout his long life. Luca was married and sired twelve children, but was never very financially successful or socially well-connected. He began writing his diary—the early part of which is really a memoir—about 1500. Luca died in Florence and was buried in the Dominican convent of Santa Maria Novella. His observations are rich in detail, and the numbers of victims he reports have the ring of truth. Girolamo Savonarola, a Dominican friar in Florence, was a preacher of reform and a prophet of the end of an age, and was executed in May 1498 for unduly influencing the Florentine people. Less than two weeks prior to his execution, with him languishing in prison, the Florentines began rousting the pestilence victims out of the hospitals and out of town, as Landucci notes. To many, these were both terrible sins against God.

DOCUMENT 12
A Florentine Diary: December 1496 to February 1499
Luca Landucci

5 December 1496 A case of plague was discovered, after there had not been one for some months. At this time the complaint of French boils [venereal disease] had spread all through Florence and the country round, and also to every city in Italy, and it lasted a long time.

1 June 1497 Many people died of fever after being ill only a few days, some in eight days and some in ten; and there was one man who died in four days. It was said that during these last days of the waning moon there were 120 cases at the hospitals and in the city together. It was also said that there was a touch of plague at the hospital. Ten or twelve cases went there each day, and 24 have died just lately at Santa Maria Nuova. At the same time there was another trouble, the spiritual discouragement and physical weakness, which caused the poor to be indifferent as to dying; and numbers of them did die, in fact. Everyone said: "This is an honest plague."

13 June There died in one day about 100, between the hospitals and the city, while the moon was at its full.

28 June It was said that there were 68 deaths a day from fever.

30 June Plague broke out in several houses in the city, and in eight houses in the [suburb of] Borgo di Ricorboli.

2 July Many were dying of fever and plague, and one day there were 25 deaths at Santa Maria Nuova.

3 July More houses infested with plague were discovered here, making everyone think of fleeing from it. At this time the price of fowls was 3 lire a pair, and of capons 7 or 8 lire a pair; there were so many sick persons.

8 July The officials of the Abbondanza [civic council on food supplies] fixed the price of corn [grain] at the corn market at 35 soldi.

9 July Plague broke out in [the Dominican Convent of] San Marco, and many of the friars left it and went away to the villas of their fathers and friends. Brother Girolamo [Savonarola] remained at San Marco, with only a few friars. At this time there were about 34 houses with plague in Florence, and there was also a good deal of fever.

16 July There was plague in about 30 houses in Florence, and there were also many deaths from fever. And it is to be noticed that all those who died were heads of families, from 20 to 50 years of age, not children. It seemed as if the prophecy of the Friar [Savonarola] were to be realized as to the renovation of the Church and the world.

20 July Many poor people fell down in the streets from exhaustion, and all day long they were picked up by those appointed to do the work, and carried in litters to the hospital, where they died.

29 July There was an eclipse of the sun and many people were dying of plague and fever, which caused the city to empty itself of its inhabitants, everyone who could, going into the country.

15 August The following case happened: At the church of San Pagolo, in the churchyard outside it, the gravediggers were burying someone, and one of them dropped his keys into the grave, and went down into it to get them; but there was such a stench that he died there before they could draw him up again.

18 October Many heads of households and worthy citizens kept dying of fever, but no women or children.

19 October At this time the plague was discovered in several houses, so that the citizens stayed in their villas.

28 October In the Mercato Nuovo [New Market], on one of the stone seats against the wall, next to the tables of the money-changers, there was a man of about 50 years of age sitting with his face in his hand, as if he wished to sleep. And whilst he sat there he passed from this life, without any of those standing by noticing it. He did not make a single movement. Presently, seeing his pallor and touching him, they found that he was dead. And so he sat there dead for hours with his face on his hand, and no one went near him, thinking that he had died of the plague, which struck down so many.

7 November The plague began at Dicomano.

15 November One morning at dawn a dead girl was found under the portico of the Spedale [Hospital] di San Pagolo here at Florence; she was discovered by those who looked after those sick of the plague, and they judged that she had not died of the plague but had been strangled. . . .

21 April 1498 Plague was discovered in many houses, in about four houses again in Via della Scala, and four other houses here round San Pancrazio, as far as the Croce al Trebbio. There were several deaths in two days, because the moon was waxing. The people near were rather alarmed.

12 May The officers of the plague went into the hospitals and drove out the unfortunate sufferers; and wherever they found them in the city they sent them out of Florence. They were actually so cruel as to place a hempen rope with a pulley outside the Armorers' Guild to torture those who tried to return. It was a brutal thing and a harsh remedy.

16 February 1498/9 During these days the plague had ceased, and was no longer spoken of.

Source: *A Florentine Diary from 1450 to 1516 by Luca Landucci*, trans. Alice de Rosen Jervis (New York: E.P. Dutton and Co., 1927), pp. 114–66 passim.

NOTES

1. For a partial translation see Rosemary Horrox, *The Black Death* (New York: Manchester University Press, 1994), pp. 163–67.
2. An Arabic (ninth century) and a Roman (second century C.E.) astrologer.
3. Earth, Air, Fire, Water.
4. A bird reputed to be chameleon-like in its ability to camouflage itself.
5. See bibliography, "Primary Sources."
6. I have translated *tenchrese* "to increase" based upon its full context in the sentence and the fact that it appears nowhere else in Middle English literature.
7. Unidentified flower.
8. That all his children die.

GLOSSARY

Anti-clericalism: Feelings or attitudes that were critical of or hostile to the Catholic Church hierarchy and clergy; often generated in the wake of the Black Death.

Apostemata, aposteme: Commonly used medieval term for bubo.

Astrology: A branch of medieval science that studied the effects of celestial bodies—especially the moon, planets, and stars—on the earth, its nations, and its people.

Bacillus: A single-celled, rod-shaped bacterium.

Bubo: From the Greek word for groin, the swollen condition of lymph nodes in the human victim of bubonic plague. These are created by the collection of bacteria and dead human cells.

Bubonic plague: Human disease caused by Y. *pestis* in which the flea-induced bacillus concentrates in and disrupts the lymph nodes, causing them to swell. Death results from toxic shock. Without treatment lethality in modern times is 40 to 60 percent.

Ciompi Revolt (1378): Uprising of Florentine woolworkers who demanded production and wages as they had been before the Plague and a voice in the government.

Commensal: Sharing living and eating space with people; true of the *R. rattus.*

Consilium: Written medical analysis and advice from one physician to another or to a patient at his request.

Contagion: Transmission of a disease by direct physical contact.

Demography: The study of the various characteristics of a human population and their changes over time.

Divine intercessors: Deceased holy people who were thought by Catholics to reside in Heaven with God and could successfully ask for God's help for people still in the world. For the Plague, Mary, Sebastian, and Roch were the most universal.

Endemic: Present in and usually common to a specific human population.

Enzootic: Present in and usually common to a specific animal population.

Epidemic: An outbreak of a disease that affects a relatively high percentage of a given human population.

Epidemiology: A branch of medicine that studies epidemic diseases.

Epizootic: An outbreak of a disease that affects a relatively high percentage of a given animal population.

Extreme unction: Roman Catholic sacrament for the dying that included one's final communion and confession.

Flagellants: Catholic laymen who joined processions in which all whipped themselves and each other in an attempt to atone to God for people's sinfulness; the movement was suppressed by the Church and political leaders.

Humors: The four fluids that course through the human body: blood, phlegm, black bile, and yellow bile. According to medieval theory, their proper balance is essential for good health.

Iconography: The cultural meaning of a specific artistic image or image type.

Immunity: The quality of an organism that allows it to encounter a normally harmful substance without experiencing the normal injury.

Lethality: A measure, usually in percent, of how much of a specific population dies of a specific disease.

Lymphatic system: The network of veins or vessels in the human body that carry lymph, a clear fluid that cleanses tissues of dead cells, bacteria, and other impurities. In places such as the armpits, groin, and neck are lymph nodes, or reservoirs where these impurities collect.

Miasma: Polluted or poisonous vapors or air; considered by most medieval physicians to be the cause of the Plague.

Morbidity: A measure, usually in percent, of how much of a specific population contracts a specific disease.

Natalism: Societal attitudes and resulting public policies that are supportive of couples having children in order to repopulate an area after the Plague.

Notary: A trained legal scribe who drew up official personal, guild, and communal documents such as contracts, wills, and minutes of council meetings. Notaries were often present at the bedsides of the dying.

Pandemic: An outbreak of a disease that affects a high percentage of people in many populations. Historians recognize three pandemics of bubonic plague, the Black Death being the second.

Pathogenic: Capable of being very dangerous to an organism.

Peasants' Revolt (1381): Uprising of rural poor and middle-class people who marched on London demanding a return to pre-Plague labor conditions and a lowering of recently raised taxes.

Plague reservoir: A widely spread population of wild mammals, usually isolated from people, among whom the Plague bacillus is endemic over a long period of time.

Pneumonic or pulmonary plague: Human disease caused by Y. *pestis* in which the bacillus concentrates in and disrupts the lungs. Primary form is caused by the victim's breathing in the airborne bacillus; secondary begins with an infected flea's bite. Lethality is about 100 percent.

Pogrom: Violent and destructive assault on a Jewish community.

Poison libel: Notorious claim that Jewish people were responsible for poisoning water wells used by Christians. Belief in this fueled anti-Semitic attitudes and actions and led to massacres in France, Spain, and Germany.

Prophylaxis: Actions taken to prevent the outbreak or spread of a disease.

Quarantine: The isolation for a set period of people, animals, or objects suspected of carrying a contagious disease.

***Rattus rattus*:** Species also known as the black or house rat and considered to be responsible for carrying the fleas that spread the bubonic plague.

Septicemic plague: Human disease caused by Y. *pestis* in which the flea-induced bacillus concentrates in and disrupts the bloodstream, causing septic shock. Lethality is about 100 percent.

Statute of Laborers (1351): Extension of English government's earlier

Ordinance of Laborers that attempted to limit workers' mobility and wage levels in light of the post-Plague inflation.

Sumptuary laws: Laws regulating the public display of wealth, including style or material of clothing and the use of excessive pomp at funerals in Plague times. Lower-class people were forbidden to dress like the upper class, and excessive display wasted resources and fueled envy.

Verjuice: A common medieval acidic sauce and marinade used in cooking to aid digestion and during the Plague for cleansing living quarters.

Virulence: A measure of the ability of one organism to injure another.

Xenopsylla cheopis: The rat flea that is considered the principal vector of the Y. *pestis* bacillus that causes bubonic plague.

Yersinia pestis: The bacillus responsible for causing the disease known as bubonic plague. It has three recognized variants: *antiqua, medievalia,* and *orientalis.* It was first isolated by Alexandre Yersin in 1894.

Zodiac: A series of twelve constellations of stars that stretch across the sky and through which the sun appears to move. Thought to possess the power to influence people and events, they were studied as part of the medieval pseudoscience of astrology.

Zoonosis: A disease, such as bubonic plague, that is generally found among animals but can be transferred to people.

ANNOTATED
BIBLIOGRAPHY

General Studies of Disease in History

Cartwright, Frederick F. *Disease and History*. New York: Dorset Press, 1972. This medical historian presents a broad overview with attention to social, cultural, and economic results of major events and is highly critical of the role of the Church in its hindering advancement of medical knowledge in the medieval world.

Giblin, James Cross. *When Plague Strikes: The Black Death, Smallpox, AIDS*. New York: Harper, 1996. Written for young readers, it presents the Black Death in a wide context of human diseases past and present. Suffers from oversimplification that sometimes distorts factual accuracy.

Karlen, Arno. *Man and Microbes: Disease and Plagues in History and Modern Times*. New York: Simon and Schuster, 1995. Provides broad context for study of human disease of many kinds.

Kiple, Kenneth, et al., eds. *Plague, Pox and Pestilence: Disease in History*. New York: Marboro Books, 1997. Series of well-illustrated essays on epidemics of different diseases from ancient to modern times. Contains brief but useful overview of the Black Death by Ann Carmichael.

McNeill, William H. *Plagues and Peoples*. Garden City, NY: Anchor Press, 1975. Classic study of man and disease from a world historical perspective. McNeill employs much conjecture for early periods, but he is on good ground for the Second Pandemic.

Wills, Christopher. *Plagues: Their Origin, History, and Future*. London: HarperCollins, 1996. Examines many types of disease; contains a chapter on recent biological and ecological research and its implications.

Zinsser, Hans. *Rats, Lice and History.* Boston: Little, Brown and Co., 1934. Though dated and often irreverent, this overview of disease and science in history is worth reading for a look at its generation's view of the Black Death, its causes, and its consequences.

General Treatments of the Medieval Plague in England and Elsewhere

Aberth, John. *From the Brink of the Apocalypse: Crisis and Recovery in Late Medieval England.* New York: Routledge, 2000. Aberth presents an overview of war, famine, and the Plague in the fourteenth and fifteenth centuries and the effects they had on English society.

Benedictow, Ole J. *Plague in the Late Medieval Nordic Countries: Epidemiological Studies.* Oslo: Middelalderforlaget, 1992. Detailed study of evidence for the Plague and its effects in Scandinavian countries that concludes that despite the climate, rat-borne bubonic plague was the primary culprit.

Biow, Douglas. "The Politics of Cleanliness in Northern Renaissance Italy." *Symposium* 50 (1996): 75–86. Links Florentine humanists' interest in the city's cleanliness with conceptions of the role of filth in the Plague.

Britnell, R. H. "The Black Death in English Towns." *Urban History* 21 (1994): 195–210. English urban responses to the Plague were usually carried out by individuals and churchmen rather than civic governments.

Cantor, Norman. *In the Wake of the Plague: The Black Death and the World It Made.* New York: Harper, 2000. Sometimes quirky series of case studies of how the Black Death affected people, relating them to larger social, political, and economic trends and issues of the period.

Carmichael, Ann G. *Plague and the Poor in Renaissance Florence.* New York: Cambridge University Press, 1986. Tightly focused study of Plague deaths in Florence, legislation and institutional changes prompted by them, and the ways these created effective social control of the Florentine poor.

Corzine, Phyllis. *The Black Death.* San Diego: Lucent Books, 1997. Aimed at a young adult audience; contains discussion of life at the time as it related to the Plague and its effects. With black and white illustrations.

Creighton, Charles. *A History of Epidemics in Britain.* 2nd ed. 2 vols. London: Cass, 1965. Updated edition of 1891 overview of epidemic history. See volume 1 on the Black Death. Certainly dated on medical aspects of the disease, but contains much of value on the effects.

Dols, Michael W. *The Black Death in the Middle East*. Princeton: Princeton University Press, 1977. Remains the only book in English specifically on the late medieval Plague in the Islamic world. Dols deals with the spread, impacts, and influences of the epidemic both broadly and with a significant level of detail.

Dunn, John M. *Life During the Black Death*. San Diego: Lucent Books, 2000. Aimed at a young adult audience; contains discussion of life at the time as it related to the Plague and its effects. Illustrated.

Getz, Faye Marie. "Black Death and the Silver Lining: Meaning, Continuity, and Revolutionary Change in Histories of Medieval Plague." *Journal of the History of Biology* 24 (1991): 265–89. Focuses on modern interpretations of the effects of Black Death and how these are influenced by modern culture.

Gottfried, Robert S. *The Black Death: Natural and Human Disaster in Medieval Europe*. New York: The Free Press, 1983. Takes an "ecological approach" to the Black Death and its recurrences, considering the 300-year Plague era as an "environmental crisis" with wide-ranging effects for Europe's population.

Herlihy, David. *The Black Death and the Transformation of the West*. Cambridge, MA: Harvard University Press, 1997. Consists of three lectures given at the University of Maine in 1985, published posthumously with notes and an introduction. A broad, critical overview of the Plague is followed by brief studies of economic effects and changes in culture.

Kelly, Maria. *A History of the Black Death in Ireland*. Stroud, Gloucestershire, England: Tempus, 2001. Study of the impact of the Black Death on Gaelic-Irish and Anglo-Irish society, economy, government, and Church that is well informed by recent scholarship.

Naphy, William G., and Andrew Spicer. *The Black Death and the History of Plagues, 1345–1730*. Stroud, Gloucestershire, England: Tempus, 2001. Well-illustrated overview of medieval plagues and modern diseases—including HIV-AIDS, BSE, and smallpox—with emphasis on the commonality of human responses to epidemic disease and the importance of the precedents of the fourteenth century.

Nardo, Don, ed. *The Black Death*. San Diego: Greenhaven Press, 1999. Collection of extended excerpts from eleven major modern scholars as well as short translations otherwise found in Horrox, *The Black Death*, which is listed in this bibliography.

Nohl, Johannes. *The Black Death: A Chronicle of the Plague*. Translated by C. H. Clarke. London: G. Allen & Unwin, 1926; reprinted in abridged form New York: Ballantine Books, 1960. Descriptive overview of major aspects of the Plague and its effects and lesser aspects such as "erotic elements," dance mania, and children's pilgrimages. Heavily reliant on primary sources, but poorly documented.

Norris, John. "East or West? The Geographic Origin of the Black Death." *Bulletin of the History of Medicine* 51 (1977): 1–24. Moves the point of origin of the Black Death from generally accepted China or central Asia to southern Russia, claiming that Asia received the Plague through India and Burma, independently of the western outbreak. This spawned an interesting response from Michael Dols and a counter from Norris, both of which appeared in the same journal 52 (1978): 112–20.

Ormrod, W. M., and P. G. Lindley, eds. *The Black Death in England*. Stamford, Lincolnshire, England: Paul Watkins, 1996. Collection of articles on social, political, religious, and architectural history of the Plague in England, especially in the fourteenth century.

Platt, Colin. *King Death: The Black Death and Its Aftermath in Late-medieval England*. Toronto: University of Toronto Press, 1996. Well-illustrated book that combines social and architectural history of late fourteenth and fifteenth century England as affected by the continuing waves of the Plague.

Schamiloglu, Uli. "Preliminary Remarks on the Role of Disease in the History of the Golden Horde." *Central Asian Survey* 12 (1993): 447–57. Reasons that despite specific documentary evidence, the Black Death played major role in transformations of the western Mongol peoples.

Shrewsbury, J. F. *History of Bubonic Plague in the British Isles*. New York: Cambridge University Press, 1970. Important treatment of Black Death in England in context of other epidemics that challenges the high death rates claimed by contemporary writers on the basis of the epidemiology of bubonic plague.

Steffensen, Jón. "Plague in Iceland." *Nordisk medicinhistorisk årsbok* (1974): 40–55. Reviews chronicle evidence of pneumonic plague in Iceland in the fifteenth century.

Williman, Daniel, ed. *The Black Death: The Impact of the Fourteenth-century Plague*. Papers of the Eleventh Annual Conference of the Center for Medieval and Early Renaissance Studies, Binghamton, NY: Medieval and

Renaissance Texts and Studies, 1982. Contains seven papers on art, literature, economics, Islamic religious law, and eschatology.

Ziegler, Philip. *The Black Death*. New York: Harper and Row, 1969. The standard history of the European Black Death in English, covering a wide range of related topics.

Rats, Fleas, and Bubonic Plague as a Disease

Davis, David E. "The Scarcity of Rats and the Black Death: An Ecological History." *Journal of Interdisciplinary History* 16 (1986): 455–70. Takes rats out of the picture of the Black Death, demonstrating that their role in spreading it was neither evident nor necessary.

Ell, Stephen R. "Immunity as a Factor in the Epidemiology of Medieval Plague." *Review of Infectious Diseases* 6 (1984): 866–79. Explores the role of natural and acquired immunity in animals and humans in the Plague's rise, demographic impacts, and eventual disappearance. Pays special attention to the role of iron in the medieval diet and the patterns of who in society had the highest mortality.

———. "The Interhuman Transmission of Medieval Plague." *Bulletin of the History of Medicine* 54 (1980): 497–510. Argues against the roles of the rat flea and rat in spreading the Plague, finding the human flea to be the more likely vector.

Hendrickson, Robert. *More Cunning than Man: A Complete History of the Rat and Its Role in Human Civilization*. New York: Kensington Books, 1983. Broad and somewhat breezy treatment of the ways in which rats and people have intersected in history. Useful but traditional section on the Black Death; better on the nature and habits of rats.

Karlsson, Gunnar. "Plague without Rats: The Case of Fifteenth-century Iceland." *Journal of Medieval History* 22 (1996): 263–84. Argues against the rat's necessity in spreading plague, conjecturing that Iceland's epidemics were pneumonic, perhaps caused by a more virulent strain of the bacillus.

Lenski, R. E. "Evolution of Plague Virulence." *Nature* 334 (11 August 1988): 473–74. Brief article presents the theory that a mild strain of *Y. pestis* was present in enzootic phases of the Plague, but "point mutations" created supervirulent strains responsible for epidemics.

Marriott, Edward. *Plague: A Story of Science, Rivalry, Scientific Breakthrough and the Scourge that Won't Go Away*. New York: Holt, 2002. Written with the verve of a novel, *Plague* recounts in detail the rivalry in the 1890s between Kitasato and Yersin for the right to claim discovery of the cause of bubonic plague.

Rackham, D. James. "*Rattus rattus*: The Introduction of the Black Rat into Britain." *Antiquity: A Quarterly Review of Archaeology* 52 (1979): 112–20. Archeological evidence for presence of *R. rattus* in Roman and Anglo-Saxon Britain.

Raoult, Didier, et al. "Molecular Identification of 'Suicide PCR' of *Yersinia pestis* as the Agent of the Black Death." *Proceedings of the National Academy of Science* 97:23 (Nov. 7, 2000): 12, 800–803. Report of experiments with tooth pulp from Plague victims that supports the contention that *Y. pestis* was the cause of the Black Death.

Revisionist Views of the Nature of the Black Death

Bleukx, Koenraad. "Was the Black Death (1348–49) a Real Plague Epidemic? England as a Case-study." In *Serta devota in memoriam Guillelmi Lourdaux, II: Cultura mediaevalis* (Mediaevalia Lovaniensia, Studia 21), edited by Werner Verbeke et al., 65–113. Leuven: Leuven University Press, 1995. Questions the "classical theory" of rats-fleas-man (bubonic plague) for the 1340s and extent of population loss in England, based on reading of quoted original sources.

Cohn, Samuel K., Jr. "The Black Death: End of a Paradigm." *American Historical Review* 107 (2002): 703–38. Challenges dominant views of nature and effects of Black Death; briefer treatment of argument presented in the following book.

———. *The Black Death Transformed: Disease and Culture in Early Renaissance Europe.* Oxford: Oxford University Press, 2002. Intriguingly revisionist view of what disease the pestilence really was and of confidence in medical knowledge; based on very wide reading of original sources.

Scott, Susan, and Christopher Duncan. *Biology of Plagues: Evidence from Historical Populations.* New York: Cambridge University Press, 2001. Zoologist and demographer carefully outline patterns of Black Death, especially in England, and conclude that it was an outbreak of a hemorrhagic virus like Ebola.

Twigg, Graham. *The Black Death: A Biological Reappraisal.* New York: Schocken Books, 1985. Carefully constructed analysis of the Plague in England as described by contemporaries rejects bubonic plague in favor of anthrax as main cause of death.

―――. "The Black Death in England: An Epidemiological Dilemma." In *Maladies et société (XIIe–XVIIIe siècles)*. *Actes du Colloque de Bielefeld, novembre 1986*, edited by Neithard Bulst and Robert Delort, 75–98. Paris: Editions du C.N.R.S., 1989. Argues against the Black Death of 1348 being bubonic plague, seeing the contrasting patterns of seasonality, incubation, and transmission of the medieval disease and modern bubonic plague as too great to ignore or explain away. Twigg sees anthrax as a reasonable alternative explanation.

Medieval Medicine and the Plague

Barkai, Ron. "Between East and West: A Jewish Doctor from Spain." *Mediterranean Historical Review* 10 (1995): 49–63. Short narrative of Jewish physician who was expelled in 1492 and landed in Istanbul.

Carmichael, Ann G. "Contagion Theory and Contagion Practice in Fifteenth-century Milan." *Renaissance Quarterly* 44 (1991): 213–56. Shows how medical theory that denied the possibility of contagion conflicted with common observation of contagion and the communal action based upon it.

Chase, Melissa P. "Fevers, Poisons and Apostemes: Authority and Experience in Montpellier Plague Treatises." In *Science and Technology in Medieval Society*, edited by Pamela Long, 153–69. New York: New York Academy of Sciences, 1985. Study of three generations of Montpellier-trained physician-authors reveals evolution away from reliance on traditional authorities and more reliance on one's own experience and observation.

Cipolla, Carlo M. "A Plague Doctor." In *The Medieval City: Essays In Honor of Robert S. Lopez*, edited by Harry A. Miskimin, David Herlihy, and A. L. Udovitch, 65–72. New Haven: Yale University Press, 1977. Brief article follows the career of Dr. Ventura, communal physician of Pavia, comparing matters such as duties and salary to those of other communal Plague physicians.

French, Roger. *Canonical Medicine: Gentile da Foligno and Scholasticism*. Boston: Brill, 2001. Extended discussion of Gentile's relation to and use of scholastic medicine, especially as found in his *commentary* on Avicenna's *Canon*. See his Chapter 6 on the Black Death.

Garcia-Ballester, Luis et al., eds. *Practical Medicine from Salerno to the Black Death*. New York and Cambridge: Cambridge University Press, 1994. Contains articles on medical astrology, Jewish medical Plague tracts, the Milanese government's Plague policies, and university physicians' Plague tracts.

Henderson, John. "The Black Death in Florence: Medical and Communal Responses." In *Death in Towns*, edited by Steven Bassett, 136–50. New York: Leicester University Press, 1992. Presenting a counter-case to Carmichael's Milan, Henderson contends that Florentine medical theory accepted contagion as possible and that communal responses reflected both popular and professional views.

Jacquart, Danielle. "Theory, Everyday Practice, and Three Fifteenth-century Physicians." In *La Science médicale occidentale entre deux renaissances (XIIe s.–XVe s.)* (Variorum Collected Studies Series, 567), edited by Danielle Jacquart, Essay XIII: 140–60. Aldershot: Variorum, 1997. Concludes that little had changed in medical theory or practice for a century after the Black Death.

Lemay, R. "The Teaching of Astronomy at the Medieval University of Paris." *Manuscripta* 20 (1976): 197–217. Links the medieval study of medicine with that of astronomy and astrology.

Ober, W. B., and Alloush, N. "The Plague at Granada 1348–1349: Ibn Al-Khatib and Ideas of Contagion." In *Bottoms Up!: A Pathologist's Essays on Medicine and the Humanities*, edited by Ober, 288–93. Carbondale: Southern Illinois University Press, 1987. Ill-titled article outlines life and views on contagion of the Andalusian physician and bureaucrat.

Palmer, R. "The Church, Leprosy and Plague." In *The Church and Healing* (*Studies in Church History* 19 [1982]): 79–99. Studies the balance of religious and medical responses, especially in Italian cities.

Singer, Dorothy W. "The Plague Tractates." *Proceedings of the Royal Society of Medicine* (History of Medicine) 9:2 (1915–16): 159–212. Despite its age, provides very useful summaries of content of the major medical tracts by fourteenth-century physicians.

Plague Tolls—Demographic and Economic Effects

Blockmans, Wim P. "The Social and Economic Effects of Plague in the Low Countries: 1349–1500." *Revue belge de philologie et d'histoire/Belgisch*

Tijdschrift voor Filologie en Geschiedenis 58 (1980): 833–63. Argues against common perception that the Low Countries suffered lightly in Black Death, and explores patterns and impacts of the Plague in late fourteenth and fifteenth centuries.

Cazelles, Raymond. "The Jacquerie." In *The English Uprising of 1381*, edited by R. H. Hilton and T. H. Aston, 74–83. New York: Cambridge University Press, 1984. Concludes that this French uprising of 1358 was conducted not by peasants, but by a slightly higher class of rural folk who were reacting to social trends that were accelerated by the Black Death.

Dyer, Christopher. "The Social and Economic Background to the Rural Revolt of 1381." In *The English Uprising of 1381*, edited by R. H. Hilton and T. H. Aston, 9–42. New York: Cambridge University Press, 1984. Explores the causes of and participants in the so-called Peasants' Revolt of 1381, noting the role of village elites and their grievances against lords who had become harsher masters since the Black Death.

Emery, Richard W. "The Black Death of 1348 in Perpignan." *Speculum* 42 (1967): 611–23. Focusing on notarial evidence, Emery concludes that the Plague toll was high and economic effects very negative but that there was little breakdown in the social order.

Gyug, Richard. "The Effects and Extent of the Black Death of 1348: New Evidence for Clerical Mortality in Barcelona." *Mediaeval Studies* 45 (1983): 385–98. Close study of Episcopal records for deaths among priests.

Harvey, Barbara. *Living and Dying in England, 1100–1540*. Oxford: Oxford University Press, 1993. A close study of the monastic community of Westminster Abbey, including medical care and the effects of the Black Death on the abbey's population.

Hatcher, John. *Plague, Population and the English Economy, 1348–1530*. London: Macmillan, 1977. Brief but detailed study of the long-term population decline of England that blames the Plague recurrences for most of the continued depression.

Henneman, John B., Jr. "The Black Death and Royal Taxation in France, 1347–1351." *Speculum* 43 (1968): 405–28. Study of fiscal effects of the fall in population and revenue on the French Royal government.

Langer, Lawrence N. "The Black Death in Russia: Its Effects upon Urban Labor." *Russian History/Histoire Russe* 2 (1975): 53–67. Examines vitalization of Russian cities as rural peasants move in during 1350s.

———. "Plague and the Russian Countryside: Monastic Estates in the Late Fourteenth and Fifteenth Centuries." *Canadian American Slavic Studies* 10 (1976): 351–68. Traces effects on rural labor force of the Plague's depopulation.

Livi Bacci, Massimo. *The Population of Europe: A History.* Translated by Cynthia and Carl Ipsen. New York: Blackwell, 1999. In his Chapter 4 demographer Livi Bacci discusses the roles of diseases of many kinds in early modern Europe, centering on the Plague and its effects.

Lomas, Richard. "The Black Death in County Durham." *Journal of Medieval History* 15 (1989): 127–40. Highlights problems of using cathedral records of tenants as demographic source for Plague toll.

Megson, Barbara E. "Mortality among London Citizens in the Black Death." *Medieval Prosopography* 19 (1998): 125–33. Brief outline of demographic effects of first epidemic.

Poos, Larry. *A Rural Society after the Black Death: Essex, 1350–1525.* New York: Cambridge University Press, 1991. Focuses on marriage, migration, employment, social unrest, and religious nonconformity as affected by the pestilence and other historical factors.

Smail, Daniel Lord. "Accommodating Plague in Medieval Marseille." *Continuity and Change* 11 (1996): 11–41. Sketches a range of issues from notarial documents: immigration, marriage, debt, property transfer, legal services.

Smith, Richard M. "Demographic Developments in Rural England, 1300–1348." In *Before the Black Death*, edited by Bruce M. S. Campbell, 25–79. New York: Manchester University Press, 1992. A good place to start in untangling demographic effects of the Plague from demographic patterns already at work in pre-Plague England.

Cultural, Social, and Religious Effects

Bernardo, Aldo S. "The Plague as Key to Meaning in Boccaccio's *Decameron*." In *The Black Death: The Impact of the Fourteenth-century Plague*, edited by Daniel Williman, 39–64. Binghamton, NY: Medieval and Renaissance Texts and Studies, 1982. Studies the moralistic lessons Boccaccio provides his readers, most important of which is the precariousness of life as proven in the realistic treatment of the Plague in the framing elements of the collection.

Bowsky, William. "The Impact of the Black Death upon Sienese Government and Society." *Speculum* 39 (1964): 368–81. Carefully researched picture of how the social classes and structure of Siena, Italy, and the communal government that led the city were directly affected by the huge death toll and the rise of new leaders.

Cohn, Samuel K. *The Cult of Remembrance and the Black Death*. Baltimore: Johns Hopkins University Press, 1992. From his study of Italian wills Cohn concludes that the second epidemic of the Plague (1362) marked the real break with traditional views of piety and family. Links the Plague to personal and family concerns in art patronage of early Renaissance.

Courtenay, William J. "The Effects of the Black Death on English Higher Education." *Speculum* 55 (1980): 696–714. Only survey in English of the Plague's impact on universities.

Dohar, William J. *The Black Death and Pastoral Leadership: The Diocese of Hereford in the Fourteenth Century*. Philadelphia: University of Pennsylvania Press, 1995. Studies the resilience of the English Church and its leadership through initial and subsequent outbreaks of the Plague, and concludes that the negative impact of the Plague on the workings and integrity of the institution in Hereford was manageable.

Mate, Mavis E. *Daughters, Wives and Widows after the Black Death: Women in Sussex, 1350–1535*. Rochester, NY: Boydell Press, 1998. Goes against the current in painting a negative picture of women's positions—legal, social, and economic—in the post-1348 world.

Palmer, R. C. *English Law in the Age of the Black Death, 1348–1381: A Transformation of Governance and Law*. Chapel Hill: University of North Carolina Press, 1993. Study of how the Black Death led to an increase in English state power through the Crown's alliance with the Church and upper nobility and the rising gentry class and use of royal statute to stabilize the lower social classes.

Powell, James M. "Crisis and Culture in Renaissance Europe." *Medievalia et humanistica* 12 (1984): 201–24. Links falling land prices to greater concentration of wealth in the hands of European upper classes and ties this to the emergence of lay cultural flourishing of the Renaissance in Florence and England.

Shirk, Melanie V. "The Black Death in Aragon, 1348–1351." *Journal of Medieval History* 7 (1981): 357–67. Brief study of the effects of the Plague on Aragonese royal and local administration and economy, based on published documents dating from 1348 to 1384.

———. "Violence and the Plague in Aragón, 1348–1351." *Journal of the Rocky Mountain Medieval and Renaissance Association* 5 (1984): 31–39. Emphasizes the social problems, especially criminality, unleashed by the destruction of the administrative and judicial structures in Aragon.

Tangherlini, Timothy R. "Ships, Fogs, and Traveling Pairs: Plague Legend Migration in Scandinavia." *Journal of American Folklore* 101 (1988): 176–206. Studies the most common ways that Scandinavian folk explained the spread of the Plague in the fourteenth and fifteenth centuries.

Wenzel, Siegfried. "Pestilence and Middle English Literature: Friar John Grimestone's Poems on Death." In *The Black Death: The Impact of the Fourteenth-century Plague*, edited by Daniel Williman, 131–59. Binghamton, NY: Medieval and Renaissance Texts and Studies, 1982. Study of the role of human moral failure in bringing about the Black Death as expressed by this late-fourteenth-century English poet.

Zguta, Russell. "The One-day Votive Church: A Religious Response to the Black Death in Early Russia." *Slavic Review* 3 (1981): 423–32. Discusses the Russian practice of communal construction of chapels in a single day during Plague times.

Jewish Massacres and the Flagellant Movement

Cohn, Norman. *The Pursuit of the Millenium: Revolutionary Millenarians and Mystical Anarchists of the Middle Ages*. New York: Oxford University Press, 1990. Strongly links mid-fourteenth-century flagellants to previous and similar movements, and to anti-ecclesiastical radicalism and anti-Semitism.

Foa, Anna. *The Jews of Europe after the Black Death*. Translated by Andrea Grover. Berkeley: University of California, 2000. Traces roots of European anti-Semitism from early Christianity and its effects on Jewish life up to about 1900. Views events of 1348–50 in terms of both historical precedents and impacts on future development of Jewish communities.

Guerchberg, Sèraphine. "The Controversy over the Alleged Sowers of the Black Death in the Contemporary Treatises on Plague." In *Change in Medieval Society: Europe North of the Alps, 1050–1500*, edited by Sylvia Thrupp, 208–24. New York: Appleton-Century-Crofts, 1965. Heavily abridged version of the French original outlines case made against and for Jews poisoning wells.

Kieckhefer, R. "Radical Tendencies in the Flagellant Movement of the Mid-

Fourteenth Century." *Journal of Medieval and Renaissance Studies* 4 (1974): 157–76. Explores later stages of flagellant movement for harsh anticlericalism, anti-Semitism, and other reasons why the authorities repressed them.

Lerner, Robert E. "The Black Death and Western Eschatological Mentalities." *American Historical Review* 86 (1981): 533–52; also in *The Black Death: The Impact of the Fourteenth-century Plague*, edited by Daniel Williman, 77–106. Binghamton, NY: Medieval and Renaissance Texts and Studies, 1982. Views European fears of the end times in a broad historical context, and sees their rise during the Black Death as a moralistic response rather than as fear of the imminent end of the world.

Rowan, Steven W. "The *Grand peur* of 1348–49: The Shock Wave of the Black Death in the German Southwest." *Journal of the Rocky Mountain Medieval and Renaissance Association* 5 (1984): 19–30. Rich article links the massacres of 1348–49 to the broader context of anti-Semitism in southwestern German areas, comparing the pattern of popular violence and its spread to the *Grand peur* (Great fear) in France in 1789.

Plague and the Arts

Boeckl, Christine. *Images of Plague and Pestilence: Iconography and Iconology.* Kirksville, MO: Truman State University Press, 2000. Provides an overview of Plague imagery from the fourteenth through seventeenth centuries in two-dimensional formats, relating it to historical events and trends and to literary sources. Well illustrated.

Cole, Bruce. "Some Thoughts on Orcagna and the Black Death Style." *Antichità viva* 22 (1983): 27–37. Revises Meiss' interpretation of the impact of the Black Death on mid-fourteenth-century painting in Florence by focusing on the decoration and functions of the Strozzi Chapel in Santa Maria Novella in Florence.

Friedman, John B. " 'He hath a thousand slayn this pestilence:' Iconography of the Plague in the Late Middle Ages." In *Social Unrest in the Late Middle Ages*, edited by Francis X. Newman, 75–112. Binghamton, NY: Medieval and Renaissance Texts and Studies, 1986. Brief but broad treatment of the evolution of Plague imagery, especially regarding the contributions of religious and scientific thought.

Lindley, Phillip. "The Black Death and English Art: A Debate and Some Assumptions." In *The Black Death in England*, edited by W. M. Ormrod and

P. G. Lindley, 125–46. Stamford, Lincolnshire, England: Paul Watkins, 1996. Rare article on English art post-1350 raises questions of relationship of quality to style shifts in art and architecture.

Marshall, Louise J. "Manipulating the Sacred: Image and Plague in Renaissance Italy." *Renaissance Quarterly* 47 (1994): 485–532. Relates numerous artistic images of interceding saints to popular need for psychological and spiritual reassurance. For Marshall, these are a sign of confidence in effective spiritual protectors, not resignation to fear.

Meiss, Millard. *Painting in Florence and Siena after the Black Death: The Arts, Religion, and Society in the Mid-fourteenth Century.* Princeton: Princeton University Press, 1979. Dated and controversial study of how the Black Death affected Tuscan painting, its subject and forms. Provides starting point for most later discussions of the subject.

Neustatter, Otto. "Mice in Plague Pictures." *The Journal of the Walters Art Gallery* 4 (1941): 105–14. Examines presence of mice in pictures related to the Plague, but finds their presence a matter of forewarning but not causing the epidemic.

Norman, Diana. "Change and Continuity: Art and Religion after the Black Death." In her *Siena, Florence and Padua, I: Art, Society and Religion 1280–1400. Interpretative Essays.* New Haven: Yale University Press, 1995; 177–96. Essentially creating a synthesis of recent scholarship in the area, Norman balances the effects of the Plague on the quality of art production and the taste and spiritual concerns of the patrons.

Polzer, Joseph. "Aspects of the Fourteenth-Century Iconography of Death and the Plague." In *The Black Death: The Impact of the Fourteenth-century Plague*, edited by Daniel Williman, 107–30. Binghamton, NY: Medieval and Renaissance Texts and Studies, 1982. Illustrated cataloguing of main artistic themes associated with the Black Death, including Plague saints and images of death.

Schiferl, Ellen. "Iconography of Plague Saints in Fifteenth-century Italian Painting." *Fifteenth Century Studies* 6 (1983): 205–25. Overview of major saints and themes.

Steinhoff, Judith. "Artistic Working Relationships after the Black Death: Sienese Compagnia, c. 1350–1363." *Renaissance Studies* 14 (2000): 1–45. Attributes apparent "retro" quality of post-Plague Sienese painting to alterations in how artists' workshops were organized and operated after so many artists and patrons died.

Van Os, Henk. "The Black Death and Sienese Painting: A Problem of Interpretation." *Art History* 4 (1981): 237–49. Agrees with Meiss that Sienese painting style changed after 1348, but attributes this to specific changes in patronage rather than to changes in religious sentiment.

Why the Plagues Ended in Europe

Appleby, A. B. "The Disappearance of the Plague: A Continuing Puzzle." *Economic History Review* 33 (1980): 161–73. Good overview of main theories.

Konkola, Kari. "More Than a Coincidence? The Arrival of Arsenic and the Disappearance of Plague in Early Modern Europe." *History of Medicine* 47 (1992): 186–209. Argues that the availability of huge amounts of industrial arsenic in the late seventeenth century and its sudden, widespread use as a rat poison were responsible for the disappearance of the Plague in western and central Europe.

Slack, Paul. "The Disappearance of Plague: An Alternative View." *Economic History Review* 34 (1981): 469–76. Responding to Appleby, credits quarantining and restrictions on trade with limiting Plague spread.

Primary Sources

Bartsocas, Christos. "Two Fourteenth Century Greek Descriptions of the 'Black Death.'" *Journal of the History of Medicine* 21 (1966): 394–400. Discusses and publishes English translations of descriptions of the Black Death by Nicephoras Gregoras, chief librarian in Constantinople, and Byzantine emperor John VI Cantacuzenos.

Boccaccio, Giovanni. *The Decameron.* Trans. Mark Musa and Peter Bondanella. New York: Norton 1977. Boccaccio's Introduction is a powerful and indispensable source for how people felt and reacted in the earliest outbreak.

Duran-Reynals, M. L., and C.-E. A. Winslow, "Jacme d'Agramont: *Regiment de preservacio a epidemia o pestilencia e mortaldats.*" *Bulletin of the History of Medicine* 23 (1949): 57–89. Translation without notes of this Catalan Plague *consilium* from 1348.

Froissart, Jean. *Chronicles.* Trans. Geoffrey Brereton. New York: Penguin Books, 1968. Contains important sections on the Black Death and the flagellants in 1348–49.

Horrox, Rosemary, ed. *The Black Death*. New York: Manchester University Press, 1994. Excellent collection of 128 translated primary sources or excerpts, most English and most fourteenth century. Arranged topically or by type with a very useful introduction to each section.

Johannes de Ketham. *The Fasciculus Medicinae*. Translated by Luke DeMaitre. Birmingham: The Classics of Medicine Library, 1988. Beautifully produced English translation of the 1493 edition of the German medical textbook with original illustrations.

Marcus, Jacob R. *The Jew in the Medieval World: A Source Book: 315–1791*. New York: Atheneum, 1979. Contains three documents relating to Jewish persecution in 1348–49.

Pickett, Joseph P. "A Translation of the *Canutus* Plague Treatise." In *Popular and Practical Science of Medieval England* (Medieval Texts and Studies, 11), edited by Lister M. Matheson, 263–82. East Lansing, MI: Colleagues Press, 1994. Mid-fifteenth-century translation of a Scandinavian medical treatise that itself was based upon the "anonymous practitioner" of Montpellier.

Useful Reference Works

Bynum, W. F., and Roy Porter, eds. *Companion Encyclopedia of the History of Medicine*, 2 vols. New York: Routledge, 1994. Useful reference source with both broad articles on medical cultures ("Chinese Medicine") and narrower ones of use to the student of the Plague.

Kiple, Kenneth, ed. *The Cambridge World History of Human Disease*. New York: Cambridge University Press, 1993. Excellent reference work containing detailed articles on various cultures' approaches to disease, as well as on specific diseases (e.g., "Bubonic Plague" and "Black Death").

Kohn, George C. *Encyclopedia of Plague and Pestilence: From Ancient Times to the Present*. New York: Facts on File, 2001. Short entries on a wide range of topics, including specific phases of the Second Pandemic.

Strayer, Joseph. *Dictionary of the Middle Ages*. New York: Scribner, 1989. Standard reference work for the medieval period.

Videotapes and DVDs

History of Britain, Volume 5: *King Death*. A&E Home Video. 2000. 60 minutes. VHS. Historian Simon Schama's exploration of the various effects on

English society of the Plague in the much broader context of English history.

History's Turning Points, Volume 3: *Black Death/Siege of Constantinople/Conquest of the Incas*. Transatlantic Films. 2002. 75 minutes. DVD. Documentary that uses dramatizations to evoke the horror and pathos of the event. Discusses it in terms of its world historical importance.

Medieval London: 1066–1500. Films for the Humanities. 1991. 20 minutes. VHS. Brief coverage of Black Death in context of London's medieval history.

Scourge of the Black Death. History Channel Films. c. 2000. 50 minutes. VHS. Covers history of man's interaction with the bubonic plague to contemporary times.

The Seventh Seal. Home Vision Entertainment. 1958. 90 minutes. VHS/DVD. Feature film by Ingmar Bergman set in post-Plague Germany: Death stalks and plays chess with a knight for the right to take him and all of his companions.

Two Thousand Years: The History of Christianity, Volume 7: *Heresy, War, and the Black Death: Christianity in the 13th and 14th Centuries*. Films for the Humanities. 1999. 48 minutes. VHS. Sets the Black Death and Jewish pogroms associated with it in context of religion and society of the late medieval West.

INDEX

abandonment: of family, 3, 74, 111, 137; of hearths, 59; of land, 8, 63, 64, 105, 106; of work, 69; of villages, 107, 115. *See also under* flight

Aberdeen, 22

Adriatic Sea, 7

Afonso, Diogo, 51

Agnolo di Tura, 58

agriculture, 62, 63, 64

air: contraction of disease via, 20, 45; corruption of (miasma), as cause of Plague, 2, 15, 16, 42–44, 48, 105, 137, 155–58; corruption of, due to earthquakes, 33, 43; corruption of, due to Jews, 82; corruption of, due to planets, 41, 43; corruption of, due to sin, 39, 46; corruption of, ordinances preventing, 110; corruption of, rejection of theory, 52, 112, 144, 172; as element, 35, 141; flight to healthier, 111, 139, 159, 162; purification of, 4, 47, 105, 110, 143, 159–62, 165 (*see also* fumigation)

Albert the Great (Albertus Magnus), 41, 43

Albert II, Duke of Austria, 85

Albi, 60–61

Albumasar, 41, 155

Alexandria, 7, 104, 105, 132, 173

Alfonso de Cordoba, 38, 47, 82

Ali-Abbas, 37

al-Ibadi, Hunayn bin Ishaq, 34

Allah, 45, 105, 107, 108, 119, 144, 172. *See also* God

al-Maqrizi, Muhammad, 9, 104, 108

Angers, 43

Apt, 61, 83

Aragon, 8, 64, 82, 83

Arezzo, 138, 139

Aristotle, 34, 37, 38, 43, 140, 155

armies, 1, 4, 6, 91, 174, 175

armpits: in art, 23, 95; buboes under, 3, 19, 21–22, 24, 44, 49, 50

Ar-Razi, Abu Bakr, 34, 37

arrows: in art, 89–90, 94; in Bible, 39, 95; as metaphor for plague, 1, 21, 93, 97, 174

astrology: and bloodletting, 49; and cause of Plague, 33, 40–42;

About the Author

JOSEPH P. BYRNE is a European historian and Associate Professor of Honors at Belmont University in Nashville, Tennessee. He has conducted research and published articles on a wide variety of subjects, from Roman catacombs to American urbanization, though his area of expertise is Italy in the era of the Black Death.